PRE-HISTORY'S CHRONOLOGY ENIGMA

Terrance F. Johnson

Cover Design by Terrance F. Johnson

Terrance F. Johnson, Author of *Our Missing Ancestors/ A Dynamic Civilization*, 2013

"Pre-History's Chronology Enigma" by Terrance F. Johnson.
ISBN 978-1-62137-808-2 (softcover).

Published 2016 by Virtualbookworm.com Publishing Inc., P.O. Box 9949, College Station, TX 77842, US.

©2016, Terrance F. Johnson. All rights reserved. No part of this publication may be reproduced, stored in a retrieval system, or transmitted in any form or by any means, electronic, mechanical, recording or otherwise, without the prior written permission of Terrance F. Johnson.

Manufactured in the United States of America.

To my parents and grandparents…

Leonard and Lois Johnson
Fred and Lillian Knoll
Fred and Emma Johnson

For my son…

Derek W. Johnson

And my wife…

Judith

Also, a special thanks to the best teacher I ever had…

Sandra Panici

"There is something inconsistent about our past, that part that lies thousands and millions of years behind us."

Erich von Däniken
Chariots of the Gods

Table of Contents

Introduction 1

Chapter 1
European and Scandinavian Glacial Cycles 5

Chapter 2
Glaciation of North America 13

Chapter 3
Maritime Knowledge of the Ancients 25

Chapter 4
The Mediterranean Mystification 37

Chapter 5
Ancient People of Europe 57

Chapter 6
Ancient People of Central America 79

Chapter 7
Ancient People of South America 93

Chapter 8
Ancient People of the Americas 113

Chapter 9
The Mound Builders of North America 123

Chapter 10
The Mystery of Red Ochre 149

Chapter 11
First Nations of North America 161

Chapter 12
The Fertile, Moist Sahara 199

Appendix 203
Footnotes 218
BIBLIOGRAPHY 223
INDEX 227

The idea of the simple linear development of society from the culture of the Paleolithic (Old Stone Age) through the successive stages of the Neolithic (New Stone Age), Bronze, and Iron Age must be given up. Today we find primitive cultures co-existing with advanced modern society on all the continents — the Bushmen of Australia, the Bushmen of South Africa, truly primitive peoples in South America, and in New Guinea; some tribal peoples in the United States We shall now assume that, some 20,000 or more years ago, while Paleolithic peoples held out in Europe, more advanced cultures existed elsewhere on the earth, and that we have inherited a part of what they once possessed, passed down from people to people.

~ ~ *Charles Hapgood*
~ ~ *Maps of the Ancient Sea Kings*

Introduction

The chapters in this book were written in an attempt to expand on and to support an *experimental hypothesis* which was set out in my first book *Our Missing Ancestors/A Dynamic Civilization* published in 2013. In that book it was brought to light that a number of prominent scientists and researchers were openly calling for a new chronology for current understanding and explanations for events, and circumstances of mankind's unwritten past. As new scientific methods are introduced, coupled with advanced technical equipment, and applied by more well trained and educated researchers, it is becoming very obvious that another, more complex and extremely controversial account is beginning to present itself for rigorous examination about what we call *pre-history*. History, in the broadest sense of the word, is a report of what has occurred or in some instances, what might have occurred. Most of what we consider to be history is derived from written accounts regardless of style, form or individual language. It is when accounts of past events cannot be substantiated with written documentation or when conditions and observations can be physically verified, but remain unsupported by written evidence that historians tend to place these phenomena into a category called *pre-history*. In order to find answers to explain the mysteries of ancient cultures and worldly civilizations, archaeology is probably still our best hope for obtaining that type of valuable information, however, many other sciences, such as, archaeoastronomy, anthropology, chemistry, and more must join the search, as well. Issues regarding paleo-humans are far too complex, just as a description of early modern man might appear to be unbelievable. Science, it seems, cannot bring itself to entertain the idea that a very early civilization actually existed that had intelligence comparable to most modern civilizations of today. Furthermore, science cannot get past 150,000 years ago for the beginning of modern man appearing almost instantly in East Africa; and then taking somewhere to around 50,000 to 60,000 years for them to walk out of Africa, and populate the world. It is understood that science requires proof in order to draw conclusions; but there is proof, which has been presented to confirm or to support many new findings of prehistory that express opposition with current perceptions. Most of these new evidentiary finds are ignored or discounted because it would require modern science to rewrite and review their beliefs, and the methods of study and research employed. Fortunately, through research and observations produced by independent amateur archaeologists, science has been forced to acknowledge some of the new information, and to reevaluate current thinking.

Archaeology is a study of life and cultures of ancient people, which to strengthen its credibility, must include a factual chronology. Chronology is a scientific measuring of time as it relates to fixed periods, with an orderly dating of events that might also include epochs. In our modern past, proper dating for monuments, civilizations, human accomplishments, and physical locations have fallen short of veracity. This definitiveness factor is in some cases, not the fault of those who carried out past research; rather it is a result of evidence not being available when the study was being conducted. It might be fair to say that the majority of our prehistorical understanding has been determined within the past fifty (50) years. On the whole, more people became educated, experienced, and inquisitive about our planet and other peoples following WW II. The United States G.I. Bill (Entitled, Servicemen's Readjustment Act of 1944) allowed for returning veterans (often referred to as G.I.s or Government Issues) to attend college or Trade Schools at no out of pocket expense to them personally. This measure allowed many Vets to enter fields of science and education, which produced a profound effect of discovering the prehistory of mankind, although still on a rather limited basis. In addition, children of the 'Greatest Generation' followed the quest to seek answers for what they saw, and what new information was placed before them. Still some others, identified as amateur researchers or independents developed to issue questions, and to point to anomalies, which caused many to think on a broader scale. The purpose of this writing incorporates a portion of these new findings, and seeks to provide an orderly intelligent clarification of what might have occurred in deep prehistory, while arranging and connecting time sensitive events to create a more current explanation for what we see today.

Because there are so many misunderstandings on the part of those who fail to follow or to learn history and science, this book begins with glaciation periods of the earth, commonly, but inaccurately, referred to as the "Ice Age." Because of this inappropriate labeling many people believe the world was totally covered in thick ice, and that only now-extinct animals lived at that time, as portrayed in cartoons by cute, friendly Wooly Mammoths. The true facts are, however, people (modern man) actually did not just reside on earth at that time, but developed through varying stages of evolution. After all, the earth's glaciation periods covered the better part of 2,000,000 years, and we know from archaeological discoveries that some form of homo species existed as far back as (from current dating) 1.5 million years. So it is the task of scientists to explain through chronological events all of the particulars necessary to account for our existence, and survival today as the reigning dominant species. This task would require an explanation as to how, where, and when events occurred to account for the development of man. This endeavor must include the entire global surface, since it has since been established that modern man has occupied space in every known modern country over many millennium, and that includes the North American continent. History can no longer accept that Christopher Columbus discovered America, and that he was first of an intelligent civilization to step foot on the American continent — discovering only half-naked savages who were only good for slaves and concubines

The overall observations, and research contained in this writing will attempt to arrange events into an orderly explication of what the prehistory of mankind might have been. It is an exertion to explain some portion of prehistory, which might allow for extended investigations to discover the true identity of a one-time reigning "High-Civilization." There can be no question of their past existence. Modern history has much evidence to prove that they did exist, and that they possessed remarkable mental and physical abilities, which could rival modern man. The only sticking point in the process might be the belief on the part of modern humans to accept the reality of individuals having the capacity and fortitude necessary to accomplish and produce such grand activities during such early times. To most people, advanced knowledge could not, and should not have existed in deep antiquity; back then man was not much more than a developed animal according to some opinions. Although, as Charles Hapgood pointed out in the quote at the beginning of this chapter, it would be very likely that an advanced civilization could, and did reside in a world where most of its inhabitants lived a less cultivated form of existence. Signs left behind by this intelligent civilization are with us today in many forms. Some examples are very obvious, such as the pyramids of several cultures, dolmens found spread out across Europe, and into the United States, artifacts discovered in burials, and in other locations, petroglyphs and pictographs evident in many worldly locations, and the shear fact of physical human beings placed at locations where circumstances designate they should not have been.

What is not so obvious is the fact that cultures thousands of miles a part — across an ocean of water during a time in deep antiquity built similar gigantic structures, which exhibit advanced astronomical knowledge common to both civilizations, while scholars negate the possibility of contact between the two cultures during those ancient times. They tell us it cannot be possible because boats had not been invented, and the people were far too underdeveloped to have had an understanding of celestial occurrences. Was it just a coincidence? Probably not. There are many other examples of similarities between cultures stretching across thousands of miles, which clearly point to an advanced people possibly having had an interaction with the local indigenous people, which they encountered. Examples of this nature clearly indicate a people much older, and more advanced than scholars care to admit.

It is also the intent of this writing to include an understanding for a chronological interpretation for peopling of the northern hemisphere prior to the people that we once referred to as Indians (once again, an incorrect assessment from Columbus). Current dogma is that Asians are responsible for all of the indigenous peoples of North America — the Asians simply wandered across a land-bridge, which formed between Siberia and Alaska some 12,000 - 10,000 years ago. Perhaps from facts and observations presented here, a new refinement of the Native American people will appear.

What makes the study of prehistory so interesting is that the entire world is involved in its all encompassing makeup. No one country can be left out of its ancient unwritten history, just as no one people can be excluded. In many cases, one culture had a formulative effect on another entirely different culture, resulting in a similar traditional conduct. If it is not evident by now that civilizations had an influencing effect on one another, then perhaps from the narrative found in these chapters that corollary might become unmistakable. The only thing then left to attend to is the dating, or correct measurement of time, for these individuals, and events to have occurred. Scholars must account for an earlier period for the existence of modern man. There are too many new artifacts, too many new dates determined by archaeoastronomy, too many more possibilities expounded by experts, and too many intricate technical similarities, which must be explained.

That will be one goal set out for this study.

The world is forever and always changing. Ocean levels have risen and fallen innumerable times over the millennia. We are just now realizing how even a seemingly minuscule change in sea level can completely alter the way we live. So why is it so difficult to believe that there once existed vast and glorious cultures that, along with their knowledge and histories, were lost to the sands of time or the depthless waters of a great flood? Most people cite a lack of any tangible evidence to support this idea, but what they don't know (or refuse to know) is that there is evidence.
~ ~ *Michael Pye and Kirsten Dally*
October 2011
Lost Civilizations & Secretes of the Past

Chapter 1

European and Scandinavian Glacial Cycles

What most people call the "Ice Age," was in reality the *Last Glacial Period*. This most recent glacial period occurred during the last phase of the Pleistocene Epoch, which ranged from approximately 110,000 BP to around 10,000 BP. The Pleistocene refers to the last glacial epoch, which commenced around 2.5 million years ago. This phase ended with melting of the solid ice packs formed during the Weichsel-Würm glacial stages in Europe and Scandinavia, and the retreat of the Wisconsinan glaciation in North America around 11,000 years ago.

Included in the Pleistocene time period were several major stages of glaciation. First, was the Günz glaciation stage, which was named after a Bavarian river in Germany. It began around 590,000 years ago, and is correlated with the Nebraskan glacial stage of North America. The Günz is also correlated with the Baventian stage of marine deposits of Great Britain, and the Menapian stage of northern Europe. Secondly, the next major phase was the Mindel glaciation of Alpine Europe, which terminated with the start of the Holsteinian interglacial. The Mindel phase preceded the Mindel-Riss interglacial, and occurred from around 750,000 to 675,000 years ago. The third major stage was the Riss glaciation in the European Alps. It commenced about 250,000 years ago, and lasted for over 100,000 years. It consisted of two stages, Riss 1, which is correlated with the Dnieper glaciation, and Riss 2 with the Moscow glaciation. Its end came with the start of the Holocene post-glacial.

It is suspected that around 20,000 years ago is when the maximum extent of glaciation occurred. Each of these thawing and refreezing stages were similar in a number of ways, but differed in many ways from one continent to another. For example, Siberia reached maximum glaciation around 18,000 to 17,000 BP; while Europe obtained maximum extent at about 22,000 to 18,000 BP. Archaeologists seem to agree it was during the Paleolithic and Mesolithic periods when carbon changes somewhat indicated the advancement, and recession of glacier activity. It is at this time when the Alps, Andes, Antarctica, and a large portion of the Himalayas were in a state of glaciation called the Würm glaciation phase.

The Würm glaciation was the fourth stage which occurred mainly in the Alps, and Pyrénées mountains, which lie between Spain and France, and consist of smaller ice caps located mainly in valley glaciers. The name for this stage came from another river in Germany, only this time in the Alpine foreland. At the height of the Würm stage, approximately 24,000 years BP, scientists have determined that Europe and Eurasia was in a phase of lebensraum (living space — without trees) or in a cold prairie / savannah environment. Permafrost was commonplace across Germany at the lower levels. At the same time solid ice fields, and glaciers could be found in the Alps; whereas, Scandinavia and most of Great Britain were layered in thick ice. Also during this time the whole of Switzerland was completely covered by the Rhône glacier (see Fig.1 at end of the chapter). The Würm stage, in total, lasted for about 60,000 years.

The next to arrive, and Europe's last glaciation spanning 70,000 to 20,000 BP, was the Weichselian glaciation stage. The Weichselian glaciation occurred at the same time as the Würm stage of glaciation. This stage is also known as, "The Last Glacial Maximum," and according to many scientists there is sufficient evidence to indicate these ice sheets only existed for a short period of time in their maximum state; lasting for only about 12,000 years. This stage of glaciers was also rated as the coldest phase of the glacial periods.

The Weichselian glaciation, which was also located southeast of the Baltic Sea, took its name from a Polish river, named *Vistula*. This Polish name also allowed the glaciation period to be known as the *Vistulian Glaciation*. This is the glaciation period archaeologists believe reached its maximum extent at around 22,000 to 20,000 BP or possibly even as late as 13,000 BP. Overall, most scientist agree on a range from 70,000 to 20,000 BP for the Weichselian stage to have occurred.

During this glaciation period it is believed the western part of Jutland was free of ice along with most of the North Sea, which connected Jutland with Great Britain. This particular area is of great interest since there has been evidence produced of possible *Homo* populations living in that area over a course of time. This may not be so unbelievable when we take into consideration that prior to this glacial phase there occurred the Eémain interglacial period, which ranged from around 130,000 to 114,000 years ago.

The Eémian phase, it is believed, had similar climatic conditions to the Holocene. It also is correlated with the Sangamonian glacial of North America. It also has tie-ins with Great Britain's Ipswichian phase, and the eastern European Mikulin interglacial stage. The name comes from Professor Dr. P. Harting (1875) who named the phase, "Système Eémien," after studying boreholes in the Netherlands. It was at the peak stage, around 125,000 years ago, when the warmest temperatures occurred allowing for warmer and wetter conditions. There is also speculation that at this time, the coast of Norway was in an ice-free state. Evidence for this temperature increase is taken from Hippopotamus remains found as far north as the Rhine River in Germany, and on the Thames River in England. In addition forests have been identified existing as far north as North Cape, northern Norway (above the Arctic Circle), which today is frozen tundra. Then at around 114,000 years ago, following an aridity pulse which lasted 468 years — and causing central Europe to undergo dust storms, brush-fires and a loss of Thermophilous trees, the glacial period returned once again.

The Weichsel-Würm glaciation was followed by the Allerød oscillation, a warm moist global interstadial, which occurred about 11,500 to 10,800 BCE. This was followed, almost a decade later, by a very rapid cold-dry period known as the Younger Dryas stadial, which produced sub-arctic climatic conditions encompassing much of Europe. Younger Dryas received it's name from an arctic-alpine wildflower the, *Dryas octopetala.* It is an eight-pedal flower of which researchers have found great quantities of its pollen in core samples dating to that time, suggesting the freeze was sudden, catching the flower either in a blooming or existing state. In total, the stadial was geologically short, lasting only for about 1,300 years.

There is a theory which exists claiming that the Younger Dryas stadial may have been caused by the collapse of the North American ice sheets. This collapse would have had a cooling effect on the North Atlantic waters which were colder than usual, at least, by a couple of hundred years prior to the start of the Younger Dryas stadial. This cooling affected almost the entire globe including the American Northwest, which was located across the North American continent from the Atlantic Ocean. The temperature change was also discovered in European and Danish peat bogs called, the Blytt-Sernander System after two Scandinavian researchers.

Following this temporary cold phase was the Pre-Boreal temperature rise around 9600 BCE, which evolved into the Boreal phase at nearly 8000 to 5000 BCE, and producing temperatures at current day levels. As temperatures increased, glaciers continued to melt away causing any artifactual evidence, of existing human populations, to be wiped away as well; although, some traces of ancient civilization have recently been recovered by fishing crews, and marine archaeologists in an area between Great Britain and the Netherlands. This area is known as *Doggerland,* and dates to prehistoric glacial and interglacial times. Prior to melting glaciers this stretch of land was probably the European version of the Siberian-Alaskan Bering Strait land bridge, which many say connected the old world with the new one (North America). This land bridge, on the other hand, connected Europe with Great Britain.

This once dry land extended along the coast lines of Belgium, the Netherlands, and a small portion of northern Germany, on the European side; then stretching over to the United Kingdom running along the coast from about East Sussex, in the south, up to around Norfolk in the north, while including Kent, Essex and Suffolk in its path. Northward, Doggerland extended to almost the southern tip of Norway, and approximately to a point at where middle-Scotland might be indicated, if extended by a line eastward out to sea (See Fig. 2-at end of chapter).

Doggerland starting at around 6500 BCE began to be effected by the melting glaciers, and by about 5500 BCE, during the Boreal phase, the area was completely submerged in what today is known as the southern North Sea. Prior to 6500 BCE, during maximum glaciation, the ocean sea levels were around 400 feet (120 m) lower than we know them to be today. This was due to the water in the oceans being used to produce snow and ice in order to create the huge ice packs, and glaciers. This action also created open land areas, which connected bodies of land to one another where once ocean sea water was all that was to be seen. Just like the Bering Strait, Doggerland could have been open and closed a great many times because of the periodic warming phases called, *Interglacials.* In support of this statement, there have been a number of articles written about such a possibility. Two articles come to mind from the web site, Science Daily. The first comes from an article dated August 12, 2009 which explained that artifacts found near Cheddar Gorge in Somerset exhibited the butchering of horses, and people around 14,700 years ago (12,700 BC). The researchers seem to think the people responsible for this followed horse herds across the Doggerland area when it was still solid ground. The second article, from the same web site is dated June 1, 2010, and contains the headline *Neanderthals Walked Into Frozen Britain 40,000 Years Earlier Than First Thought, Evidence Shows.* Once again, if accurate, it would mean there was another glacial period, which allowed for the Doggerland passage to be navigable by foot, which was later covered over by the onset of an interglacial.

At about 8000 BCE (Mesolithic Era) Doggerland, according to some researchers, might have been a very rich region for hunting and fishing. It is now known, and accepted, that at least one ancient population resided in that location as evidenced by ancient artifacts, such as flint tools retrieved by fishermen, and later by marine archaeologists. More recently some vague news has become known that researchers have dredged up artifacts of Cro-Magnon in the Doggerland crossing. However, not much of the information has been made public.

It has been hypothesized that by around 6200 BCE the remaining visible portion of land remaining from rising ocean waters, which once was Doggerland, was completely submerged by a tsunami caused by a gigantic landslide, which broke away, and slid into the sea off of the Norwegian coast line. This coastal landslide is referred to as the *Storegga Slide*. This slide completely swamped what remained of Doggerland after persistent flooding from melting ice packs, and entirely separating Great Britain from the European continent.

Following the Younger Dryas stadial (sometimes referred to as the *Big Freeze*) at about 12,000 years ago, geologists and archaeologists have named this current, and first interglacial of the Holocene Epoch the *Flandrian interglacial*. The first phase of this interglacial was noted by rapid rises in sea levels, and called the *Flandrian Transgression*. This phase also had a correlation with the Fenno-Scandian, Laurentide and Cordilleran glaciers melting intervals. The rising filled Scandinavian coastal areas creating fjords where none had existed before. Rising seas from this interglacial might lend credence to the *Ryan-Pitman* theory, which was mentioned in my first book (*Our Missing Ancestors*). Ryan-Pitman put forth a hypothesis, which states water from the rising Mediterranean Sea was forced into the Black Sea through the narrow Bosporus at about 5600 BCE. The theory also claims that the water levels climbed about six inches per day. This episode resulted in turning the Black Sea from a fresh water landlocked lake into an inland salt-water sea. Further, some scholars believe this rising sea action is what was explained as the Great Deluge of Biblical times.

Also at around 6000 to 5000 BCE a Neolithic *Wet Phase* came into existence, which caused rains to occur in what is today northeastern Saudi Arabia, Iraq, and southern Iran. This wet phase triggered a greening, and fertilization of the area. People then moved into the region, and began developing an agricultural lifestyle. Some people believe this was Eden or more specifically, the *Garden of Eden*. This event coincides with the rising sea levels of the Flandrian Transgression since water began filling the Persian Gulf, and then reaching today's current levels at about 4000 BCE, and eventually covering the area referred to as Eden.

It might be clearly seen that the so called Ice Age was not a consistent perpetual phenomenon at all. Rather the entire epoch was filled with melting and freezing periods, which allowed for human life to exist, and establish cultures in places where many individuals today believe only glaciers stood as kings. Today's research and sciences seems to be documenting the reality of human existence interacting with the various stages of earth's glacial period. We know from scientific means that Neanderthals lived in Europe for thousands of years prior to the arrival of Cro-Magnon some 35,000 to 40,000 years ago. This understanding alone testifies that it was possible for humans to live in some European areas, and develop civilizations during the continuous reoccurring phases. It should remove any misunderstanding about how humans populated this world, and as to when. Even the aforementioned artifacts of Doggerland having produced flint and bone fragments, indicating a more advanced culture of Cro-Magnon living there at one time, which remains unaccounted for by prehistory.

One other mystery to be researched pertains to the *Pay Basque* culture of the Pyrénées. From studies, and research efforts there is some strong evidence (mainly through blood groups) that perhaps can confirm the Pay Basque were the original Cro-Magnon that settled and remained in Europe since the very beginnings of human evolution. If this is true, then we must question how these people survived, and developed during the number of reoccurring glacial phases; especially when we now know that the Würm glaciation affected their area in the Pyrénées Mountains, which lies between the current countries of France and Spain. One must question if they were there prior to the Pleistocene Epoch or did they arrive at some point during the continuous thawing and refreezing stages. If they did — then how did they survive, and where? Further, why aren't these people taken into consideration when speaking of man's evolution?

As we look back through the various stages of the Pleistocene Epoch we gain a clear understanding that people, members of the *Homo* genus variety, have been around a lot longer than current science cares to admit. It is somewhat obvious that humans could, and did, exist and survive through the worst, and best of times in the European environment while adapting to the changing cycles of glaciation. In my first book, it was pointed out that water was no obstacle to the ancient prehistoric people. Now it appears that weather was also not an obstacle to these hardy and creative adventurers. With the varying amounts of time involved between the glacials, and interglacials it would be quite possible for a civilization to have existed long enough to have formed themselves into very highly intelligent cultured people. Perhaps some skeptics will view this observation with words of rejection. They may deny the possibility of people living near or on frozen ice sheets, and being able to survive. If this might be the case, it would be necessary to point to modern civilizations living quite happily in regions such as, Canada, Alaska, Siberia, and Scandinavia; then ask the skeptics if they detect any hardship or deprivation of these people. If these modern people can survive, and prosper in frozen regions — what would hinder or stop a group of individuals in prehistoric times from banding together, utilizing their intelligence, and resources to create themselves or to develop into a *High Civilization*? This seems to be a question, which many researchers fail to ask.

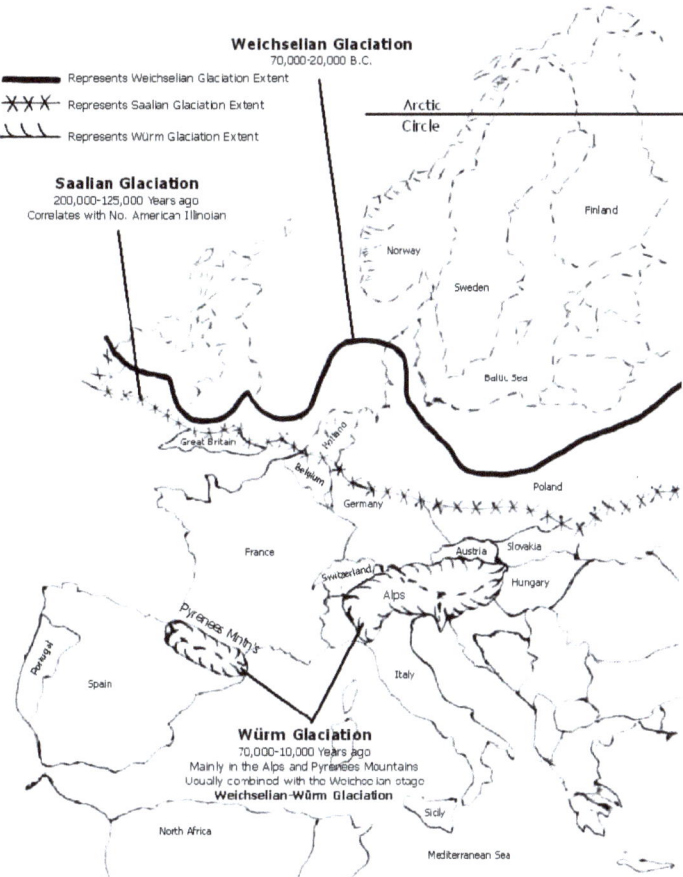

EUROPEAN GLACIATION PHASES

Fig. 1

Figure provided by Terrance F. Johnson, 2013

Weichsel-Würm glaciation-approximately 50,000 BP
Northern Germany and Denmark are free of ice on the west side, but is ice covered in the east.
Image from Wikimedia

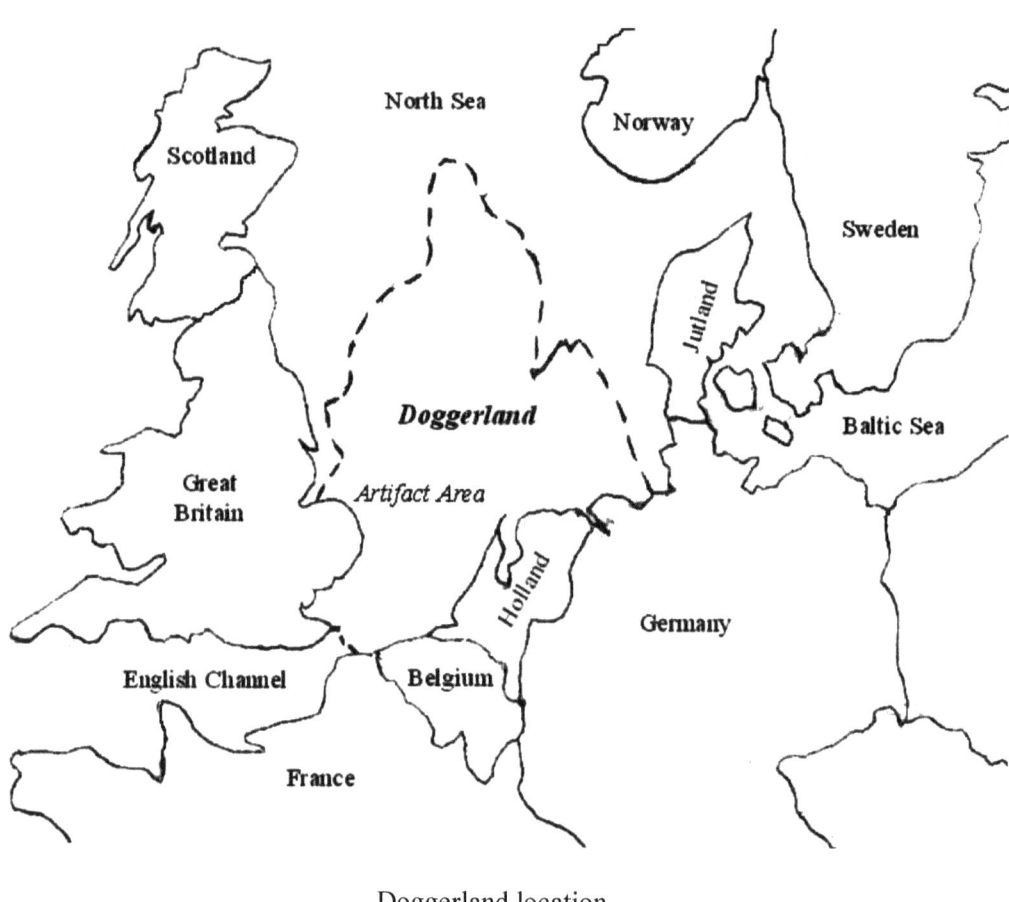

Doggerland location

Fig. 2 Figure provided by Terrance F. Johnson
2014

Those newly arriving Ice Age American, trekking in from Siberia across the Bering land bridge, would have faced the most appalling conditions between 17,000 and 10,000 years ago. It was then that the Wisconsin glaciers, all at once went into their ferocious meltdown, forcing a 350-foot rise in global sea levels amid scenes of unprecedented climatic and geological turmoil. For seven thousand years of human experience, earthquakes, volcanic eruptions and immense floods, interspersed with eerie periods of peace, must have dominated the day-to-day lives of the New World peoples.

~ ~ *Graham Hancock*
~ ~ *Fingerprints of the Gods*

Chapter 2

Glaciation of North America

Approximately 18,000 years ago nearly 35 percent of the worlds land masses were covered with some form of ice. The magnitude of this event spread across Greenland, Iceland, Great Britain, the upper portion of Europe covering all of the Scandinavian countries and stretching over into Siberia, Alaska, Canada, and down into an area now known as the lower forty-eight states of America. In addition to this amount of northern global land, some portions of land south of the equator also experienced the effects of the last glacial period. Most of these locations go unnoticed or unmentioned when speaking of the last 'Ice Age'. Locations like Antarctica or alpine area glaciers of the Andes in Bolivia, Colombia, Peru, Chile, Venezuela, and Argentina. The South American events were much different and less drastic then the glacials of the northern hemisphere. Further, glaciers of South America were of a wetter nature than those in the north, and generally confined to mountainous regions. This was not the case in the northern hemisphere.

Similar to the European events North America also experienced phases of glaciation, but not as many as on the European side of the ocean. North American glaciation phases are divided into two major events. First, the Illinoian glacial, which created the greatest maximum advance, and secondly, the Wisconsinan, which was the final stage. Prior to the Illinoian glaciation there were other stages, which have been reassigned by researchers, and placed into a category labeled the Pre-Illinoian stage. Included in the Pre-Illinoian stages are the Pre-Nebraskan interglacial (1.6 million-800,000 years ago), the Nebraskan glacial (800,000-600,000 years ago), the Afton interglacial (600,000-480,000 years ago), the Kansan glacial (480,000-230,000 years ago), and the Yarmouthian interglacial (230,000-170,000 years ago).

Scientists have established that around two million years ago the temperature in what is now referred to as the United States of America to be somewhere near 56° F (13° C), just about 3° F (-16° C) warmer then our current day temperature. As time went along the North American continent experienced the Pre-Nebraskan stage, which was estimated to be a warmer version of normal glaciation. This phase began nearly 1.6 million years ago, and persisted up to about 800,000 years ago. This phase was also called the *late Blancan* or White Rock stage. The name was derived from the numerous faunas found in the state of Kansas during a site inspection tour near one of its rivers. The researchers pointed out that the condition of the fauna samples indicated that the climatic conditions were not extreme enough to force these animals to flee to a more southern location.

At about 800,000 years ago the glacial Nebraskan made its appearance, and had the distinction of being the oldest glaciation in North America. Deposits from this glacial have been discovered in Nebraska, Iowa, Kansas and Missouri. It ended around 600,000 years ago.

Following the Nebraskan stage was the Afton interglacial, which seems to be a very minor stage when compared to most glacial and interglacial stages. This phase was mainly placed around southern Iowa, and in some respects it is logged in as a drift along with the Kansan phase rather than an independent glacial stage. This period ranged from 600,000 to 480,000 years ago, and it was considered a warm phase.

The Kansan glacial event came next at around 480,000-230,000 years ago. Deposits from this glacial seem to be more obvious in southern Iowa, which connects to the Afton stage then in other areas; even though, deposits of this phase can be found in Kansas. The Kansan glacial has been described as extensive, however fauna in and around its pathway seem to be diverse, and plentiful. There were also signs that forests in Indiana were full and healthy, which is evidence of moisture. Also discovered, during this phase, was an ash bed residue in the Midwest thought to be the result of volcanic activity produced by the western cordilleras.

The Yarmouthian interglacial followed the Kansan stage at nearly 230,000 years ago, and this phase has much controversy associated with its credibility as an actual phase. It seems that there are numerous questions about the volcanic activity associated with the time of the phase. Some scientists think that prior volcanic activity should have been included into the time frame for this phase in order to present accurate facts. Perhaps this is one reason for this phase to have been included into the category of Pre-Illinoian stages. Nonetheless, most scholars seem to agree that this phase ended at about 170,000 years ago.

Toward the end of the interglacial Yarmouthian, temperatures dropped to below 0° F (-17° C) at a very rapid rate. Within about 10,000 years the temperature reached 26° F (-3° C), which is the approximate average temperature of a normal northern Illinois winter. Scientists are still seeking answers for the sudden rapid drop in temperature, speculating the cause might have been created by a change in the tilt of the earth or maybe even a variation in the earth's natural orbit. The temperatures remained low causing snow storms to occur, and not having the time to melt away it continued to compact the snow into layers of heavy ice. As this cycle persisted over the years massive glaciers were formed, some estimated to be three times higher, or more, than the Empire State Building in New York City. The excessive weight of the glacier caused it to move under geological ramifications.

Our land surfaces on planet earth constantly float on top of an ever moving soft mantle called the, *Asthenosphere.* Thus, when a massive amount of weight is forced down upon a land surface the areas below the glacier sinks down producing rising of the ground in other areas. This action allows for the glacier then to move in a particular direction. The amount of weight has a determining effect on the direction in which the glacier will travel. This is much the same as when a human foot steps into soft mud. The foot will sink down displacing the mud area, while causing ridges to develop around the edge of the imprint. In some cases the slippery mud can cause the foot to slip toward a certain direction. This is very similar to what happens when a huge ice pack bears down on land floating on top of the soft underlying mantle. Because of the deformation of the earth's crust, movement can be in any direction. As one example of directional variation of glaciers, it has been determined that the glacier, which covered a large portion of Illinois, came into the area moving from a northeastern to southwestern direction. Proof of this came from markings on stone located in a stone quarry near Champaign, Illinois. Conversely, the markings in stone located in Central Park, in New York City, showed that a glacier once located there, moved from northwest to southeast. These examples also proved that the glaciers were not one gigantic massive ice sheet; but instead they were individual ice packs, which moved separately. This information nullifies any assumptions that the glacier simply slid southward into northern parts of the United States from Canada because of its size, as believed by some individuals. In fact, during the Pre-Illinoian phases, glaciers moved into the Illinois area from both east and west. Some scientists have calculated that these glaciers moved at a rate of about two feet (0.061 m) per day. Perhaps this was a great rate of speed for such an enormous object.

The glacial Illinoian was the first, and most devastating of the North American glaciation periods. It advanced further south than any of the other glaciers.

This glacial period commenced at around 170,000 years ago, and ended somewhere near 120,000 years ago. The farthest point south of the advancement was in the state of Illinois. Approximately 85 percent of Illinois was covered with a glacial residue (See Fig. 1). Scientists have established that the Illinoian started at the North Pole, and built its way southward over tens of thousands of years allowing the thick layers of snow and ice to form itself into a colossal glacier. The constant build-up of ice caused water from the oceans to be drawn-up into the growing glaciers, and consequently created a lowering of the sea levels around the globe to be near 300-400 feet (120 m) lower than levels of today. It should be noted, sea levels have varied from higher to lower each time one of the events occurred. This was a normal part of the glaciation process, and what we are experiencing today.

Scientific studies have learned that some glaciers in Illinois were nearly 2,000 feet (610 m) thick in certain areas. In others, the ice thickness was only around 700 feet (213 m) thick. These massive ice structures totally rearranged the lay of the land. They leveled hills, and filled valleys. They carried gravel and boulders, some from thousands of miles away, and deposited them at the end of their advancement or dropped them during the recession stages. Scientists refer to these boulders as an *erratic* stone, a stone which should not be in a particular location. The material accumulated, and carried along inside of the glacier eventually became deposited at the leading edge of the glacier once it had stopped advancing. The conglomeration of sediment and boulders is called a *moraine*, and it is used to plot where the glacier finally stopped its advancement, and it also allows the researchers to identify the areas from where the erratic stones had been brought. This helps researchers to plot the direction, and overall distance the glacier had traveled.

During an event of one of the glacials, which moved into Illinois, the Mississippi River was relocated from approximately the middle of the state, to where we now know it to be. An advancing glacier formed an ice-dam near the old river location, which resulted in a large lake to be created. The build-up of the lake caused it to overflow into a new area about eighty miles west where the river flows today. The force of water ultimately carved out the earthen crust necessary to allow the great river to form and flow normally all these thousands of years. It is not unusual for large rivers to change locations in the course of historical events. The grand Nile River in Egypt, as one example, once stood at the feet of the Sphinx, which is twelve miles west of where the river is now located.

Between the two major glacial maximums in North America, there occurred the interglacial Sangamonian. The interglacial followed the Illinoian glacial, and preceded the Wisconsinan glacial phase. This phase is placed at starting at about 120,000 years ago, and concluded roughly around 75,000 years ago. The Sangamonian has been correlated with the Eémian interglacial stage of Europe.

Although there are differences between the two stages, it is understood that the two phases occurred at around the same time.

The Sangamonian interglacial is thought to be the warmest interglacial on record. It is believed, by scientists that during this phase temperatures triggered a significant melting action of the northern polar ice cap. The huge melting action initiated sea levels to rise once again to levels much higher than previously experienced. Documentation by researchers revealed artifactual evidence of alligators as far north as the State of Missouri and Cypress trees growing as far north as Illinois, while spruce trees normally native to northern states, encompassed Illinois.

The final glacial Wisconsinan started forming in the northern polar region around 70,000 years ago, and began advancing southward until about 75,000 years ago when it finally became a fully recognized glacial period. This time period of the Wisconsinan glacial is noted as the *Early Wisconsinan* (75,000-53,000 BP), followed by the *Middle Wisconsinan* (53,000-23,000 BP), and the last stage the *Late Wisconsinan* (23,000-10,000 BP). This North American glacial correlated with the European Weichselian-Würm glacials (See Fig. 2). The advancement of the Wisconsinan did not move as far south as the Illinoian advancement, and it is estimated that it advanced to near the 45-degree north latitude boundary. Ice covered northern Washington State, over to northern parts of Montana, extending into the Upper Midwest regions, and continuing over to just north of the Ohio River, and on into the New England portion of the United States. This phase of glacial activity, as with the Illinoian phase, managed to modify the landscape of the lower forty-eight states. A number of new rivers were created by the glacial meltwater flow. The Mississippi River, as previously discussed, was one of these newly created rivers. The action also reformed, and shaped the Ohio River from what was once the Teays River. One other well known river, the Niagara River was affected by the glacial events, which underwent a diversion into different channels caused by damming of the existing river flow. The directional change produced the, now famous, *Niagara Waterfalls* of upstate New York. As a side note, there are a total of three waterfalls located on the border of Canada and the United States, which make up the Niagara Waterfalls Honeymoon location.

Lakes are also a result of the meltwater action from the glaciation stage. All of the now famous Great Lakes are the product of the Wisconsinan melting phases. They formed from pooling waters trapped in rock basins fashioned by scouring action of the moving glacier. The small stone fragments being carried by the glacier polished the bedrock, which created erosion and deepened the rock-basin locations. This glacier's meltwaters, and its movements are also responsible for the many lakes in the State of Minnesota. The State's motto is, *Land of 10,000 Lakes.* All of the lakes created by continued meltwaters eventually overflowed their banks, and massive flooding became the end result. One significant flood caused by these meltwaters is the *Kankakee Torrent,* which is dated at around 15,000 years ago. The Kankakee River today begins in the State of Indiana, and flows westward into the State of Illinois ultimately joining with the Des Plaines River and forming the Illinois River, which flows into the Mississippi River. The city of Kankakee is located about fifty miles south of Chicago, Illinois, and sits on the banks of the Kankakee River. During the melting stages of receding glaciers Kankakee was just south of melting glaciers in the north around the Great Lakes, and west across the lake area in what today is the State of Michigan. For a short period of time the moraines from the receding Wisconsinan glacier blocked the flow of melting waters which formed into vast lakes. Quickly, due to great amounts of incoming water, the moraines were broken down, and water rushed south towards the Kankakee River valley. Many scientists believe the Kankakee Torrent to be one of the greatest floods during the Pleistocene Epoch, causing significant effects to many noted landmarks today. The flood impact affected areas as far south as southern Illinois, and as far as the northwest portion of Illinois carving out the Starved Rock State Park, while leaving "sand prairies" along its movement in the form of sand dunes. The sand prairies are large deposits of sand piled up at the end of the flood waters movement. The Kankakee River is unusual in the respect that it is known for 'hanging tributaries' a term used by geologists to describe water flowing into the Kankakee River from tributaries entering over waterfalls. One such tributary is Rock Creek, near the city of Kankakee, and is now part of the Kankakee River State Park. Rock Creek is one of the waterfall tributaries, which has a canyon cut into it by the waterfall forces. The area exhibits steep cliffs leading down, in one locality, to a very enjoyable swimming hole once carved out by forceful waters. The author is quite familiar with this area since Kankakee was once home, and the Rock Creek and State Park locations were sites for exploration, camping, and swimming.

The affected areas from the Kankakee Torrent did not end in Illinois. As a result of the massive rushing waters along many miles of the Kankakee River, which extend eastward into Indiana created momentous consequence for moving the now, Ohio River (once called the Teays River) location, further south into the Tennessee River Valley, where it remained to link up with the Mississippi River. Then, on the west side of Illinois it helped to move the Mississippi River further west from its position in the middle of the State, while having a deep cutting action on both the Illinois and Mississippi River channels.

One other area of concern is the western United States. As clearly presented, the glacials of North America did not seem to have any substantial bearing on the lower western states, at least not as great as the regions of the Midwest, and eastern portions of the United States. Still, there was some effect associated with the glaciation phases in terms of mass flooding.

One location, which experienced glaciation effects, was in the Sierra Nevada Mountains, which run along the eastern edge of the State of California. This region was subjected to three glacial maxima stages. First, was the *Tahoe* stage, which ended at about 70,000 years ago, secondly, was the *Tenaya* stage, which scientists and researchers know little about, and third, was the *Tioga* stage, which began about 30,000 years ago, and ended around 10,000 years ago along with the Wisconsinan glacial phase. Of course, there was glaciation in the Rocky Mountains, which extend out of Canada, and stretched southward the entire length of the United States ending near the northern border of Mexico.

Even though the American west did not incur extreme glaciation, it did suffer the effects from the various glacials and interglacial cycles. The effects were mainly in the form of winds, waters, and permafrost (permanently frozen subsoil) attributable to the many glacial events. Many times throughout the glacial events enough ice blockages of rivers, and drainage systems occurred to alter the normal course of some rivers – just as rivers of the Midwest, and the eastern section of the United States were reshaped, and rerouted. The sloping land demarcation of the glacials blocked normal flow from west to east. This forced the water from these locations to flow southward, creating new river systems. The Missouri River is but one example of this flow variation. The Missouri once flowed northeast; but due to ice blocking the normal drainage flow it was forced to change to its existing course. Today the Missouri begins flowing in Montana west to east, with a slight northerly slant until it reaches middle North Dakota — then bending south where it continues covering much of South Dakota. At this juncture the river turns southeast, and proceeds on to form the South Dakota and Nebraska border, then flowing south to form the borders of Iowa and Nebraska. As this explanation clearly indicates, the Missouri River still attempted to maintain its original easterly flow.

Any geological record of effects from the Illinoian glacial phase, across the Great Plains, does not exist. Any tills identified thus far cannot be connected with the Illinoian stage with any certainty. Any evidence once produced by the glacier probably would have been covered over by the advancing and receding Wisconsinan glacier. Then again, this would most certainly have occurred in the northern part of the country near Montana, Washington, North Dakota, and other northern locations since neither of the glacials advanced very far south into the Great Pains area.

Another ramification of the glacial period on the Great Plains and far western states is major flooding caused by glacial meltwaters, and rising sea levels. Each had a profound effect on the landscapes of the American west. Previously we learned of ice blockage causing rivers to overflow, and change the directions of ancient rivers during the recession phase of the glacial Wisconsinan. Another important phase of landscape change came from huge lakes, such as Lake Bonneville, which was a late Pleistocene lake located in the States of Nevada and western Utah. In size, it is estimated to have been around 22,000 sq. miles (58,000 km^2). About 15,000 years ago something caused this large lake to overflow its holding-basin, and expel massive volumes of water northward into the State of Idaho. This massive flooding had a great effect on the present day form of the Snake River. It also left behind, in Utah, two modern day remnants, the Great Salt Lake, and the famous Bonneville Salt Flats. When the overflow dried up due to warmer developing temperatures the Salt Flat was created, while at about the same time water filled a shallow lake basin forming the Great Salt Lake.

Death Valley is another famous location, which was once a giant lake. Geologists point to around 16 million years ago as the time when the Farallon Plate under the Pacific Ocean, began a moving action which would force itself below the North American Plate causing an upwelling of mountains and volcanoes creating a basin around 2 to 3 million years ago. Lake Manly nearby, was a large lake listed as 80 miles (128 km) long with a depth of 600 feet (130 km), and its main function was filling the Death Valley basin with water during each glacial cycle from about 240,000 to 10,000 years ago. After recession of the final glacial activity, approximately 12,000 years ago, water was blocked by the Sierra Nevada mountain range from flowing into the valley area. Thus, producing Death Valley as we know it to be today.

Scientists working in many fields today are still questioning the cause, or causes, for the end of the glacial period. Some geologists point to earthquakes as the main factor for producing an end to glaciation. As mentioned earlier, the massive weight from huge ice packs bearing down on the earth's crust has a deforming effect on land surfaces. So too does the excessive weight have a distorting effect on the entire globe. For example, if a finger were pushed into an inflated balloon it would produce an indentation of the surface. When the finger is removed, the balloon would return to its natural round shape. This shape recovery, in effect, is what the globe underwent in order to reshape itself from the heavy pressure caused by the gigantic ice sheets, which once developed on surface areas. The release of pressure produced reactions to occur with the earth plates and soft mantle, which flows beneath the land crust sections. It is believed by some scientists that the earth is still trying to reshape itself from the last glacial periods. Some geologists attribute the ending of glaciation, and natural global recovery of the earth's shape to earthquakes occurring in many global locations, including Canada.

The decreasing pressure on the layers of the earth not only can cause earthquakes, but volcanic development will also occur. Melting cold water from the glaciers will sink deep to the ocean's floor, especially when an immense amount of this water is expelled in a short period of time — forcing it downward as it attempts to expand outward. The cold water, which contains sediment is drawn or pushed into the oceanic plates, and then forced deeper into the soft hot mantle layer. The location where this action takes place is called *subduction zones* and this is where, in laymen's terms, the exterior elements of the earth are reclaimed by the earth's interior subsurface layers. The salvaging procedure produces magma by adding water into the hot mantle layer. This type of volcanization is referred to as *convergent margins,* and it is capable of setting tsunamis, landslides, and volcanic eruptions into progression.

Divergent margins are yet another type of volcanism, and usually occur underwater. During the divergent margins process the crust is pulled apart causing rock within the mantle to melt. The melting portion of the process is magma, which pushes up to form basalt rock. The process is much less horrendous than the more visible seismic volcanic eruptions seen on our television screens. Even though, geologists state that the divergent type of volcanism is the one most common, and it is responsible for the majority of magmatic eruptions.

One cause, which might be a factor for the end of the last glaciation period could be the appearance of CO_2 (carbon dioxide) gas in the atmosphere. As we have observed the last glacial period, along with all the others, was very unstable with constant advancements, and recessions of glaciers accompanied by climatic warming, and cold phases. With all of this constant activity the earth has had numerous opportunities, and an immeasurable amount of time to allow for exterior components of crust material to be forced down into the hot mantel layer for a reclamation of the material, and then for a releasing action of the material to be drawn up into the atmospheric layers of the planet. The reissuing process of the elements could have been by means of either the convergent or divergent types of magmatic volcanism.

Crust material being drawn into the mantle layer contained carbon. The material moved through a geothermal gradient, actually cooking the material, and returned it back to the surface in the form of lava through volcanic eruptions and lava flows from a slow exuding of basalt lava from ridge-cracks on the ocean floor. Eruptions, of all types, include the process of degassing. Degassing is applied to describe the release of carbon dioxide (CO_2) into the atmosphere during a volcanic eruption. The CO_2 gas is formed during the dissolving of carbon being processed by magma, resulting in instability. This instability creates pressure of the liquid, resulting in it being forced out of the fluid into the atmosphere. It is well understood, in scientific circles, that large amounts of CO_2 will have a warming effect on our planet, a condition, which our planet is now currently experiencing with the excessive use of burning fossil fuels. As more and more CO_2 is pumped into the atmosphere, the planet forms what is called the 'Green House Effect'. The condition traps heat in our thin layers of atmosphere, and causes massive warming. It is this type of climatic warming, which might have sparked the many recessions during the last glacial period. It is a strong possibility volcanic activity was not only present and active toward the end of the last glacial phase, but magnified many times by the break-up and melting action of the existing glaciers. In one sense we could ask — which came first, the chicken or the egg? In this case we must ask — which came first, the earthquakes or seismic volcanic activity? Based on a personal observation, it seems quite normal that earthquakes were continuous events combined with the typical functioning of the Lithosphere and Asthenosphere layers of earth. It is most probable earthquakes were a routine occurrence since the early formation of our globe, and they continue to this very time. Since scientists have identified the layers of our planet, they have calculated how these layers interact with each other and how this interaction affects day to day happenings in our observable world. Therefore, it would be quite understandable to believe the earthquakes were the original factors to be accountable for the extended warming activity. The movement of these earth layers have never stopped. It appears quite clear that the volcanic phases were a result of interaction between the exterior materials of the world, and the continuous natural movements of the sublayer-particles, introduced when sediment and cold water were forced down into the sublayer (soft hot mantle) of the earth.

Should this observation be considered legitimate, it would then indicate normal volcanic action was present prior to the major meltdown of the last glacial period. The volcanic eruptions put CO_2 into the atmosphere causing a certain amount of climatic warming, which affected the ice sheets to gradually begin to melt. As these ice sheets melted faster, more cold water and sediment along with boulders were washed into the ocean. These phenomena could have occurred on both coastal areas of North America at the same time, multiplying the melting performance of the glaciers many times. As this meltwater action continued, and increased more carbon dioxide gas was placed back into the atmosphere at a faster rate, which ultimately produced more exterior material, and cold water to be forced down into this frenzied geological cycle.

The perpetual accelerated cycle would also have been responsible for the colder Atlantic sea temperatures, dating to around 11,500 years ago at the start of the Younger Dryas glacial period in Europe. The colder water temperatures have been suspected of being one source for the start of the Younger Dryas phase. This observation may confirm that theory.

If such a rapid meltdown of the glacial ice sheets was the result of extensive earthquake, and volcanic activity it most certainly would have developed over many years. Of course, the process would have been accelerated, at least by double, with volcanic eruptions happening on both sides of the North American continent at the very same time. Perhaps Graham Hancock is correct in his statement (at the start of this chapter), when he pointed to 17,000 years ago when the volcanoes became a factor in the glacial meltdown of the last glacial period.

Given the harsh climatic conditions of glaciation, and the tremendous ramifications resulting from the various stages (just as those times in Europe), the majority of the landscape was quite capable of supporting life. We see this proof in the form of fauna remains after glacials and interglacials had passed. Would it not be possible for humans to have survived the same forces, and conditions as those of the animal kingdom during those tumultuous times? Hancock believes so, since he pondered the day-to-day lives of the unnamed people living in North America, as stated in his quote at the beginning of this Chapter.

North American glaciation stages

▪ Represents maximum advance of galaciation during the Wisconsinian stage
▨ Represents maximum advance of glaciation during the Illinoian stage

Figure provided by Terrance F. Johnson, 2013

Fig. 1

Final glacial advancement of the Glacial periods of the Pleistocene Epoch (2.5 million years-11,500 B.C.)
Last advancement included the Weichselian and Würm stages of Europe, the Devensian of Great Britain the Midlandian glaciation of Ireland, and the Wisconsinian glaciation of North America.

 Represents glacial coverage during the last world glacial advancement.

Figure 3 Provided by Terrance F. Johnson, 2013

Fig. 2

When he examines the huge heap of shells along the shores of the numerous arms of the Baltic sea, composed of individuals of large size, select and full-grown, of several species, commingled with rude implements of stone and bone, with also the bones of the codfish, and compares them with the diminutive specimens he is able to procure from the same waters now, it is an inference most reasonable, that when these heaps were piled up around the miserable huts of the ancient fishermen, the waters of the Baltic were not so fresh as now. The presence of the bones of codfish gives some evidence of skill in navigation, for they must be caught in the open sea.
~ ~ *A. J. Conant*
~ ~ *Foot-Prints of Vanished Races*

Chapter 3

Maritime Knowledge of the Ancients

As the quotation above illustrates, early man had used the sea as a source to supplement his food supply. Artifactual evidence substantiates the fact that early man, as believed by many, was not landlocked, and ignorant of methods of navigation, either by land or on the sea. Man, by nature, is an inquisitive creature capable of learning by a number of different methods. Through man's developed brain functions he was able to learn by simply watching, and associating movements, and developing concepts to meet his physical and mental needs. It might be that the old saying, "Where there is a will, there is a way" is most accurate when it is related to the needs, and wants of mankind.

As one example to support the statement above, comes from the book *The Earliest Ships,* by Conway Maritime Press, and edited by *Robert Gardiner.* This book brings to light that there is every indication boats were being used in northern Europe around 8000 BC to follow, and hunt the reindeer for food and clothing. It seems while following the herd, ancient man recognized that the reindeer could swim, and they would lose their quarry to water. By using his developed brain he recognized logs, like other debris, floated in water, and ultimately he was able to adapt these instruments into a water going apparatus so he could follow his prey even across the water. Evidence of this practice was scratched into stone by early hunters following reindeer herds into Norway at around 8000 BC as the glaciers receded north. These stone carvings also showed the boat design as resembling the reindeer, which they were chasing. These oldest forms of boat images depicted that they designed the bow of the boats to look like a head of a reindeer, obviously to camouflage their craft to blend in, and slay their intended target. The crafty hunters were very precise in their camouflage depiction of their prey, by adding a small white stub tail to the stern of the craft in order to complete the illusion of another reindeer.

Boat building in Europe was much earlier than 8000 BC as expressed in the same book, *The Earliest Ships.* The editor explained that hunters would fish from the banks of a river or lake using their hands to grab or flip the fish out of the water, and onto the shore. From archaeological sites fish hooks, harpoon tips, and fishing spears made of bone were unearthed. In addition, on one spear tip was found the pattern of a net embedded so clearly that it showed how fish could be caught in the net. The artifactual findings were dated to be around 16,000 BC. It was clear from the findings that some form of water-craft vessel was placed into service by ancient man prior to the end of the last glacial maximum period. Because the water-craft were built using perishable materials, artifacts of these objects cannot be available for researchers to find at the ancient sites. Logically it could be suspected that if ancient hunters used water-craft vessels, it would be natural for them to have used these floating objects for exploration, and travel. Such activities would surely have produced more sophisticated river boats, and possibly sea worthy vessels.

It probably is clear that placing a carved head of some creature on the prow (bow) of the boat or ship is a very ancient tradition; and that pronounced visual *figurehead* placed on the bow is possibly the result of ancient German reindeer hunters from before the end of the last glacial maximum — over 10,000 years ago. This traditional symbol was not only adopted by the later Viking seamen, but also by almost every seafaring nation sending ships out to sea. There were variations involved with figureheads for example, the Egyptians painted eyes on the prow so they could see their way across the water while turning the figurehead facing inwards. Later the Spanish ships used religious symbols to decorate their prows, and many British ships placed full body figures or heads of women on the prows of their ships during the 1700s.

According to archaeology, it appears that boat building did not develop as quickly in the southern to middle portion of Germany as it did in the northern areas. This observation is made because of lack of artifactual evidence to support a theory, which would confirm advanced methods of construction. What has been found by researchers are variations of boat building, which exhibited neither German nor Norse characteristics. Some experts have termed these examples as *Celtic* style since the planks of the boat were joined edge-to-edge by clenched iron nails. Most of these plank types of boats are dated to the time of the Roman occupation of Europe.

One-paradox which science and archaeology encounters is simply a lack of history of the Europeans prior to the Roman invasion. The Romans seem to be the only historians of the tribes, and of the knowledge of the people in the area prior to their arrival. Further, it would be safe to conclude that the Roman observations might have been biased, not to mention incomplete. At least through maritime archaeologists we have an opportunity to test any Roman comment, and to piece together the sea-going exploits of the Europeans as a whole. As stated in my first book, in the deep prehistory of Europe no countries existed; boundary lines were determined by tribes or confederacies or by opposing armies. There was a great amount of mixing of the European peoples. Thus, transfer of information surely did ensue as exhibited by boat building methods, and designs.

Most maritime archaeologists probably accept the fact that boats began as a log dugout type canoe design. These dugouts were probably produced to carry one or two people, and they were intended to be used on rivers, streams, ponds or even small lakes. The main functions for these types of craft were to chase their quarry or to fish from. They were simple, but functional. This type of small water-craft was also used in the Americas especially by the native indigenous peoples of North America. However, there are challenges to the theory about log boats being used in Europe because trees were not in abundance during the glacial period or during its end.

With an absence of trees for building primitive boats in the north, there were many tribes located south of there who probably had access to timber, and the ability to create some form of water-craft for varying purposes. More than likely, the first water-craft to appear was the crude raft consisting of logs, and tree branches bound together with vines or scraps of material from animal hides. In some areas of the world bamboo or local reeds were used, bundled together, and lashed with animal skin or gut material from domesticated animals or in some cases manufactured cord from area grass species.

The northern Germanic tribes were not alone in their ability, and desire to use and create some type of floating platform, in water, which they could control and use for a number of different needs. Although not abundant with artifactual evidence, the Frankish tribes in the southern lands were noted for their seafaring exploits. The Bructeri, and Usipi were two independent tribes who became part of the Frankish confederacy later in the third century. However, they did have an interest in water-craft long before that period. The Canninefates, Batavi, and the Frisian were also active tribes, at that time, who also attempted to build, and sail various types of boats. The Frisians were a more northern people who lived west of the Chauci tribe in northern Germany, and eventually would become the Dutch people of Holland. The Bructeri, and Usipi were more middle German tribes, and would have probably had access to timber before the northern tribes as the glaciers melted, and climatic conditions changed allowing for the growth of trees in the north. Evidence of this currently does not exist since most material of that time has long become mulch or decay. The only records of the Frankish naval exploits comes from a report by the Romans, who wrote of a group of Bructeri (once a Germanic tribe) attacking a sea expedition along the North Sea coast of Germany in 12 BC led by Drusus, stepson of Emperor Augustus, and father of future Roman Emperor, Claudius. It is quite evident the ancient Bructeri tribe must have been very advanced in boat building skills to be able to attack a Roman squadron of ships both well armed, and well manned. The tribe lost that battle, but it does not dampen the fact that the Bructeri did have the technology, and skills necessary to produce hulks of ample condition to be used as a platform from which to do battle with the renowned Roman forces. This knowledge or design of the craft did not appear overnight. These skills were learned over a long period of trial and error preceding 12 BC. Furthermore, it is probably safe to conclude that if one ancient tribe of people was proficient at naval activities, then most likely all the other tribes were as well. These examples infer a time period much farther back into prehistory than people might care to believe. Most people point to the Vikings as the masters of the seas, since it seems to be where most historians and movie producers tend to pin-point the ancient history of naval awareness. John Haywood pointed out this misconception in his book *Dark Age Naval Power* when he wrote:

> Though the importance of Viking seafaring in European history is undeniable, this concentration on Viking activities has resulted in a distorted view of European maritime history, with the Vikings occupying a far too prominent position: they were in fact only the last in a long line of barbarian pirates to harass western Europe.[1]

Another point of clarification about a lack of trees in northern Europe comes from Eske Willerslev, a Professor at the Center for GeoGenetics, at the University of Copenhagen. The Professor believes the historical views about the trees of northern Europe, and Scandinavia in particular, should be modernized. Current perception about trees in northern Europe, specifically Pine and Oak trees is that they were destroyed by the many glacial stages in that portion of Europe, and today there are no Pine and Oak trees in northern Europe especially in Denmark, who claim the Beech as their national tree. However, there are currently Oak trees with bracket fungus in Danish National Forests, which came about after the last glacial. Prior to the end of the glacial impact Professor Willerslev has determined that some species of conifers (pine trees), and some species of spruce (one of 30 + species of conifers) might have survived in ice free pockets of the glacial areas, and from there propagated normally as the glaciers regressed. If his observation is correct that would mean ancient civilizations would have had wood to build water-vessels. The Oak tree is not mentioned by the Professor, so it is probably safe to believe that Oak trees were wiped out by the last glacial maximum, estimated to be around 22,000 years ago.

A. J. Conant, author of *Foot-Prints of Vanished Races* seems to confirm the loss of the pine and oak trees of northern Europe, and adds a confirmation that early man did live in those locations of Europe during that time period. Conant wrote:

> When the peat-bogs of this same country are examined, they present a record reaching far back of the historic period. These depressions in the natural surface of the earth-sometimes to the depth of thirty feet, disclose three distinct periods of arborescent vegetation. At the bottom are the stately trunks of the pine trees; above these the oak, which once grew upon the sides of the pits, and when their full maturity was reached, fell inward. The oak was succeeded by the beech and birch which now flourish-and have flourished during all the period of history-throughout the land. The pine and oak have never been known during the historic period in the native forests of Denmark. In these bogs, beneath the layers of pine, are found the rude implements of the ancient inhabitants. Man lived, then, when the pine forests were in their glory, and at that time also piled up the shell heaps along the shore; for in these are found in great abundance the bones of a bird whose food is derived from the pine.[2]

The observation, by Conant, clearly states ancient man not only lived in Jutland, now Denmark, in prehistoric times, but that he also fished in deep waters — for shell fish, inferring a knowledge of seamanship, and navigation over 20,000 years ago. It must also be surmised that these ancient people had access to wood in order to build sea craft for their fishing expeditions. In order for them to catch crustaceans it would have been necessary to fish in deep waters of the Baltic Sea. Some forms of clams and crabs could have been procured from the shorelines, but shrimp, scallops, mussels, and many other types of mollusks must be acquired from the sea. We have been informed that ancient hunters were constructing boats around 8000 BC to hunt reindeer across the waters, but it might now appear that early prehistoric man was using boats much earlier for fishing expeditions. Since artifactual evidence indicates that man lived during the time of the pine and oak trees of Jutland, it might indicate prehistoric man could build log dugout canoes, rafts, and possibly one other type of sea going vessel — that of a wood framed boat, which some variations are still in use today. It has been determined by some archaeologists that wood-frame, skin covered boats did not make an appearance until trees had once again developed in northern Europe. Now from the information contained in the peat-bogs of Denmark, it just might be that wood-frame craft could have existed far earlier in prehistoric times. This concept is not so far out of line when we consider that early man had thousands of years to develop, and to design such a craft to be seaworthy and functional to support his purposes. Conant, also comments on the presence of man in Europe when he wrote:

> Now it is considered certain by the best informed, that man existed in Europe at the commencement of the quaternary period.[3]

From Conant's observation above, possibly modern man had hundreds of thousands of years to expand on Naval engineering since the Quaternary spans from 2.5 million years ago. Therefore, why should we believe man would have been incapable of designing, and building a wood-framed-skin-covered sea vessel? This production method would require knowledge of connecting two pieces of wood together, and locking them into position for a strong, consistent hold. Skill required to accomplish this feat could have been easily adapted from working with animal bones or antlers. In fact, it is quite a strong possibility that those types of materials, from hunted animals were incorporated as framing stock for these skin-clad sea craft.

It seems the concept that hollowed out tree logs could not be used since trees were not in existence until after the glacial period ended, may not be accurate. From the peat-bog evidence, early man had many trees to use, and probably the skills to produce a water craft made from a hollowed out tree log. These type of crafts could have been used long before the last glacial maximum began. As far as the question of — did early men have the ability to use stone implements to hollow out logs or to gouge holes, and make grooves necessary to insert a pointed bone for holding power— one would only need to examine stone tools used by early man for hunting, and animal skin modification for clothing. After all there are stones much harder than wood, and these stones could have been sharpened by a flaking method used to produce spear, and arrow head points. Furthermore, if pine or spruce were the chosen material selected for the dugout or for the frame of a skin-clad boat, these wood species are of a soft, porous nature in comparison to oak, maple, birch or other hardwoods. The workability of these materials would have been much easier to carve. No evidence has so far been found of these type of craft being produced during such a deep prehistoric time, but perhaps in some northern European bog in the future, one of these crafts may be unearthed — since we now know that early man fished for a living. It might also be that archaeologists will uncover, in that peat-bog time span, artifacts of harpoons, fish-hooks, scraping blades of stone and bone, along with well-worked antler tools. Perhaps also, they will find the smoothly worked wood for hunting bows, arrows, spears, even maybe bones used for needles to make clothing, and skins for the wood/bone frames for their fishing boats. At present, marine archaeologist have identified the oldest log dugout at 6300 BC, and found in the Netherlands at Pesse. By the fifth millennium BC dugouts were about 32 feet (10 m) long, and were made with a separate board in the stern providing a watertight joint between two pieces of wood.

> *I went down on the sea in a ship of one hundred and fifty cubits long and forty cubits wide, with one hundred and fifty sailors of the best of Egypt who had seen heaven and earth, and whose hearts were stronger than lions.*
> ~ ~ *Derived from Ancient Egyptian texts*
> ~ ~ *The Shipwrecked Sailor, ca. 2200 BCE*

The passage above is not about a fictional Sinbad type sailor setting off on an adventure, and somehow becoming marooned on an island filled with dangers and extrication. Instead it is the oldest story, on record, about a shipwrecked sailor from ancient Egypt's maritime period. The story is dated at 2200 BCE, but the story took place prior to that time — as to exactly when is not known. What we can understand is that the ship described is 221feet long (67 m) by 59 feet wide (18 m), and that it was manned by a crew of 150 sailors, which was quite a large and exceptional water vessel for that time in ancient history. Although the ship's proportion is not a surprise to marine archaeologists, and scholars since many today point to Egypt as perhaps the leader of naval accomplishments. Lionel Casson a noted researcher, agreed with the premise of Egypt being an advanced seafaring nation in early antiquity when he expressed quite clearly in his book, *The Ancient Mariners*:

> Yet, in the light of what follows... , it seems most likely that the first true sea voyages were made by Egyptians who worked northward along the coasts of Palestine and Syria or southward down the Red Sea, and by Mesopotamians and Indians, who sailed between the Persian Gulf and the northwestern coast of India.[4]

Another example of advanced naval capabilities by Egyptians is Pharaoh Sahure, in 2450 BC, when he assembled a fleet of transport ships to move his entire army to the Levantine coast. Casson further cites an older example still, which gives evidence of Egypt's ancient naval past:

> But the words of his scribe remove all doubt; some three thousand years before the birth of Christ a fleet of forty vessels slipped their

moorings, sailed out of a Phoenician harbor, and shaped a course for Egypt to bring there a shipment of Lebanese cedar.[5]

The Egyptians must have used, and sailed their ships to Phoenicia for cedar trees long before 3000 BC when the large shipment of cedar trees was sent out from the Phoenician port. Cedar has been found in tombs of pharaohs in the form of sawdust, which probably was used for burning offerings to ensure a happy afterlife. Also, cedar resin was used in the mummifying process of the pharaohs, and their family members. Furthermore, Lebanon cedar was used for Egyptian ship and Nile river boat building material.

Cedar is a member of the evergreen family of *Pinaceae* (a coniferous). The Cedars of Lebanon were derived from the mountain range at Sannine, Barrouk, which was once almost completely covered with the large cedar trees. Cedar was selected as a ship building material because cedar's *lignin* (the wood's natural binding agent) is an organic polymer, which fills the cell wall space, and strengthens the wood; moreover the polymer acts as a natural preservative with strong antifungal, and bacterial properties. Cedar wood, in general, naturally resists humidity, insects, and extreme temperatures; and as a result resists rotting. The Egyptians must surely have understood the benefits of the chemical properties of cedar wood since they used it to mummify their dead. Thus, the qualities and value of cedar trees from Lebanon must have been known, and understood for sometime prior to such a large order being placed. It was used as far back as the Old Kingdom in pre-Dynastic graves, and at least as far back as the fourth millennium BC. So when Khufu (Cheops in Greek) built the largest pyramid at Giza, Egyptians were at that time using cedar from Lebanon. This order might also have confirmed that Egyptians had used cedar in the past for boat building, and were possibly continuing their seafaring expeditions along with their other established uses for cedar.

Cedar for Egyptian ships probably originated from Nile river boats. Most scholars hold to the belief that the first river boats used on the Nile River were reed boats made from local papyrus reeds. The boats were made-up of bundles of papyrus reeds bound together by some form of rope. Most often these type of boats were used by fishermen; they were propelled, and steered using a long pole, which was pushed off from the river bottom. Later, as determined by archaeologists and others, the Egyptians developed wooden boats, possibly made of cedar wood, to use when moving megaliths down the Nile River from the city of Aswan. These boats were sturdy, and durable for moving giant obelisks, many weighing approximately 300 tons (3000 kg) or more. One possible extreme example of the weight these river boats had to carry is expressed by the obelisk now standing in St. Peter's square at the Vatican in Italy. Caligula, then emperor of Rome, ordered the megalithic monument moved from its location in Egypt, to a new destination in Rome in AD 40. The obelisk is 130 feet (40 m) tall, and weighs almost 500 tons (453 kg). This megalith was moved from its quarry location near Aswan, in Upper Egypt, to its place in Lower Egypt by means of Egyptian wooden river boats. However, for the Romans to move the great stone from Egypt to Italy they employed a transport ship called a *leviathan,* which was specially built to haul this obelisk, and it was designed to carry 800 tons (727 kg) of lentils — producing a total carrying load of around 1,300 tons (907 kg).

The Egyptian wooden river boats were built much differently than sea going ships. The river craft were built with flat bottoms, no keel, and no rib structures. Because of a lack of a keel, the boats could not use a mast for a sail. These types of craft did not have to contend with sea like conditions of strong winds, and high waves. Their main function was for transport of goods, passengers, and megaliths up and down the Nile River.

In comparison to ancient German boats, and ships of northern Europe there are some strong similarities between the two countries. As we now know, cedar is a species of pine with numerous qualities to be very suitable for the construction of sea-crafts. Further pine, cedar, and many other types of trees do not grow in Egypt; yet the Egyptians had early ancient knowledge of cedar, and its various qualities. We might recall, Conant pointed out that ancient man resided in northern Europe at the time of the pine tree forests, which preceded oak stands of trees, and prehistoric man had knowledge of, and access to fish, and crustaceans from deep waters. This only means that ancient man could build crafts to carry him out into deep water where he could fish, and return safely to shore from where he began, signifying a competency of navigational skills. This example also implies, again from my first book, that ancient seafarers already possessing knowledge of pine trees for making seaworthy vessels, could have imparted this knowledge to a civilization of Egypt in deep antiquity — possibly prior to the final advancement of the Weichselian glaciation, or about 30,000 to 40,000 BC when the pine, and oak forests of northern Europe were still in full forestation. Gardiner, in *The Earliest Ships* points out that it was in the fifth millennium when ancient boatbuilders in northern Europe figured out how to place two pieces of wood together to form a watertight seal on the stern of a dugout type craft. He then clearly stated:

> ...boatbuilders were already capable of constructing watertight joints between two wooden parts, even though it has to be admitted that boatbuilding in Egypt was already much more advanced by this time.[6]

The early Anglo-Saxon ships became larger, resembling the beginning of the long ships made famous by the Vikings of the 9th century AD. Still at this building, and design level the craft was built without a keel, instead employing a bottom plank reinforced by a strengthening lath on its underside. This building procedure could not have supported a mast. Earlier models like the Sutton Hoo German Angle ship, and most early Norse ships, were built with light flexible hulls, which did not support the stress of a sail, and its rigging. These types of ships were more suited for rowing because they did not track well with their rounded bottoms, and were more suitable for shallow waters.

The same is almost true of the Egyptian initial attempts to build seaworthy ships. The early designs of sea ships were created from designs of their river boats, which did not include a keel. As with all sea-going vessels sails are required for long range expeditions for trade and military endeavors, and in order to use sails a ship must have a mast to support the use of a sail. Thus, to support the mast and sail, a keel is necessary. The Egyptians did eventually develop the appropriate design structure for a sailing vessel very early, deep in their prehistory. This is evident from a picture of a ship on an Egyptian vase, dating to 3500 BC. This predates the beginning of Egypt's Dynastic period of 3100 BC when kings/pharaohs began to rule Egypt. This date, according to many Egyptologists, would have been prior to the building of the pyramids at Giza. What is even more astonishing is there is evidence of Egypt using a square sail on ships earlier than 2600 BC. Gardiner in *Conway's History of the Ship* explained:

> By 2600 B.C. the Egyptians were building big vessels and fitting them with a sizable spread of canvas, a single square sail that — and this is a feature typically Egyptian—was spread by two spars, a boom along the foot as well as a yard along the head. The boom was heavy, on larger ships heavy enough to support the weight of a man, and hence required a line of lifts to hold it up; they run from points all along the boom to the top of the mast.[7]

The date of 2600 BC is about the time of the building of Khufu's Great Pyramid, dated by Egyptologists at around 2650 BC. Further, we also know the square sail was used exclusively by Viking long ships, which were developed from the German Saxon ships. Could there be a connection between the two cultures? Most definitely so. The ship designs are also strikingly similar with the upward curving prows and sterns (See Fig.1 at end of chapter).

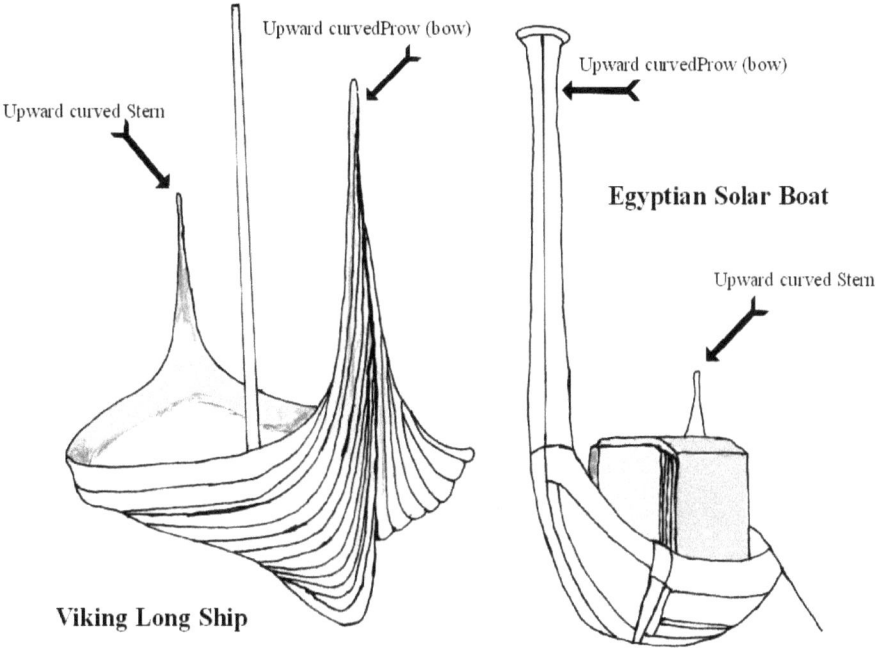

Figure provided by Terrance F. Johnson, 2014

Fig. 1

In the Mediterranean where states of any size had to depend on overseas sources for food and the only feasible long distance comunications were by water, sea power was paramount.
~ ~ *Lionel Casson, Author*
~ ~ *The Ancient Mariners*

Chapter 4

The Mediterranean Mystification

The Mediterranean Sea seems to hold the key to many mysteries of ancient man's prehistory. One special area of interest is the *Levant*, the one time cultural, and economic portion of the eastern Mediterranean Sea. The coastal areas within this well defined area were home to many well formed, and still growing civilizations. The quotation above explicates these civilizations depended on trade, and resources from other countries. The main question is however — who was the first to sail the Mediterranean, and to establish trading contacts, and alliances?

To answer the question above, we must first ask the question — how long has the Mediterranean Sea been in existence? We know that it has not always existed from the beginning of time. So the most recent information we have is that some scholars credit the Messinian Event (or, Messinian Salinity Crisis) with the formation of the Mediterranean Sea. This event occurred in the later stage of the Miocene Epoch, which is placed at around 5.96 to 5.33 million years ago. The last portion of the later stage of this event is labeled the Lago Mare event, meaning that it is this time when the Mediterranean Sea nearly dried up completely. A geological study of the sea has determined that about 5.96 million years ago, what is now known as the Strait of Gibraltar, closed off the Atlantic Ocean for the first time. This process is probably related to the formation of a glacial stage in progress. This action allowed the sea to partially dry up, but was periodically subjected to incoming ocean waters as the blocked strait was exposed to rising waters. Then at around 5.5 million years ago, the sea basin began to receive fresh water from inflowing rivers, which formed various lakes. One of these rivers was the Nile, flowing out of Africa, but today it flows into the Nile Delta, and was known in earlier times as the *River Styx*. During its entry into the Mediterranean Sea basin, the River Styx made a bend westward just after exiting Africa, and eventually flowed into low-lying areas creating lakes south of Greece, and continuing on west to drain into the Atlantic Ocean through the Pillars of Hercules (or Strait of Gibraltar). It was at the dry period when the basin became a rich, fertile valley populated with towns, and people. Just recently marine archaeologists have discovered ancient stone ruins on the bottom of the Mediterranean Sea, many in the form of cities complete with streets, and buildings with upper stories. It has been estimated that there are somewhere around 200 submerged ancient towns, which lie in the entire basin area of the Mediterranean. Such cities could have been possible since during this dry Lago Mare phase, the Mediterranean valley was positioned nearly 2 to 3 miles (3 to 5 km) below the world's ocean sea levels, and blocked off across the Strait of Gibraltar.

Further still, we are knowledgeable of what are referred to as cart-tracks on the island of Malta, which are not yet specifically defined, that goes on for miles, and run into the waters of the Mediterranean Sea disappearing beneath the water's surface. On the island of Malta are sites very ancient, and extremely well constructed displaying advanced technical megalithic knowledge. Also, let us not overlook the giant megaliths of Carnac in France, where once again the giant menhirs extend down into the waters of the Morbihan Gulf. There is clear affirmation for intelligent cultures residing in the Mediterranean basin for thousands of years before sea water once again came over the wall at Gibraltar and flooding the basin, some 5.33 million years ago. As a result of it's closed in condition the Mediterranean Sea has a higher salt content than other oceans of the world since it does not have a chance to blend, and mix with other fresh waters, which wash into the seas, such as, the Mississippi River into the Gulf of Mexico.

What people were living in the Mediterranean Sea basin during the Lago Mare phase are unknown. Some researchers, such as David Hatcher Childress, speculate that these people were the Egyptians of the pre-Dynastic period, which he refers to as the Osirian Civilization. It is this ancient civilization, which Childress credits with building megalithic structures, such as, the Sphinx or the Osirion at Abydos in Upper Egypt. If this is correct, then we must consider these people to be part of the Early Predynastic phase (there are four phases in all), which ranged from approximately 5500 to 4000 BCE. Just recently, Professor Robert Schoch, of Boston University, dated the Sphinx conservatively at about 5000 to 7000 BCE. The Osirion at Abydos (in Greek), Abdu in Egyptian, is considered to be much older. The one time underground chamber is thought to be more ancient than all of the Egyptian ruins. It is here, Egyptians believe the head of Osiris is buried. Osiris, god of the afterlife, the symbol for resurrection, god of Agriculture, aficionado of wine, who was murdered by Seth (Set Animal), his brother, over jealousy and greed, and then restored by Isis, his wife and sister, piece by piece. The site ruin at Abydos was built using large blocks of red granite, some weighing upwards of 100 tons (901 kg). On one red granite block there is inscribed with what has been named, "The Flower of Life," which is so precisely cut that it resembles modern day laser etching.

Osiris was one of the original nine gods who are believed to have ruled Egypt in deep antiquity. Some scholars believe Osiris was not Egyptian, but rather he was once a king of the lost continent of Atlantis. Egyptian mythology, on the other hand, states Osiris was born of the Earth and Sky who served as the first king of Egypt. Much like the white gods of Central and South America, Osiris taught civilization, agriculture, worship of the gods, and he set up laws to guide society. Having achieved all of that, he set off on a journey to help other, less fortunate civilizations. This leads to some speculation that perhaps, Osiris could have possibly been one of the white gods (or 'the white god') who came from the east, and landed on the shores of Mesoamerica. While Osiris was gone Isis, his wife/sister ruled on his behalf. However his brother Seth (Set), and brother-in-law of Isis, became disruptive and scheming, plotting to kill Osiris upon his return, and marry Isis taking the kingdom for himself. Upon the return of Osiris, Seth did trick Osiris into getting into a custom sized box, and then locking down the lid, trapping Osiris inside. The box then was covered with lead, and dropped into the sea ultimately washing up on shore at Byblos in Lebanon. There Seth retrieved the box, and hacked Osiris' body into fourteen pieces, scattering the fragments in all directions around the countryside. Isis, upon learning of this murder sought out the pieces of Osiris' body, and buried each piece in an undisclosed location. Egyptian myth explains these body part burials are the locations where temples to Osiris were built.

After the death of Osiris, his son Horus (a parallel to the Norse god Odin) sought out, and killed Seth to avenge his father, aided by the mighty god Thoth. Horus, in Egyptian mythology, appeared as the one-eyed hawk-headed god, and the last true god to rule Egypt. The total amount of time the nine original gods ruled is 13,900 years. Following Horus' rule, Thoth (son of Ptah, and half brother to Ra) ruled for 1,570 years. Thirty Demi gods reigned for 1,255 years after the gods (Path, Ra, Shu, Geb, Osiris, Isis, Seth, Horus, and Thoth). The *Followers of Horus* came last after two additional lines of kings. In total, the historian Manetho calculated the time to be about 25,000 years from Ra to Menes, the first dynastic Pharaoh. Author John Baldwin seems to concur with a more ancient Egypt than modern history's interpretation. Baldwin stated:

> Before the times of Menes, Egypt had a civilization which must have seemed old to those acquainted with it. This is apparent to all who have studied the antiquities of the country. Sir Gardner Wilkinson refers to "the great mathematical skill of the Egypians in the time of Menes," evinced by the change he made in the course of the Nile, and says; " It

may be inferred, from their great advancement in the arts and sciences at this early period, that many ages of civilization had preceded the accession of their first monarch." [1]

Perhaps Childress is correct in his theory that the one time Mediterranean people were, in deed, the Osirian Civilization. This might be supported by the stages of the predynastic period. Each time-line phase was determined by variations of cultures along the entire length of the Nile; and the Nile River is considered to be the longest river in the world.

In some respects this author concurs with much of the facts, and mythology of the Egyptians; however somehow there must be some deeper time, in Egypt's past, when the Giza pyramids were constructed. The mysterious symbols of a once great powerful civilization must have been built prior to much of the city dwellings, which now lay submerged under the waves of the Mediterranean Sea. Had the same people who built the famous pyramids, built the ancient cities of the Mediterranean basin, then the architecture and grandness surely would have reflected such creativity and skill. Although the megalithic greatness at Carnac, and Malta are not considered mutually exclusive when related to the megalithic construction of the Giza Pyramids. Based on the activity, and size of the stones there must have been a physical connection between the sites. The sites, as it appears, were constructed over time, in stages, by different groups with totally separate purposes in mind. At the Carnac site in France these large megaliths, some weighing more than 20 tons (181 kg), totaling 4,000, are dated to be 5,000 to 6,000 years old, by some archaeologists. However, recent studies indicated they are much older, and were positioned prior to the Gulf of Morbihan being filled up with sea water — starting some 5.33 million years ago. Many of these gigantic stones were larger than the stones used to build the Giza pyramids of Egypt. In his book *The Ancient Alien Question,* author and researcher *Philip Coppens* commented about the largest stone at Carnac:

> There is one standing stone that was 60 feet high, weighed in at 340 tons, and was moved over a distance of 4 miles to its present location. It should come as no surprise that this stone is no longer standing. But this stone does underline the knowledge and technology of this culture which erected stones on a scale not seen anywhere else.[2]

Coppens also brings to light that most archaeologists now believe there once existed, at least, 10,000 stones at Carnac. There are many explanations for the disappearances of these additional stones, one being vandalism. Fortunately, more were not destroyed before researchers could have the opportunity to study these mysterious rows of standing stones. Coppens does mention in his book, that during WW II the invading American forces almost destroyed these ancient megaliths because they thought the layout was a German defensive obstacle.

In comparison to Carnac, the island of Malta brings new awareness of megalithic inclination with a combination of many unexplained ruts running parallel to each other, a monolithic temple, and an elaborate multi-roomed cave system complete with acoustics, and a ventilation system, which was supposedly carved out by people using hammers, as stated by some archaeologists. Erich von Däniken, in his book *Signs of the Gods* describes the ancient wonders of Malta in great detail. In regard to the Monolithic temple of Hagar Qim, von Däniken wrote:

> There they lie, the gigantic monoliths. The millennia have passed over them. Have weathered and split them. When we look at the ruts, we think about how much rain has poured down on them, how many hundreds and thousands of times cold and burning heat have worked on them. Did they originally lie deeper in the ground? Have they been pushed upwards? Only one thing is definite: they were there before the Mediterranean reached its present-day level. Does this mean that the temples, too, should be dated to before the Ice Age? We do not know, but the assumption seems likely.[3]

Von Däniken quotes from the 1975 *Lexicon der Archaeologic,* by *Reinbeck* in his book, which stated:

> 'More emigrants from Sicily came to the island around 3200 B.C. An astonishing number of megalithic temples were constructed between 2800-1900 B.C. The still extant temples, some thirty in number, exhibit a highly developed plan and superstructure...[4]

The dates, like others we have seen, predate the Giza pyramids, if we use the dates set by current Egyptologists. These dates also place the time after the Mediterranean had been replenished with sea water during the glacial meltdown phase. These dates come into question when it is known Egyptians were sailing the Mediterranean in the fourth millennium BC. During this time, it is unlikely the Egyptian people were engaging in any megalithic building on the scale of the Giza pyramids or monolithic temples as discovered on Malta. These ancient sailors of the fourth millennium were involved with trade, location and procurement of minerals, jewels, and many other valuables to enhance the economy of their nation. Further, it does not account for the so called cart-ruts on the island of Malta, which disappear into the sea. More than likely, just as the Giza pyramids and the Osirion at Abydos, these ancient sites were also extant at this period in time. The age of building large had already vanished deep into man's past: just as this portion of deep antiquity is "ancient history" to modern people, it was ancient history to the Egyptians of the Mediterranean Sea. The Osirian Civilization had become the next generation, the modern day Egyptians of that period.

Egyptian prehistorical artifacts and writings are scarce if not completely missing. It is known that sometime before 7000 BC agriculture developed by people residing in the Levant where farming communities had been formed. It was during this time history shows a vast use of the Nile for fishing, hunting waterfowl, and other assorted game, while acquiring wild sorghum and other useful plants from the river banks. Crops of wheat and barley obtained from countries in the Near East were developed by farmers, which clearly shows Egypt was engaging in trade with foreign countries prior to 7000 BC. The domestication of animals such as sheep and goats also became part of the farming, and civilizing processes. Egyptian society was mainly oriented around the Nile River where resources were more abundant than in the desert locations with excessive heat, and water shortages. Author *Marc Van De Mieroop,* in his book *A History of Ancient Egypt* commented on the prehistory of the Egyptian people when he stated:

> From 5400 to 3000 is a very long time, but developments in Egypt were rapid when compared to other prehistoric societies. They include a shift in subsistence from hunting and gathering to farming, and the evolution of a social and political structure with a clear hierarchy of power and wealth that culminated in the Egyptian state. Throughout these two-and-a-half millennia we do not see abrupt cultural changes or the sudden appearance of populations that brought new practices with them, so the evolution must have been indigenous, albeit with influences from the outside. The processes of formation of the Egyptian state accelerated around 3400...[5]

It was the time from 3000 to 3250 BC when writing is said to have begun by the Egyptians in the form of hieroglyphs. In those early times Egypt was known as Misr, and did not become known as Egypt until it was modified from the Greek term *Aegyptos.* This occurrence did not take place until sometime after 900 BC. The Greek society, as we know them to be today, did not occur until 900 BC. Prior to this time Ionia was the predominant influence in that area. Ionia, now Turkey, was the original home of Herodotus and Pythagoras, and it is claimed that all scholars, prior to the formation of Greece, studied in the institutions of learning in Egypt, and in Phoenicia. Greeks inherited science and art from the Ionians (who were the product of an earlier civilization still unidentified), Phoenicians, and the Egyptians. Over all, the Greeks are a very young civilization, and culture when compared with most other Mediterranean civilizations. What seems to tie the Greeks to the Egyptians is the influence, and power brought into Egypt when Alexander the Great (the young Macedonian king) invaded Egypt in 332 BC. The Macedonians ruled Egypt until 30 BC (the Hellenistic period) until Octavian (future Roman Emperor, Augustus) established Egypt as the Roman province *Aegyptus* following the death of Cleopatra (last Pharaoh of Egypt, and daughter of Ptolemy XII, a General in Alexander's army), and Marcus Anthonius (Roman military commander, and third member of the Second Triumvirate of Rome and commander of Rome's eastern lands).

One important civilization, when discussing the Mediterranean Sea, and the Levant is the Phoenician culture, now Lebanon. For many years the Phoenicians were overlooked by historians, many stating information not being available. However, within the last few decades archaeologists have been able to develop evidence of the Phoenician ancient history. One recent study of blood conducted in 2004 by Spenser Wells and Pierre Zallous, clearly identified the Canaanite people of Biblical awareness, as the direct ancestors of the Phoenicians. There had been early speculation that Phoenician origin came from around the Erythraean Sea (or Persian Gulf). The study produced results, which indicated those people classified as Phoenician, lived in that location for at least 12,000 years. This finding, of course, does not rule out any immigration of other people entering their country, and producing any additional effects; it simply shows that the Canaanite people were the originators of the blood line for the Phoenician civilization.

The early history of Phoenicia depicts the country as a peaceful place with the largest city being a sleepy little seaport where the Lebanese mountains end along the sea shore. The name of this small fishing village, located there, was Byblos. Byblos starting at around 3200 BC was suddenly changed by the seafaring Egyptians who came to Lebanon to purchase cedar lumber for their seagoing ships, and river craft in quantity form. The Egyptians used cedar from Lebanon in much earlier times, but in much smaller quantities, as discussed earlier in Chapter 3. This economic windfall caused sudden growth in housing, public buildings, and new cities being built, by the Phoenician people, and ending the status of Byblos as a sleepy fishing village. This expanded need for cedar clearly indicated that the Egyptian sea trade was producing excellent results, and that they expected to expand into other lucrative markets. This also explains that the Phoenician culture did not precede the Egyptians as the dominant sea force in the Mediterranean. Evidence of this statement is supported by the large fleet of ships sent to Lebanon to collect a large order of cedar in 3000 BC. It wasn't until later times as the Egyptian economy, and its interior power base declined somewhat, that the Phoenicians gained control over trade in the Levant, and in the Mediterranean. This bit of history of the Phoenicians enlightens us to the fact that the Phoenicians learned ship building, and open sea sailing from the Egyptians, not the other way around. As we will observe later in this book, there is evidence of Egyptians, and Phoenicians sailing together as a united crew.

The name of Phoenicia, as with many other countries, was determined by the Greeks. What the original name was we do not know — other than, Canaan from the Bible. As wealth accumulated through their business enterprises with Egypt, Phoenicia began to expand their own trade routes into the Mediterranean. In the mean time, they created two new cities, Sidon, 47 miles (77 km) south of Byblos along the coast, and Tyre located on an island, which was about 23 miles (38 km) farther south of Sidon. Ultimately, Tyre became the principal city in Phoenicia, replacing Byblos in about 2759 BC as the center of influence.

Early trade routes had been established by the Egyptians. The main route for sea trade was called the 'circle route' because it extended out from the end of the Mediterranean Sea — the eastern portion of the Levant, to the Island of Crete, and back again. This route produced a number of pieces of evidence to support that claim. In later site inspections, archaeologists found imitations of Egyptian designs, along with numerous Egyptian objects. Similar Egyptian type burials were also discovered on Crete, along with Egyptian architectural designs. At a later time when the Phoenicians gained superiority in sea trade of the Mediterranean, they too carried Egyptian trade goods to their customers. They also expanded trade to Anatolia (Turkey) and beyond. From Tyre, the Phoenicians negotiated in silver, tin, lumber, copper, pottery, and probably many other items, from which they could easily trade and realize a profit.

The Phoenicians designed, and built the *Bireme*, which was an early galley with two tiers of rowers on each side of the ship in order to accommodate the oversize loads they encountered on their trading expeditions. By this later time, the Phoenician trade routes had expanded to Sicily, Italy, Lybia, Carthage, and out through the Pillars of Hercules to the Iberian peninsula, where they established the city of Gades (now Cadiz) in southern Spain. From here they reached Britain, and also circumnavigated Africa. More recently new investigative research efforts might point to their arrival in North America. There is knowledge, which indicates that in many instances these sailing excursions consisted of crews made up of Phoenicians, Nubians, Egyptians, and Carthaginians. Further exploits might also connect the Phoenicians with the Baltic Sea. Some researchers attempt to connect the name Baltic to the Phoenician fertility god *Baal*. The ancient temple ruins at Baalbek, in Lebanon, is named in honor of the god Baal. The ancient site at Baalbek is dated to around 9000 BC, and it contains blocks of stone 60 feet (18 m) long by 13 feet (4 m) high, and they are considered to be the largest blocks ever created for this type of construction, and it is almost impossible to calculate their weight.

As an independent observation to the gigantic megaliths at Baalbek, it just might have been reality for someone other than the Canaanites, or Phoenicians, to have constructed a complex structure of this magnitude. Why? First, earlier

Canaanites and Phoenicians were common ordinary farmers, goat herders, and fishermen. They lived a simple life, and they were not known for megalithic construction. Secondly, Phoenicia had close ancient ties with Egypt, who did have a past history of megalithic building sites — hence, the Giza Pyramids. We know that Egypt was obtaining cedar trees, and possibly other items from Phoenicia in deep antiquity: so it might have been through payment of debt or as prepayment for future material that Egypt constructed this astounding ancient temple using their technical building knowledge, and refined mental skills. As with other megalithic sites, Baalbek was probably built further back in time than 9000 BC.

The Carthaginians' god Cronus, was considered to be an incarnation of Baal, probably introduced to the people of Carthage, in North Africa, during trade interactions. In about the 5th century BC, the god *Baal Hammon* was considered the supreme god of the Carthaginians.

When we speak of chronology, writing must be included as a main topic for consideration. The Phoenicians seem to receive much credit as the culture who developed the alphabet, and writing. This credit for writing seems to stem from logs, and clay ledger items used for their record keeping purposes. One theory, which exists is that when customers of the Phoenicians saw that the symbols were being used for business purposes they wanted to learn the system too, so they could know if they were being treated fairly by the merchants. Thus, the writing form spread throughout the Mediterranean trading area. Perhaps, if this is the method by which writing, and the alphabet, originated we must keep in mind that this occurrence came about after 3200 BC. Since prior to that time, the Egyptians controlled the shipping lanes of the Mediterranean Sea until sometime before 2181 BC when the Egyptian economic system fell upon hard times due to famine, disease, destruction of monuments, and a division of the ruling classes. This 'Dark Age' period lasted until 2046 BC when a Theban king named, Menuhotep united the country, and became known as the first pharaoh of the Middle Kingdom. Following Menuhotep, were other pharaohs, such as Hatshepsut, and Thutmose III who contributed greatly to Egypt's sailing expeditions; but as a controlling entity of trade on the Mediterranean Sea Egypt never regained their one-time superiority.

The term *alphabet* is best described as symbols representing verbal sounds. When these different symbols are assembled in various ways it produces *writing*, which represents speech in a visual form or in the case of the hearing impaired, Braille — a tactile form. Some various forms of symbolic writing are first, *Pictographs* representing an object or a number of objects similar to primeval cave paintings, secondly, *Glyphs* a carved, scratched or engraved symbol, possibly in stone, and third, *Hieroglyphs* used by the Egyptians to represent a form of writing through individual pictures or a sequence of pictures denoting a concept, sound, or an action. If we accept these examples as the basis for writing, then we cannot state accurately that the Phoenicians were the first to create, and use the alphabet. Instead, we must look back to Mesopotamia where the earliest form of writing there was discovered in 1930-1931 during an archaeological dig. What was found were clay tablets with circles, wedges, triangles and ovals impressed into them. They further determined that each symbol represented a phonetic feature. By placing these symbols into various patterns words could be formed expressing thoughts verbally, which is a form of alphabet creating a written message. The clay tablets are placed at the fourth millennium BC — with the start set at around 3500 BC.

To move one step backward, David Diringer, a British Palaeographer commented:

> I propose that the antecedent of writing was not an earlier script, but a counting device. What had been missed — or dismissed — were, the humble tokens that had been used for centuries and that were, I argue, the immediate precursor to writing.[6]

With Diringer's observation we can include incised bone artifacts retrieved from the Kebara limestone cave in Israel, which shows clearly a series of parallel notches grooved into bones dating between 56,000 and 46,000 BC. This might be the earliest counting symbols found thus far. What were they counting, and why? Further evidence has been produced showing bones with parallel engravings have been found in locations from Iraq to the Mediterranean Sea.

The next important transition in counting symbols are tokens, which made their appearance in the Near East, and consisted of clay objects such as cones, disks, ovals, cylinders, and many other designs, each hand made. The earliest use of these clay tokens can be traced back to the eighth millennium, and were usually found in plain form with a few exceptions including vessels, or animals — some with eyes, ears, and mustaches. The main use of these tokens in the eighth millennium was for food production. Later, in the fourth millennium, the use gradually changed over from agriculture to big business, and governmental purposes. Further, the use of clay for communication developed into the clay tablet forms with markings impressed into the soft clay tablet, and then allowed to dry and harden. One good example of this technique is the clay tablets, which Moses brought down from the mountain containing the Ten Commandments.

Another example of an ancient writing form called *Vinča* has been unearthed in a number of countries located in the south-east section of Europe, and it is dated to be from 6000 to 4500 BC. The symbols have appeared in Greece, Romania, Hungary, the former Yugoslavia, the southern Ukraine, and at the site of Vinča near Belgrade on the Danube River. Also at a prehistoric settlement at Tărtăria-Gura Luncii, in Western Romania on the Danube, another ancient script was found, which was called the *Danube Script,* and its dating predates the Sumerian cuneiform writing, which is thought to be around 6,000 years old, and the oldest known writing in the world. Sometime later it was determined that the

Danube Script was a product of the Vinča culture, as well. (See examples of Vinča symbols at end of chapter (Gimbutas font) after archaeologist, Marija Gimbutas.

Archaeologist Marija Gimbutas is credited for identifying the pre-Indo-European culture. Many scholars were stunned to find civilization existed in southeastern Europe (the Balkans) in prehistoric times around 6500 BC. More recently in 2007, archaeologists uncovered an ancient site in southern Serbia believed to be at least 7,000 years old, and that they were skilled in the manufacturing of bronze items, which might mean archaeology will be required to reassess the dating for the Bronze Age. Currently, archaeologists place a date for the southeastern European Bronze Age at between 3500 and 1100 BC. Some also say that this script predates the Egyptian hieroglyphs. In the opinion of this author, that assumption is incorrect. It is the belief of this author that most of the ancient Egyptian buildings, containing hieroglyphs, were built further back in deep Egyptian prehistory than what is currently being stated as intelligent fact by Egyptologists. This time period might pre-date dynastic Egypt, but it does not account for pre-dynastic times.

The next Mediterranean civilization we need to speak about is the Minoan people. The Minoan civilization, in comparison with the Egyptian and Phoenician cultures are like the Greek civilization, a younger nation. The current acknowledged date by researchers for the Minoans is from 1950 to 1450 BC, which precedes the modern Greeks. According to British archaeologist, Colin Renfrew, Minoan society developed from growing wheat to expand into cultivating olives, and grapes at the end of the fourth millennium BC. However, no evidence of this could be obtained; so overtime a number of researchers debated, and hypothesized as to why the Minoan civilization developed and grew into a noted sea going people. The solution they seemed to agree on was 'Trade' from the outside. As discussed earlier, there is much evidence of Egyptian, and Phoenician influence of Crete, and the Minoan people. Some of the artifactual pieces date the trading time to have started around the beginning of the third millennium BC. This time period can only mean that it was the Egyptian sailors who were responsible for introducing these items to the island of Crete, since it predates any Phoenician contact. The Minoans developed, and changed into a prosperous society after 2000 BC, forming itself into groups of centralized states with ruling entities. Martin Bernal, author of *Black Athena* noticed the building of palaces around 2000 BC signaled an expansion into the southern Aegean Sea because of a growing social system, and a developing economic order, which had established itself for over one millennium. So there seems to be some corroboration of outside trade interaction beginning at around 3000 BC. Lionel Casson in *The Ancient Mariners* stated:

> As far back as the days of Snefru and Sahure there was trade
> contact between Minoans and Egyptians.[7]

The Minoan ships came later to the Mediterranean Sea routes of trade. The designs of their ships resembled the Egyptian ships with upward curving prows (bow), and sterns. They, like the Egyptian ships, were built using a center mast extending to about 52 feet (16 m) in length, and made of oak, which was placed into a reinforced structure so that it could be removed. A single boom of about 32 feet (10 m) was attached to the mast to hold the single square or rectangular sail similar to the Egyptian Ships. The main lumber used to build the Minoan ships was selected single tall Cypress trees, unlike the Egyptian ships, which were made from Lebanese cedar. Cypress wood, like cedar, contains natural weathering, and aging prohibitives.

The Minoans not only created and operated a profitable sea trade, they also developed, and operated a successful naval fleet. They controlled the sea power in the Mediterranean for many years. Albeit, the Minoan decline came quickly once the Mycenaeans controlled Crete at around 1450 BC. It is unknown if the downfall of Crete, and the Minoan civilization was due to a land war or one final naval battle. In any case, the Minoan hay-day ranged from about 1800 to 1500 BC.

The Minoans also are credited with having a writing system. In fact, the Minoans, over time had three different writing systems, starting with *Cretan Hieroglyphs,* which is believed to have developed from non-linguistic symbols, and it is related to their second form of writing called, *Linear A.* Many scholars who study epigraphy believe that Cretan Hieroglyphs, and Linear A might be the same writing system expressed by two different script forms. The Linear A form still remains somewhat of a mystery for researchers because it is based on an unknown language. Although, efforts are being made to understand Linear A by relating the symbols to the third form of writing, *Linear B.* Linear B was used on Crete between 1500 to 1200 BC, and it is the oldest record, to date, of the ancient Mycenaean language of the old city state of Mycenae, once the kingdom of Agamemnon of Greek history, and mythology. This language is more easily understood since it is derived from an archaic dialect of Greek origin. The two writing forms share approximately 80 percent of the same symbols, possibly demonstrating that the Mycenaean invaders adapted their language to Linear A, causing change variations to the Linear A system. Nonetheless these three writing, or a variation of these, systems were in place, and being used by the Minoans on Crete prior to, and during, the arrival of the Phoenicians. Therefore, if the Minoans used, and learned the Phoenician alphabet it probably would have been a secondary language for business purposes.

Like Egypt, they appeared to arrive as a full-blown megalithic culture without a gradual rise from a primitive state.
~ ~ David Hatcher Childress
~ Lost Cities of Atlantis, Ancient Europe & The Mediteranean

The quotation above refers to the Hittite Civilization who once resided in northern Anatolia (Turkey), from around the 18th century BCE. The people spoke an Indo-European language, which was interpreted by using a Hittite stelae written in both Hittite and Phoenician. Some experts believe the Hittite language was derived from a group of languages, such as, Greek, Latin, Celtic, and Germanic. Some even speculate that these people immigrated in from the Balkans, of southeastern Europe, and from the Bosphorus (part of the boundary between Europe, and Asia). The Hittites are an ancient people, and they are cited in the Bible. Childress points out that some German archaeologists believe the Hittites to be Indo-Germanic, and the "Sons of Heth." He also mentioned that the Hittites placed a double-headed eagle on the monuments, which is still used in Germany today. Although, Arthur C. Parker, an American anthropologist, wrote in his book *The Double-Headed Eagle and Whence It Came* that there is a Mesopotamian precursor to that of the Hittites.

The Hittites also have very close ties with the Egyptians. For example, they acknowledged the god *Bes*, who was a hunchbacked dwarf with a thick beard, and an erect phallus who played the flute. He was a god of fertility, and protector of sailors. Bes is also acknowledged by Phoenicians, Egyptians, Greeks, and there are also rock paintings in the American Southwest, called 'Kokopelli', which depict this god character who is also considered as a god of peaceful trade, and fertility by the Hopi, Zuni, and the Anasazi (the 'Ancient Ones'). The southwestern petroglyphs are dated to be 3000 BCE. The Zuni tell of the legend of the "flute player" during ceremonies being encircled by young virgin maidens. He begins to play his flute, and when he stops playing, the young maidens are then required to run away as fast as they can — chased by the flute player. The flute player then captures, and rapes one of the young maidens, eventually releasing her. If the young girl becomes pregnant because of her ordeal, she is then killed by her fellow tribe members. In New Mexico and Arizona, people today can purchase Hopi, and Zuni jewelry with the flute player featured on their work.

One other bit of information regarding the Zuni people is that they have a language, which seems to be based on North African Libyo-Egyptian elements resembling Coptic; according to Harvard Professor Barry Fell, author of *America B.C.* Fell explained his conclusion:

> The Libyan language, as I have shown elsewhere, is basically Egyptian combined with Anatolian roots introduced by the Sea People who invaded Libya, while the written form of the language is like that of the Phoenicians, alphabetic but using only consonants.[8]

The Hittites, just as the Egyptians used the sphinx or lion statues to guard their main city gates. Similar to the Egyptians, the Hittites built large stone structures, but not on the scale of the Giza pyramids or on the scale of the Phoenician temple of Baalbek. Instead their construction technique was that of large irregular-shaped polygonal blocks fitted faultlessly together to form collossal walls. This form of building is sometimes called cyclopean construction, and it is quite common at ancient sites in South America, along with other archaeological site's world wide. Earlier we spoke of the Hittites connection with the Zuni (A:Shiwi, meaning *The Flesh*). So it might not be surprising to discover many other Hittite, and Egyptian signs in North America of their ancient presence. One such article of evidence was the Newberry Tablet, which was made of unbaked clay, along with some statues, now known to be written in Hittite, and containing Egyptian hieroglyphics. When sent off to be confirmed by the Smithsonian Institution, all items mysteriously disappeared. This tablet, as determined by Barry Fell, was of a boustrophedon pattern, which is a pattern read twice, once across and once down or vertically and horizontally.

The writing form used by the Hittites was hieroglyphic in nature, and also resembled the Linear A and Linear B scripts used by the Minoans on Crete. The Hittite script still remains undeciphered today, and was read in a boustrophedon pattern.

Further it is known that the Hittites used a cuneiform text for diplomatic, and commercial use. It has also been established that in their one time capital city of Hattusas, at least eight different languages have been identified, which were once used in their various trading endeavors.

Unfortunately we do not have a lot of detail regarding Hittite naval history. We do know that they were inland from the sea, and had access to the Halys River, which flows through central Turkey, and into the Black Sea. We also are aware of their extensive trading enterprises, that they covered an extended area, possibly into North America. How they arrived at such far reaching destinations can only be surmised that they had help or possibly a business partnership with the Egyptians, and Phoenicians. Once again, as an early Mediterranean Sea power they do not place in that category. They were late comers to sea type sailing just as were the Greeks.

As one possible answer to this dilemma might rest with Egypt. Over the years of sailing the Mediterranean, and conducting trading enterprises the overall grandness of the Egyptian naval experience had weakened in some respects. Although the Egyptians did maintain their far reaching ventures, some changes to their expeditions have had to occur. One such change came in the form of manpower for crews to man their ships. We discussed earlier that Phoenicians replaced Egypt as the dominant sea traders on the Mediterranean Sea as Egypt's interior condition weakened due to various factors. Later though, Egypt made a naval/trading comeback. Since there was a time span between the naval hay-day, and Egypt's enhanced return to the sea there probably occurred a shortage of qualified seamen to participate in these new sailing ventures. So the next step would naturally be to hire sailors to fill the void. Some of these newly hired people could have been from the Hittite people since they held a close relationship. We already know that Phoenicians joined Egyptian sailing excursions, so why not the Hittites? David Childress addressed this issue when he stated:

> The Egyptians had a large navy, one that apparently traveled all over the world. This navy was often a hired one, however. The Egyptians were well known for hiring Libyan (North African) and Phoenician seamen to go on long trading voyages.[9]

An even older civilization perhaps, than the Egyptians are the people of Kush (Cush), but not exactly thought of as a Mediterranean civilization. The land of Kush, was once known as Ethiopia, today known as the Federal Democratic Republic of Ethiopia, and Aethiopia from the Greeks in more ancient times. The name Kush came from an association with Ham's son, of the Old Testament. The Hebrew texts applied the name Kush to identify Nubia.

Kush/Ethiopia is often thought of as the location in East Africa where the first signs of Homo sapiens sapiens first emerged, and began their journey out of Africa. There may be some truth to this hypothesis since a recently discovered specimen named *Homo Sapiens Idaltu* was found in 1997 by Tim White, an American paleoanthropologist, at Ethiopia's Middle Awash site. The name *Idaltu* denotes "elder," and the specimen was found in layers of volcanic ash dated to be between 154,000 and 160,000 years old. Another specimen in 1967 and 1974, was unearthed by Dr. Richard Leakey, son of the famous Louis and Mary Leakey, near the Omo River in southeastern Ethiopia, and dated to be around 195,000 years old.

Movements of the Kushites have been placed in India, Iraq, Egypt, and in Phoenicia. The Kushites have never been noted as a sea going civilization; however, they have also been placed in locations of western Africa, Libya, and now maybe, even in the Baltic Sea area. Since the Kushites had contact with the Phoenicians it might have been possible some of these Kushites became crew members aboard Phoenician ships, and eventually sailed up to Scandinavia. It was Sir John Lubbock, a British scientist and Polymath, who first recognized images appearing on a Tumulus found in Norway during the late 1800s to be Phoenician and Egyptian looking. On one other stone Lubbock found it had an image of an obelisk symbolizing what appeared to be a Baal festival. In his book *Pre-Historic Nations, John Baldwin* commented:

> The festival of Baal, or Balder, celebrated on midsummer night in the upper part of Norway, reveals the Cushite race, for the midnight sun did not originate in that latitude. This festival of Baal was celebrated in the British Islands until recent times. Baal has given such names as Baltic, Great and Little Belt, Belteburga, Baleshaugen, and the like.[10]

The references to 'Belt' in the quotation stems from the Swedish *Balt,* also meaning belt, Latin — Balteus. It is further speculated by Baldwin that the Kushites presence in old Iberia was much earlier than the Bronze Age.

The Kushites were also a nation with ancient writing systems. During the Napatan Period, hieroglyphs from Egypt were used. Then during the 2nd century BC an alphabet with 23 forms used in hieroglyphic, and script form made up a separate Meroitic (Meroë-Kush's capital) structure of writing. Currently, scholars still have not deciphered this language since, like the Linear A used by the Minoans, it is made up from an unknown language.

From this review of civilizations, and cultures located in the Levant area of the Mediterranean Sea in ancient times, every indication seems to point to the primeval culture of the prominent Egyptians as the dominant populace to have perfected megalithic building methods, formed and maintained a rule of law, developed organized religion, created farming communities that produced advanced strains of crops imported into their region along with grain storage facilities for large harvests. In addition they designed, and built river boats, later seafaring craft, in order to explore, fish, and to enhance their economic system through trade with other civilizations.

As we continue to look back into deep antiquity of the world, and at the Egyptian culture as a whole, we find no other people of that time to match the skills, knowledge, tenacity, and accomplishments of those impressive people. The Egyptian empire, throughout their existence, has had a notable effect on many other civilizations, which researchers are finding difficult to deny. As many scholars previously have stated, Egypt is a very ancient civilization, so old in fact, that even to them their history is ancient, and unknown. Egyptian civilization must go farther back in time than what is currently identified. From visible evidence of their extant megalithic structures, in relation to other worldly megalithic manifestations, there seems to be no other conclusion than there was once a common connection among all of those enigmatic displays. The similarities are too great, the mathematics are too prevalent, the purposes are obvious, the construction methods too defining, and the need for such wonders, undeniable. Are we to believe that all of these individual cultures, worldwide, developed the same expertise, and abilities to create gigantic, earthquake proof, artistically designed, functionally efficient, scientifically accurate structures using megaliths brought into the site location from miles away using only brute strength, determination, and crude ancient tools?

It is evident that what modern day researchers are finding is that most, if not all, of the megalithic structures known to archaeology today are from a time much more ancient than we place them to be. When science speaks of 10,000 BC, it should be interpreted as merely a short measurement of time into man's past. Within the past few decades research has gathered evidence of ancient civilizations once inhabiting locations on what is now the bottom of the Mediterranean Sea. These towns made of stone could not have been built, and societies developed after 10,000 BCE because of meltwaters occurring from glacial recession. Therefore, only one conclusion can be drawn, and that is those structures were built by people prior to the end of the last glacial period. Civilization existed during glaciation periods, and possibly before. When we hear of scientific researchers speculating that an entire megalithic city, like Tiahuanaco, could possibly have been raised to about 11,000 feet (3353 m) into the Andes Mountains because of powerful waters supplied by glacial meltwaters and other geological phenomenon, then it is time to reconsider what we know about man's prehistory.

Egyptologists must stop and reassess their current views, and hypotheses about the chronology of the Egyptian empire. It is no longer consistent with the facts. Even ancient writings give evidence of Egyptian antiquity, which does not coincide with current historical dogma. David Childress points out that Plato in his writing *Critias* tells of Egyptian priests describing Greece, and its area before 9000 BC. Childress included one passage from Plato's work, which supports the ancient age of Egypt when he wrote:

> Hence, in comparison of what then was, there are remaining in small islets only the bones of the wasted body, as they may be called; all the richer and softer parts of the soil having fallen away, and the mere skeleton of the country being left. But in former days, and in the primitive state of the country, what are now mountains were regarded only as hills; and the plains, as they are now termed, of Phelleus were full of rich earth, and there was an abundance of wood in the mountains. What is clearly being said in the *Critias* is that the many small islands of Greece were once the mountaintops of a large, fertile country that was well wooded and with a larger population than Greece had in Plato's time.[11]

This passage cannot be interpreted in any other manner than to state that the Egyptians were there during the dry period of the Mediterranean Sea, and that they actually witnessed the landscape and the terrain of Greece. This information was in their ancient libraries. This also might support Childress' theory of the Osirian Civilization for being the dominant people in the Mediterranean basin during the dry times. It possibly also explains the stone construction work found on the island of Malta along with the menhirs of Carnac, and the temple of Baal in Phoenicia; all of them a megalithic wonder.

These megalithic structures were not conceived by a society which lacked writing forms. As presented in this chapter, almost all of the cultures located in the Levant had some intelligent, and somewhat advanced form of writing and communication. Just as our civilization today conducts business, education, literature, and prose, so did the ancient prehistorical societies.

Perhaps these ancient societies had knowledge of metallurgy, laser technology, levitation through sound, stone softening workability techniques, and maybe even flight capabilities in addition to written language, which we are just now learning to understand. Our knowledge of the ancients is quite basic, and incomplete both on an academic and scientific level. Therefore, we cannot rule out such colossal possibilities. If we consider ancient efforts so archaic, and underdeveloped or even impossible — then why have we not solved all of the mysteries, which are associated with their visible remnants?

We have taken for granted, and accepted the findings of earlier researchers who have, for one reason or another, come to incorrect conclusions or at best incomplete observations. We have been told for decades that the Sumerian people in Mesopotamia were the oldest, and most advanced civilization of all prehistoric time. Now we have learned of a culture from southeastern Europe which might predate the Sumerians, and it is quite possible they had a writing system far older than Sumerian cuneiform. Further, it is a strong possibility that this civilization had an earthen pyramid larger than any one of the three pyramids at Giza. Yes, there are questions, and objections as to the validity of the built-up areas actually being pyramids. Recently though, in 2008 an International Conference met to discuss the claim of pyramids in Bosnia, and they concluded:

> Work at the archaeological location "Bosnian Valley of the Pyramids" in Visoko, Bosnia and Herzegovina, is an important geo-archaeological and epigraphical research that requires further multidisciplinary scientific research which should answer the origin of the Bosnian pyramidal hills and the extensive underground tunnel network as well as other archaeological sites in the vicinity.[12]

We should be pleased, and grateful to the people of that International Conference for not merely ignoring the possibilities of the structure actually being a man-made pyramid form. The call for a multidisciplinary research effort to seek truth, and understanding is a positive beginning for future archaeologists, and for scientists working in other related fields. With the professionally trained scientist working alongside of the amateur researcher there is great hope for more complete, and accurate information. Perhaps in the near future scholars will not have to withhold views and findings from the public, and their associates for fear of committing 'career suicide'.

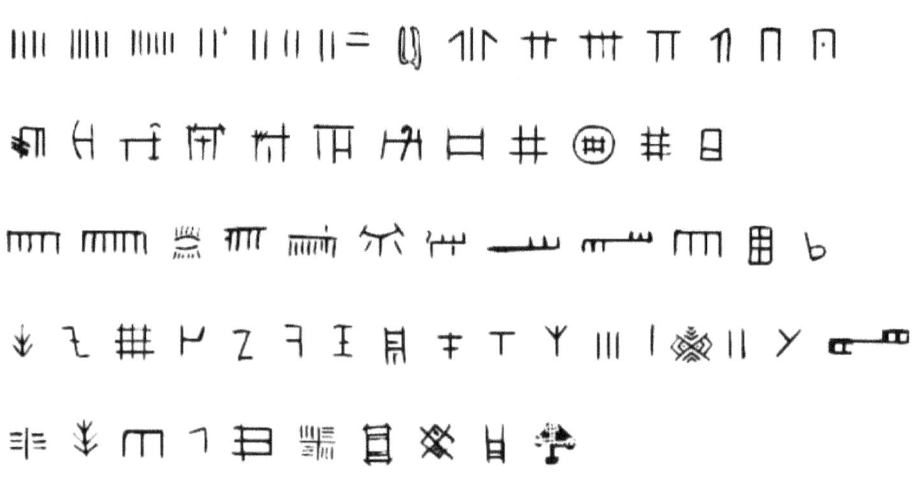

Vinca symbols

Figure provided by Terrance F. Johnson, 2014

Fig. 1 — Maria Gimbutas font

It is more likely that primitive humans were present in Europe during the Lower Pleistocene, just as they were in Africa, and certainly a proportion of the specimens from the sub-crag deposits appear to be humanly flaked and cannot be regarded merely as the result of natural forces. Implements from below the Crags would however, be not Early (Lower) Pleistocene but at least Late Pliocene in age.
~ ~ *Louis Leakey, 1960*
~ ~ *British Palaeoanthropologist*

Chapter 5

Ancient People of Europe

Louis Leakey, noted and respected anthropologist, is telling the world in the above quote that Europe was not one of the last continents to be inhabited by the species *Homo*. In fact, Leakey points out that man have occupied portions of Europe since, at least, from the Late Pliocene or around two million years ago (Table 1). Leakey's comments are directed toward ancient forms of stone tools known as industries, which reflect displays called flaking caused by chipping away small pieces of the stones surface by using another harder stone and creating marks similar to gouges on the face of the stone being worked. These various types of tools are usually made by members of the homo species, according to many archaeologists. Of course, in regard to Leakey's quote many will contend that it was not Homo sapiens sapiens who created the above noted flake scars, since modern man has not been around until 150,000 to 200,000 years ago. If it were not the Homo sapiens creating the tools — than who? If skeptics or scholars suspect it to be *Homo sapiens neanderthalensis* then they must remember also, that Neanderthals are dated from 350,000 to 400,000 years ago, still well short of the two million year date. The next likely candidate would be Neanderthal's ancestor *Homo heidelbergensis,* who also roamed the European continent. However, once again when we consider the time line for this species of homo we learn that Homo heidelbergensis is placed at between 600,000 to 1,300,000 years ago, which still does not meet the two million year mark for the Late Pliocene age. One other relative, *Homo ergaster* ("Working man"), is questionably listed as the ancestor of Homo heidelbergensis, and possibly African Homo erectus and Homo erectus in Asian regions. The only drawback to this homo member is that they are listed as residing in Africa only, and not having a connection with Europe. In addition, Homo ergaster is dated to be 1.3 to 1.8 million years old, again not reaching the two million year figure. As a reference date for the Pliocene, it was when the first hominins the *Australopithecus Africanus* species, the anthropomorphic-semi-erect-walking-primate-group-hunters entered the archaeological record. The reader might recall, archaeologists have placed man's exodus for Out of Africa to have been in two stages, the first, placed around 60,000 years ago, and the second, placed at about 50,000 years ago. These dates, as presented, do not coincide with those stated by Leakey. Furthermore, evidence of stone tools manufactured by a homo species in Europe two million years ago is completely contrary to all anthropological teaching put forth so far.

Even more eye-opening are the discoveries at the Red Crag formation, uncovered by J. Reid Moir, of the Royal Anthropological Institute, and president of the Prehistoric Society of East Anglia, which are considered far older than two million years, and were made by modern man. These were the conclusions drawn by M.C. Burkitt, of Cambridge University when in the 1920s, he examined the artifacts found by Moir. Burkitt in his 1956 book, *The Old Stone Age* stated:

> The eoliths themselves are mostly much older than the late pliocene deposits in which they were found. Some of them might actually date back to pre-pliocene times.[1]

Cremo and Thompson in their book *The Hidden History of the Human Race* elaborated on Burkitt's statement when they wrote:

> In other words, he was prepared to accept the existence of intelligent toolmaking hominids in England over 5 million years ago. Because there is much evidence, including skeletal remains, that humans of the fully modern type existed in pre-Pliocene times, there is no reason to rule out the possibility that Moir's implements from the below the Crag formation were made by *Homo sapiens* over 5 million years ago.[2]

In addition to the tools Moir itemized, several other signs signifying human occupation at the Crag site, were reported:

The finds consisted of the debris of a flint workshop, and included hammer-stones, cores from which flakes had been struck, finished implements, numerous flakes, and several calcined stones showing that fires had been lighted at this spot ... if the famous Foxhall human jaw-bone, which was apparently not very primitive in form, was, indeed, derived from the old land surface now buried deep beneath the Crag and a great thickness of Glacial Gravel, we can form the definite opinion that these ancient people were not very unlike ourselves in bodily characteristics.[3]

More examples of artifacts from deep prehistory are quite numerous; some consisting of bone notches thought to be made by early hunter-gatherers, footprints interpreted to be complete with leather shoes, tools of flint, fire scars, necklaces formed from sea shells, and human bone fragments, such as arm and leg bones intentionally broken to obtain marrow, and skull pieces along with human jawbones. What all of these artifacts have in common are that they originate from a time period prior to when modern man is supposed to have existed, and in places where modern man should not have been for, at least, another millennium or more in some cases.

One example of the ancient artifacts involved a piece of the skull, now known as the Vértesszöllös occipital fragment, extracted from a site in Hungary dated to the Middle Pleistocene or about 781 to 126,000 years ago. The occipital bone is a curving-compound bone, which forms the back, and a portion of the base of the skull. Then in 1972 David Pilbeam, an American anthropologist commented, after examining the skull bone that it did not appear to be from Homo erectus or archaic man, rather it resembled a section from early modern man. Pilbeam then placed the time range for the artifact at between 250,000 and 450,000 years old. This might not be so out of the question since archaeologists have since discovered an ancient civilization in the Balkans dating to possibly before the Sumerians of 6000 BC. This dating also connects to the evidence produced in England, France and Germany offering attestation of earlier modern man than currently acknowledged by today's scientific community.

Of course, many of these artifacts have been downgraded or ignored by leading scientists because the evidence does not fit the time line. Many of the skeptics simply refuse to make any effort to seek out a possibility of truth or change for a position of archaeology. Nevertheless it is a fact that Europe is a very old continent, and contains a wealth of unwritten prehistory. We know hardly anything of Europe's people prior to the written records of the Romans. The impression of all tribes of the northern regions from Rome, of being barbaric-illiterates, seems to have been the overall description of the northern European people. Albeit, we now know that such a description of those early people is not correct. The Germanic (paleo-Norse) tribes were building boats to hunt and to fish in rivers, and out into the open sea using knowledge of celestial navigation. Later, we know they had knowledge of metallurgy for tool and weapon making. Their societies were formed, and operated under well organized local government systems, and they had language, and other skills very common to that period of time. So what is missing about these people, and the landmass which they occupied, is merely a well documented, and honest written chronological history. This, unfortunately, might be more difficult to gain, than stated.

Graham Hancock, is seeking signs and remnants (as is this author) of an unidentified ancient civilization that most likely originated from the mountains and valleys of the European continent. A civilization who once designed, built, and used boats for water highways, and later built long ships with a square-rigged sale and oars to seek new lands for trade, minerals, ores, and even prime land for farming to raise families. A chronology for such an ancient civilization will run deep into antiquity showing only minute and most often misunderstood pieces of their one time unique dynamic civilization, and culture. Hancock stated:

> My view, ... is that we are looking at a common influence that touched all of these places, long before recorded history, a remote third-party civilization yet to be identified by historians. A wide range of natural evidence and recorded human experience points to the existence of such a civilization. Etymology, the study of word origins, postulates that a prehistoric Indo-European language must have existed to account for the deep similarities in the world's languages.[4]

Our discussion about ancient maritime knowledge brought some awareness of European tribes who existed before the Romans had arrived in Europe. We mentioned the Chauci tribe, who occupied an area along the northwestern shoreline of Germany somewhere close to today's city of Bremen, a river port city near the North Sea. Their name "xabukaz," meaning hawk is derived from Proto-German; in today's Low German, *Habicht*. We also briefly spoke of the Frisians, who inhabited the area now known as the Netherlands, and the Frisian Islands plus Helgoland an island located in a German Bay in the North Sea close to Schleswig-Holstein.

The Bructeri tribe settled into an area of northwestern Germany just south of the Teutoberg Forest, in what is today the Rhine-Westphalia a German Bundesland with a capital city of Düsseldorf, and its major city — Köln.

Conversely, the Burgundian tribe was an eastern Germanic tribe probably originating from the Old Norse island of *Burgundarholmr* (today- Bornholm). These people eventually migrated to the mainland of Germany and made their way westward into the Rhine Valley.

In addition to the tribes mentioned, there existed many other independent tribes who were well organized, and self-sufficient. Some of these tribes were the Marsi, Chatti, Franks, Vandals, Canninefates, Bavaria, Cherusci, and many others.

One other tribe which cannot be overlooked, are the *Angles* (from *Angeln*, today Schleswig-Holstein). This tribe lived quite close to the Chauci in the area once called Jutland (Denmark or Danemark in German). Their origin is vague, at best. The name is thought to have stemmed from the root *eng*, meaning narrow (perhaps narrow waters), also the root *angh*, meaning tight; so these base words might refer to a possible land area having a sharp bend, such as an inlet or bay waterway on the North Sea or Baltic Sea, since they resided on the Baltic side of Schleswig-Holstein. Located also in that area were the Jutes, hence, Jutland. The Chauci later transformed into the Saxons, and combined with the Angles to explore and settle into what is now England, so named for the variations in spellings of the name Angeln — *Englan or Englaland.* The 'E' in modern Low German, which is descended from Low Saxon, is pronounced as — a/aa/ah.

It is believed by anthropologists that these northern Germanic tribes shared a common ethnic origin, a common religion, and spoke in a common dialectic form. Although not united politically, they did share some common bonds of survival, and protection alliances. These tribes eventually blended together to form an extensive ethnic group referred to as the Germanic peoples of northern Europe. The name German means "Spear Man," (*Gar* (Ger), means *Spear — man*, means *man*) derived from another separate tribe from the northern regions of Europe. Their religious beliefs can be seen as part of the religion, and mythology passed along to the Scandinavian tribes who developed out of the northern Germanic tribes. Over all, the Germanic peoples were the most immense ethnic population of Europe. The Germanic peoples ranged from as far south as northern Italy, east into the one time country of Czechoslovakia (the Sudetenland-segment of southern and western Bohemia, in addition to Moravia close to the Sudeten mountain range), west over to Luxembourg-Belgium and up to Holland (the Netherlands), out to England, Scotland, Iceland, Greenland, and the Faroe Islands then stretching north to the Arctic regions of Norway, Sweden, and deep into Finland.

Unlike many ancient tribes the factions of Germanic people of northern Europe were more settled, and adapted to an agrarian form of existence, which included animal domestication and farming. We also know they were fishermen, and probably maintained hunting skills for additional sources of meat. It might be determined that agriculture had existed for an extended period of time, as indicated from the discovery of a man thought to be about forty-five years old, nearly 5 feet 5 inches tall (1.65 m), and lived about 3300 BCE. His well-maintained corpse was found in the Ötztal Alps at an elevation of around 10,500 feet (3200 m); thus, he was named Ötzi. Some other names have been assigned to this mummy such as, "Frozen Fritz" or the "Iceman." It has been determined through autopsy results that he ate his last meal approximately eight hours prior to his death, which consisted of Red Deer, barley, and a bread mixture without yeast, made from einkorn wheat not native to Europe, but grown in his farming community once located about 50 miles (80 km) north of Bolzano, Italy. Einkorn wheat is thought to have originated between 5,000 and 15,000 years ago in the region of the Fertile Crescent, of the Tigris and Euphrates river valley. It is the first species of wheat grown by man more than 12,000 years ago, but it produced low yields with a gluten type, which made bread-baking difficult. So probably, Ötzi's bread was more like a thick biscuit, possibly much like modern hardtack.

Of course, it is well known that these bands of Germanic tribes were boat builders, and seamen. This accounts for, at least, some portion of their societies to have remained semi-nomadic in nature. The reason for their nomadic ways might have developed from a need, or lack of employment to be more accurate. Since the Germanic tribes ultimately produced the Scandinavian people, they might have also formed the family inheritance traditions used at later times by the Swedes, and Norwegians. In agricultural communities, of ancient times, it was the eldest son who would inherit the land, and all contents of the family farm leaving the other sons to either work for their brother or to fend for themselves. In many cases, the farm property was not large enough to support more than one family. Therefore, many of the men not in line for inheritance, set off on exploration ventures or turned to fishing as a means for earning a living. This inheritance dilemma, as described by *Vilhelm Moberg* author of *A History of the Swedish People*, was the main reason for the appearance of the later age Norse Vikings.

Some experts tell us that the Jutes, of Jutland, and many other northern Germanic peoples moved into those areas around 5000 BC long after the last glacial period was in its final stages. This conclusion might be correct for some of the tribal people, but not all. As we have seen, the history of glacial stages extended in time back to nearly one million years with warming, and refreezing stages occurring as the time-line progressed. It has been determined from petroglyphs found to be from, at least, 10,000 BC that the people now known as the *Sámi* had lived in the Arctic regions of Norway, Sweden, Finland, and the Russian Peninsula of Kola in Northwest Russia, which makes up the Murmansk oblast (region). There is much argument among scientists as to the validity of humans living north of the Arctic Circle or anywhere close to that location in such prehistoric times. Moberg points to Oscar Montelius, a Swedish archaeologist who attempted to establish foundations for a prehistoric chronology for Sweden. Moberg wrote:

> Our great 20th-century student of prehistoric times, Oscar Montelius, has asserted that 'our-fair-haired, tall, dolychocephalic ancestors' have

been living here since the end of the Ice Age; or for about 15,000 years. Biblical history apart, this archaeologist has arrived at his view by applying evolutionary doctrine to his own science. Montelius has been our first historian to read Sweden's history in her soil, revealing her secrets with the spade.[5]

Additional support for early inhabitancy of far reaching Arctic lands can also be drawn from an ancient map, which was brought to the attention of the public in Charles Hapgood's book, *Maps of the Ancient Sea Kings.* Hapgood presented what is known as the Zeno Map, named for Nicolo Zeno, a descendant of the Zeno brothers who were sea traders and adventurers from Venice. Hapgood referred to a map, which shows Greenland not covered entirely by ice. Based on the shapes of the islands drawn on the map, Hapgood thought that it could have come from the Zeno collection discovered by Nicolo as part of his inheritance. In addition, the map also showed the southern portion of Sweden still in a glacial state of development, and considered by Hapgood to be an accurate cartographic presentation of the area more than 10,000-plus years ago. The accuracy of the maps, Hapgood points out, might have been the work of Angelino Dulcert (1339 ?) who produced maps based on compass directions, and port and harbor locations referred to as the Portolanos. Of course the contours of this map could only have been plotted, and drawn accurately by someone actually doing this work while at that exact location, some 10,000-plus years ago. It is unknown who these ancient cartographers really were, but it does clearly confirm that some intelligent, tenacious, hardy race was there for an extended amount of time pinpointing precise locations, and land-features of that terrain. Very easily, the people creating the cartographic works could have been the Sámi people, who are sometimes referred to as *Lapps* or *Laplanders.* The name Lapp is not easily defined. In Swedish lapp denotes 'patch' possibly relating to the type of clothing worn by the Sámi. The term Lapp is usually the most accepted description among many of the Nordic countries. The Laplanders are a very old civilization, which extended into Russia, Finland, Sweden, Norway, Germany, and the Niederland (or, lowlands-Holland). They have inhabited these areas for at least 5,000 years, as the best calculation. Prior to this time period the Komsa culture, ancestors of the Sámi, roamed the Arctic regions beginning about 6000 BC. They are officially identified as a Stone Age culture of the Sámi, and there are similarity connections between the Sámi, and a culture known as the Suomusjärvi from near the Ural Mountains. Ancestors of the Komsa were the Fosna culture, stretching further back to around 8000 BC or earlier. The earliest evidence for the Fosna culture might be found at the Bremsnes Cave of the region Møre and Romsdal, along with the nearby island of Averøy in Norway. This area has been estimated to have been occupied by the Fosna culture for more than 10,000 years (8000 BC). Other early artifactual evidence has been uncovered all along the coast of Norway because it is thought that during the glacial recession, between 11,000 and 8000 BC, this area was clear of ice sheets first, allowing the Fosna people to follow the clear areas. From about 13,000 BC areas of Denmark, Scania, in southern Sweden, and parts of the Norwegian coast was ice free, as described in the Zeno map discussed earlier. What is currently unexplained is how the Fosna and Komsa people arrived in the Scandinavian locations, and when. They are known as a circumpolar indigenous people — could they have traveled across the snow pacts from the Ural Mountains? Or, could they have moved west during one of the interglacial periods?

The Enigmatic Pays Basque

Of all of the mysteries surrounding cultures and civilizations of ancient Europe it is the Pays Basque who make their home in the Pyrénées Mountains, which separates the countries of France and Spain, who seem to draw the most attention. John Baldwin, in *Pre-Historic Nations* referred to the Basque people as the first people to have occupied Spain or people once known as the Iberians. He further classified them as a fragmentary group of mysterious people who simply disappeared. In addition, he pointed out that their language does not have a connection to any other known languages. Yet these people who exist today maintaining a traditional mode of attire, complete with the large black beret worn by the men since before the Romans, speaking their native language called *Euskara,* and still creating spicy dishes with their own locally grown assortment of peppers, such as *Le Piment d' Espelette, Gernikako Piperra, and the Langostinos Ibarra* to mention but a few, are still a mystery to archaeologists, anthropologists, and other scholars working in related scientific fields.

Some strides have been made to, at least, understand who these people are, and from whence they came; not an easy task, as it may appear. There is a great deal of speculation that the Basque people were the original Europeans (Cro-Magnon) who, it is believed, entered the European continent some 35,000 to 40,000 years ago migrating out of Africa. Over the many centuries which history has been written, some speculation has been brought forth to place the Basque wandering down through Italy, and locating on the islands of Sicily, and Sardinia. But at the same time, the first written evidence of the Basque was in 218 BC, two centuries after the arrival of the Romans into Europe. No reason has been offered for why it took the Romans so long to recognize, and to write about these people of the mountains. Just as any other civilization of ancient times, the Basque left no written records of their history or any petroglyphs to ponder.

The Basque, as we know, lived in the mountains as they still do today. However, they had access in ancient times to the Bay of Biscay, which is a gulf on the Atlantic Ocean encompassing the coastal areas of southwestern France and northwestern Spain. The area known as *Basqueland* also had access to two major rivers, the Adour River a boundary separating it from France, and the Ebro River, separating it from Spain. Albeit, not much evidence has been produced denoting the Basque as a sea-going nation of great stature. There are stories of the Basque being a fishing society, and there is one hypothesis currently what states that the Basque were the people who, during the 'Age of Exploration', connected Europe with North America, South America, Africa and Asia. However, it appears that the Basque exhibited most of their seafaring prowess during the Middle Ages, having ties to Christopher Columbus, ship building skills, and whaling and fishing expeditions, which they were notorious for keeping secret so as not to expose the best areas for obtaining the most bountiful catch.

Language of the Basque is as unique, and mysterious as the people themselves. It is not related to any other language of Europe, and it is thought to have arrived ahead of the Indo-European languages, but from where is yet unexplained. Most researchers argue for support of Proto-Basque as the earliest language form used, ultimately conforming itself into Aquitanian or into a group of languages called Vasconic (a precursor to Basque). In the 20th century Dené-Caucasian was offered as basis for the Proto-Basque, and included Sino-Tibetan, North Caucasian, Na-Dené, Yeniseian, and Vasconic. Later on this theory was viewed as doubtful. The next group of languages to be proposed is the Dené - Yeniseian languages, which includes Yeniseian languages native to central Siberia, and the North American Na-Dené languages of Canada's Northwest, now widely accepted by Philologists. Navajo, of the American Southwest is also included.

Once again we observe a connection with an area of the Russian Ural Mountains, as was the case with ancestors of the Lapps / Sámi people of the Arctic regions. There have been a number of theories starting mainly in the 1800s, which relate the Aryan race with the Nordic, and Germanic peoples of northern Europe based on physical appearance, and specific characteristics of those people. For research and understanding purposes, this book will not include the 20th century Nazi views of Aryan propaganda.

It is fairly well accepted by researchers today, that the Aryan people originated from a location somewhere in southern Russia. This belief might have developed from a theory in the 1880s proposed by Theodor Porsche, a German-American anthropologist, who argued for the origin of the Aryans to have been in the vast Rokitno or Pinsk Marshes, once part of the Russian Empire; now an area of Belarus and northwestern Ukraine. Porsche, in 1878, published a book on the Aryan people relating them to the Indo-Europeans by physical characteristics; describing them as being fair-haired, blue-light eyes, tall, and having slim-fine lips with a prominent chin. One other factor, which prompted his selection for that region as a home-land for the Aryans, is within that area there have been numerous cases of *albinism,* also known as achromia or achromatosis. The albino designation denotes an organism with complete absence of melanin (a complex polymer produced by an amino acid called, tyrosine) in their skin pigmentation, while Albinism is a result of a recessive gene received through inheritance.

Somewhat later, Joseph Deniker, a Russian-born French anthropologist, coined the term *nordique* (northern in French) to describe an "ethnic group" defined by their physical characteristics (comparable to Porsche's observations), as fair, possessing wavy hair, light colored eyes, with reddish skin, having a tall physique, and a dolichocephalic skull.

Since the Yeniseian languages have an origin in Russia near the Ural Mountains, and the Dené languages are described as an aboriginal people who lived in the Boreal and Arctic regions of Canada, it has been proposed that the Basque be included into the Dené - Caucasian group of languages. This connection provides for theories arguing for an ancestral correlation between the Basque and Scandinavian races. It is well understood that the Aryan people migrated on a grand scale in many different directions. Possibly one of those directions was to northern Russia into the Ural Mountain range, ultimately meeting up with members of the Suomusjärvi people, and from there trekking westwards across the northern tundra to Scandinavian, and European territories, thus, linking up with members from the early Basque population.

The matter of physical characteristics of the Basque race is not only enigmatic, but also very fascinating since it not only relates to the northern Germans and Scandinavians, but back into the times of Cro-Magnon. There are theories, which argue since the Basque language does not relate to any known or Indo-European language, they must have arrived first in Europe as the Cro-Magnon species, and then developed and spread out across the continent from that point. Of course, for those believers of Atlantis, there is a theory which argues for the Basque people to be the survivors of the once highly advanced island, which sank into the sea in one night from some unknown cause.

A study conducted by *Miloš M. Bogdanović and Marija Lj. Bogdanović,* entitled *Reconstruction of Speech and Language of the Cro-Magnon Man,* listed 5 feet 10 inches to 6 feet $4^{3}/_{8}$ inches (1.7 to 1.9 m) as an average height for male members of the Cro-Magnon species based on skeletons uncovered in 1868 from a cave in France. The findings also confirmed that the specimens found were well-built, had a strong jaw bone, with big hands, a long head-skull and short broad face; and an appearance very similar to the northern German and Scandinavian peoples.

The study also listed findings of Cro-Magnon skeletons found in the oldest cultural layers of Lepenski Vir in Serbia. In comparison with the skeletons found in France these specimens also ranged in height from 5 feet 9 inches to 5 feet 10 inches (1.7 m) tall. The study also indicated that after these skeletal findings were made, physical attributes of the Cro-Magnon was identifiable with living people in certain European areas. The Bogdanovićs stated in their study:

In the anthropological literature one can read that the living Cro-Magnon dwelt in North-West Germany, in Westphalia, on Dalmatians islands in the Adriatic sea in South Europe, and also in the mountain area of central Balkans.[6]

As support for their observation, the Bogdanovićs point to the Encyclopedia Britannica, which confirms that the Swedish county of Dalama, today, is populated by persons with almost pure Cro-Magnon characteristics. The study results also stated:

Consequently even today in mountain areas of central Balkans we find a considerable number of individuals having prominent characteristics of Cro-Magnon race. Undoubtedly they seemed like giants to various barbarian tribes of short growth as they were taller at least by a head.[7]

Many other studies, involving skulls of the Cro-Magnon, conducted in the 1800s have related the skulls to not only Germans and Laplanders, but with Magyars, Tartars, and the Turks.

The next major area of study with European cultures, and the Basque is a unique blood history of the Basque when compared against other people throughout the rest of the European continent. It has been proven through research studies, that the Basque people have a propensity to inherit the blood type 'O'. During the early part of the twentieth century science was able to identify three main blood groups, A, B, and O. The Basque population exhibits more than 50 percent of people with blood type O. Further, it had been determined that more than 27 percent of the Basque population carry an O Rh negative blood type, which in most cases can be fatal to a fetus, ultimately causing a poisoning reaction. It wasn't until 1940 when Karl Landsteiner and Alexander Wiener discovered the Rh blood types, called the *Rhesus factor* — named after the rhesus monkeys used to produce the antiserum for typing blood samples. The Rhesus factor has two groups, Rh negative and Rh positive, and when these two groups are brought together it can create complications for the fetus, which might cause "Blue Baby Syndrome," a result of having two different types of blood in the baby's body, circulating around at the same time. The rest of European populations are found to be more equally mixed with the Rh negative, and Rh positive blood groups. Later on in 1947 English physician, Arthur Mourant, carried out a study involving a group of both Spanish and French with Basque heritage, and concluded each group possessed a high frequency of Rh negatives, which could be classified as the highest in the world. This finding also caused Mourant to conclude that the Basque were descendants of the original inhabitants of Europe; placing all other European people — to have been a result of a mixing process of the originals, and from later arriving emigrants of the Near East.

Additional findings relating to the unique blood history of the Basque people connect with the homo species of Cro-Magnon, most notably the original inhabitants of Europe. It seems that the blood group O is also attributable to Cro-Magnon. There have been studies carried out, which also indicate there are areas where Cro-Magnon's presence had been significant, which presented findings of blood type O in higher frequencies, along with higher Rh negative occurences, as in the Atlas Mountains of Morocco, Algeria, Tunisia, and on the Canary Islands off the coast of North Africa in the Atlantic Ocean.

Further, as mentioned earlier, the people of Dalama County, Sweden are identified as possessing almost pure Cro-Magnon characteristics, and it is probably no surprise that people living there have a high prevalence of O blood type. The O blood type is caused from a mutation, or a deletion of the 258 nucleotide guanine of the blood type A. Some experts then claim that people having blood types A or B cannot have originated from Cro-Magnon. If this finding is correct, then that leaves most of the European people probably having originated from other groups migrating into Europe from other areas.

> *But the Solutreans did leave rock art, which showed a diamond-shaped flat fish in delicate black etchings. It looks like a halibut. A seal also appears, an arrow-headed line stabbing through it.*
> *~ ~ Dennis Stanford*
> *~ ~ Smithsonian Institution anthropologist*

The Solutrean culture, a somewhat recent addition to the archaeological record gained recognition beginning in the 1970s, not in Europe, but instead at a location in the State of Virginia, in the United States of America. The Solutreans are named after a site in eastern France, which was discovered in the mid-1800s called Solutré, near the district of Mâcon (Saône-et-Loire). The culture found there was labeled as upper Paleolithic who were mainly hunters, and who produced a unique form of spear heads known as *Biface*. The style of the bifacial tools was created by means of lithic reduction percussion, which is created using a hammerstone to flake away pieces from the stone being worked in a sequenced manner. This distinctive form of tool-making is unique to the Solutrean civilization. A spearhead of this design was discovered near the remains of an extinct mammoth, dated to be around 24,000 years old, in Virginia, U.S.A. We will discuss this extraordinary find, along with other interesting facts about the

Solutrean people in Chapter 9. For now, we will look at the European findings relating to these people.

The archaeological site also produced other kinds of tools made by the Solutreans such as, scrapers, boring tools, stone hammers, stone blades, and tools made using bone and deer antler. Another type of bone instrument, which was found at the site, were needles with an eye cut into one end, allowing for some form of thread material to be passed through for sewing purposes. The most obvious use for these needles might have been to make fitted clothing apparel. Still one other speculation, these needles could have been employed in order to stitch hems for sails to be used on boats for fishing, hunting and exploration. According to the quote by Dennis Stanford, above, they had access to seals, and fish resembling halibut, which is a deep water species of fish requiring a boat, and some knowledge of navigation. These ancient pictures are a sign that these people were not a 'land-locked' civilization. Still further, the fauna found in and around the site area indicated that these people lived in a somewhat cold climate, perhaps not too far away from existing glaciers. This might be possible since dating for this culture is placed at between 26,000 and 15,000 years ago, prior to total recession of the last Glacial Maximum ending around 10,000 BC in northern latitudes. Some scientists and researchers now believe that it was about 50,000 years ago when cultures were capable of supporting themselves in extreme colder climates, much like the Eskimos. This theory might also account for cultures such as, the Sámi, and their ancestral cultures, previously discussed.

Other bone implements uncovered at the site in France consisted of bone points with a groove carved into its base to receive a wooden thrower used to hunt land animals, awls (made also of stone), a bone flute, and bone beads made into necklace or bracelet bijouterie along with pendants and anklets, and fishhooks created with bone. These creative people were skilled in the entire ancient tool making industries, including the use of antler for making harpoons, also probably used in conjunction with a wooden shaft (found in Spain and France) to launch the harpoon for greater speed and accuracy. Another use for this tool will be discussed later.

The Solutreans demonstrated their creativity by display of art work in the form of cave paintings, carvings on bone pieces, paintings done on flat stones or stone friezes, and bas reliefs. All of these items along with other artifacts have been unearthed at locations in Spain, southern France, Portugal, and at Derbyshire, England. Then at around 15,000 BC the Solutrean tool industry disappeared from Europe, replaced by stone tools produced by the Magdalenian culture.

It suggests that the Aryan people, whose influence in Western Europe created Keltica and the Keltic tongues, were Pelasgians from Italy. These Pelasgians found in those Western countries a people of

another race, who, long before their arrival, had been civilized by the Arabian Cushites. What happened in England at a later period, when the Saxons and Norman French were brought together in that country, must have occurred in this case, with results still more remarkable, for here the peoples were not of the same race.
~ ~ *John D. Baldwin, Author*
~ ~ *Pre-Historic Nations*

The Celtic people, though very well known, have an obscure past with many unsolved variations, such as the origin of their language. Sometime ago, Philologists arranged the identified tongues of the Celtic language into two different divisions. The first division, is Gadhelic, which encompasses Irish, Gaelic, Scottish, and the dialect found on the Isle of Man. The second division is Cymric, and includes Welsh, Cornish, and the Armorican of Brittany, France. Today those divisions have been revised to be, the Insular Celtic Culture — the Gaels (Irish, Scots, and Manx – Isle of Man), and the Brythonic Celts (Welsh, Cornish, and Bretons – Lower Brittany in France). Insular Celtic can be confirmed back to the beginning of the 4th century CE, which was probably used prior to that time. By the middle of the first millennium AD the expansion of Rome, coupled with the Great Migrations of the Germanic people of Europe, induced the Celtic culture to become more isolated in Ireland, and into the western and northern regions of Great Britain. The individual cultures located there banded together to create a somewhat concordant culture by forming a common religion, sharing a linguistic and artistic heritage, while eliminating the use of the Continental Celtic languages by the late 6th century CE.

Celtic history in Europe is also somewhat muddled by lack of facts and evidence. There are some who recognize the Celtic culture to have developed in central Europe, east of the Rhine River, in what is today southern Germany. This culture, from there, expanded into Austria, the Czech Republic, Slovakia, and into Hungary. Conversely, since the Celtic language has been designated as an Indo-European language, some researchers believe the Celts originated much further back in time to possibly around 2700 BC or before.

From John Baldwin's quote above, he credits the Aryan peoples of Europe for creating the Celtic people, mainly occurring through the Pelasgian civilization of Italy. The Pelasgians are listed by some as the ancestors of all Indo-European peoples having their origins from a place north of Arcadia (central mountains of modern day Pelopónnisos), thought to be near the location of the Aryan peoples. They settled in Arcadia prior to the Dorians, they were ancestors of the Hellenes (Greek) civilization. The Pelasgians educated the Greeks on the religion of Hera, metallurgy, writing, and the cyclopean form of stone architecture. As discussed in Chapter 4, it has been determined by many that Phoenicians were responsible for introducing the alphabet to the Mediterranean

Sea coast civilizations. However, it now appears that the Pelasgians pre-date that theory along with the other cultures, which we reviewed earlier. The Pelasgian language and writing style is connected very closely to the Albanian language, who some claim are descendants of the elusive Illyrians — an ancient Balkan tribe, which would make them the modern descendants of the Pelasgians.

The Pelasgian explanation for the Celtic origin is quite contrary to the theory that the Celts originated in Germany and, hence, spread southward. If we are to agree with Baldwin's observation, then it would be necessary to agree that the Celtic culture developed from the south and moved into central Europe; and at the core of this progression is the Pelasgian civilization. The name *Pelasgian* denotes from the sea, and also hairy. It seems, in deep antiquity, a bearded group of people from the north arrived by way of the sea, settling into the Peloponnesus (the southern peninsula of Greece — the *Peloponnesian Peninsula*). These sea people along with ship building skills, were also master stone masons; they worked large individual cut stones into thick sturdy walls unlike any previous architecture in that location. This resulted in much larger buildings replacing smaller antiquated hovels. From this locale they continued their expansion both by land and sea, projecting north into the Balkans and beyond to what is today, Italy. As Baldwin pointed out in his book *Pre-Historic Nations,* there had been no Aryan presence in Europe prior to the arrival of the Pelasgians into Italy. The arrival of the Pelasgians into Italy was also noted by Pliny the Elder (a Roman historian, 23-79 CE) when he wrote, "It is said that the first dwellers of our Italy were the Pelasgians," [8] when confirming observations of 1st century BC Greek historian, Diodorus. The arrival of the Pelasgians is placed at around seventeen generations prior to the Trojan War (1194-1184 BC) — allowing for a generation to be twenty years — that would then be about 1534 BC. The blind Greek poet Homer (around 800-700 BC) was the first to tell of the Trojan War, if it did actually occur at all.

After their arrival into Italy the Pelasgians founded the city of Cortona, in what is now the north-central region called Tuscany. According to the study *The Enigma of Pelasgians and Etruscans,* Tuscany's name derived from the southern Albanian city named, Toskeria. Arrival of the Pelasgians was preceded by the Eturia, now Etruscans, and in Greek, Tyrrhenia. The Tyrrhenia must have inhabited the area sometime after 1180 BC. During the year of 1180 BC the Egyptian Pharaoh, Ramses III, was attacked by what he called northern people who joined with the Libyans to attack Egypt by land and sea for the third time. Ramses destroyed their fleet, and for the third time claimed victory. To proclaim his victory for the historical record, Ramses had his scribes list all of the enemies who joined together in this final attack. Some on the enemies list were the Peleset (Philistines), Libyans, and the Tursha (Tyrrenians) from Asia Minor, not yet having gone to their new home in central Italy.

The Pelasgians referred to the Etruscans as the Tyrrhenia, and their people were known as the Siculi, Umbrians, and Tyeehenes. The leader of the Pelasgians was Œnotrus, and from this the Pelasgians were called Œnotrians. However, there might have been an earlier arrival by some of the Pelasgians led by a king named Italus, later succeeded by King Morges, thus, resulting in the Pelasgians being known as both Morgetes and Italians.

The later Pelasgians fought many bloody battles with the Tyrrhenes ultimately capturing the city, which they renamed Cortona, from the Umbrians. The Umbrians were ancient people who arrived long before either the Tyrrhenia or the Pelasgians. It is believed the Umbrians originated from ancient Kushite explorers, some 3,000 years earlier. During these bloody times the Pelasgians conquered many towns from the Tuscans, while driving the Siculi out of Italy over to the island of Sicily, which at the time was occupied by an Iberian tribe called the Sicani.

Eventually the Pelasgians became war weary; also probably short on funds from waging so many continuous wars, began to decline in power and strength. This situation prompted many of the Pelasgians to return to Arcadia while some of the others moved westward into European locations. Still, those remaining behind settled mainly in Latium a region of west-central Italy where they helped to establish the city of Rome. It should be noted that during this time any knowledge of Celts or evidence of the Celtic language has not been found.

Before we continue with the origins of the Celtic people we need to be aware of one other possibility regarding Aryan appearance in Europe. The reader might recall that Aryan presence in Europe was brought there by the Pelasgians, probably sometime after 1200 BC. Now Baldwin from his accounts in *Pre-Historic Nations* points out another scenario for Aryans entering into Europe when he stated:

> There is no record or tradition that tells when the first group of the Aryan race appeared in Central or Western Europe. The people represented by the Lithuanians and the Letts appear to have been the earliest immigrants; the old Prussians belonged to this group. Next probably came the Slavonians, who settled in Poland and other countries of Central Europe. The Teutonic family, including several distinct groups, came later to the countries where history found them. It may be that all these immigrations preceded that of the Pelasgians into Spain and Gaul, but it does not seem probable that any group of the Teutonic family appeared in Sweden, Denmark, or even Germany, previous to the beginning of the Keltic age.[9]

The above statement by Baldwin, contains many agreeable observations, which seem very plausible for the existence of the Aryan race into Europe. Most philologists tend to agree that it is the Lithuanian language, and the language of the Letts (Livonians) that resemble more closely the Aryan language than any of the other European languages. However, Baldwin's statement about members of the Teutonic families not being in their historic areas of record must be challenged. We have already discussed ancient evidence of Proto-Germanic tribes and to some extent their development. Germanic languages derived from Proto-German long before 1200 BC. The full-Celtic designation did not occur until about 800 BC. With all due respect to Mr. Baldwin, it is this author's opinion; Baldwin's observation on this particular point is incorrect.

According to the Greeks the Pelasgians spoke a language, which they identified as "barbaric." However, during their time in Italy, the language of the Pelasgians blended in with the, ancient Kushites, Umbrians, and Etruscans — all thought to have blended with the old Arabian Kushite civilization that settled in Italy some 3,000 years prior to the Pelasgians arriving. Although, researchers have admitted that the Etruscan language has, as yet, not been identified much like the Basque language. Some philologists believe that the language may be a western variation of a Greek alphabet, brought into Tuscany by an ancient Greek culture that might have resided on the island of Euboea, the largest island after Crete. The language is quite similar to Lemnian, a language once spoken on the island of Lemnos, located in the northern part of the Aegean Sea. The Etruscans referred to themselves as the Rasna, which might have some connection to Raetic, a language once spoken only in the Southern Alps. Nevertheless, the Etruscan language apparently seems to have some unknown Mediterranean origin.

As the portion of reorganized Pelasgians moved out from Italy to escape the remnants of harsh wars, their first stop is said to have been in Bohemia where they connected with the Urnfield culture during the Late Bronze Age period. It was at this stage researchers designate them as Proto-Celtic. The Urnfield culture received their name from the ritual of placing the cremated remains of an individual into urns. This culture was first identified around 1200 BC in northern Italy, and in east-central Europe. The Urnfield culture migrated extensively to the Ukraine, down to Sicily, up to Scandinavia, and over to the Iberian Peninsula. In all, the culture existed for more than 1,700 years.

By the beginning of the Iron Age (800-450 BC) archaeologists considered this culture to be fully-Celtic in structure. During this step of development, the full-Celtic were combined with the Hallstatt culture near the Austrian village of Hallstatt in the Austrian Salzkammergat (Salt chamber locker or Salt Mine) area southeast of Salzburg, Austria. Even though this culture was located in Austria, the Hallstatt enterprises was divided into two zones; first, an eastern zone, which encompassed Austria, Slovakia, western Hungary, Slovenia, Croatia, and the Czech Republic, and secondly, a western zone covering northern Italy, southern Germany, Switzerland, and eastern France. The main enterprise of this culture was salt (Salz), mined and shipped throughout all of Europe since before 7000 BC using the grand waterways such as, the Danube, Lech, Mur plus other rivers and tributaries as their main highways. The salt business was so profitable that it financed their second major enterprise — iron works, consisting of weapons, tools, and ploughs. In general, they participated in profitable industries consisting mainly of salz und eisen (salt and iron). We know the Celts also built boats, which were of a different design, and construction method than those built by the many tribes of central and northern Europe. Some parts of these crafts were uncovered by archaeologists in, and around, France and dated to the time of the Roman's occupation of Europe. Perhaps now we know why some of these crafts were built, and how they were used as shipping vessels for salt and iron products.

Pottery was one other business on a rather minor scale when compared to the salt and iron industries, which helped to identify the Celtic presence within these various cultures. Some of the cultural time-lines overlap to some extent. For example, during the early Proto-Celtic phase (Late Bronze Age) these people were also connected to the Bell-Beaker culture (2800 to 1900 BC). The Bell-Beaker people are believed to have arrived in Europe about 2900 BC, but from where has not been determined. They are noted as an ancestor culture of the Celts, and they are known for making two unique styles of pottery, the cord-impressed version called — "All Over Ornament," and the "Maritime" type with decorative bands made using combs or cords. At the later time of the Hallstatt culture, pottery with early Celtic designs were produced using both Greek and Etruscan artistic designs, most likely derived from their earlier inhabitance of Italy.

By end of the Iron Age (450 BC) the Celts (Insular Celts) had expanded migration from their locations in Bohemia over to central Europe, in southern Germany, France, and on into the Iberian Peninsula, all prior to the Roman arrival (see Fig. 1-end of Chapter). However, during the third century BC the Celtic tribes, which inhabited southern Germany were attacked by the Alamanni, a Germanic alliance of tribes living around the upper Rhine River, and pushed out the people who relocated to the area. The Alamanni were a fierce, aggressive people who remained bitter enemies of the Romans. Roman Emperor Caracalla, between 211 and 217 BC, made a pledge to be their 'defeater' — he failed! The Celts were still not a complete civilization; rather they remained divided into individual tribal units. During the time of the attack by the Alamanni, there existed also, in those locations, mixed Germanic and Celtic tribes.

Then by around the early sixth century BC five Celtic tribes arrived, and inhabited the Atlantic coastal peninsula region of Gaul (France), named Armorica by the Romans when they came into the area. This coastal region was of great strategic importance to the Romans, since it would allow them to cross over the English Channel, into Britain, by shorter routes. The Armorica region is also what is known today as Brittany, which also is the location of the giant menhirs of Carnac, France, on the Gulf of Morbihan. The Celtic people who once resided in that area are in no way the builders of the site at Carnac. Many archaeologists consider the site to have been built about 5,000 years ago; but more recent studies conceivably put forward dates much further back in time for their creation and placement (See more details in Chapter 7 of *Our Missing Ancestors*). As we have seen, the Celtic tribes did not arrive in the area until near the 6th century BC, or around 501 to 600 BC, which is far too late for these people to be considered as the builders of Carnac.

The five main Celtic tribes of Armorica are first, the Curiosolitae who lived near the present day French town of Corseul, which was founded in 10 BC by the Romans, calling it Fanum Martis (Temple of Mars). The second tribe was called the Namnetes, and they lived north of the Lorie River, in today's wine country of Centra-Val de Loire a region of north central France. The third Celtic tribe is the Osismii, and they occupied a portion of western France from Lannion on the east, to near Dinard in the west, today known as Côtes-d'Armor, and Morbihan. The fourth tribe is the Redones, once occupying the location of today's Rennes, (named for the Redones) France, which lies in northwestern France of east Brittany, and today the capital city of Brittany.

The fifth tribe, but not the last of Celtic tribes in the area, is the Veneti who dwelt near today's city of Vannes (name derived from Veneti), France. Vannes is located on the Morbihan Gulf at the mouth of the Marle and Vincin Rivers. There is much debate and speculation about who the Veneti really were. Some researchers recognize them as a sea-going race, and others believe them to be a Slovak tribe, ancestors of the full-Celts. However, no concrete proof has been produced in order to substantiate either one of these theories. Other less prominent tribes, residing in the Armorica region, also members of an "Armorican confederation" delving into the trade of tin were the Ambibarii, Unelli, Caletes, and the Lemovices.

On a broader scale of European landscape there was the Transalpine Gaul or the Gallia Transalpina, by the Romans, who marched in on 121 BC to defeat the local Celtic tribes. The area known as the Transalpina was bounded by land north and west of the Alps up to the Pyrénées, over to the Atlantic Ocean, north to the Rhine River, into parts of Belgium, Germany, Switzerland, and the Netherlands. An additional four major Celtic tribes lived within this defined land area named the Aedui, in central Gaul – now Burgundy, theAllobroges, in today's city of Geneva between the Rhône and Isère rivers, the Senones, from today's city of Sens, and the Sequani, who held the area between the Rhône and Saône rivers in what is today's city of Besançon. The term Galli was given to the European Celts by the Romans, which was a variation on the name Gauls.

The Romans also considered the land south of the Alps, occupied by Celtic tribes, as Cisalpine Gaul, meaning "on this southern side" of the Alps. On both sides of the Alps during Roman times there were possibly as many as 100 tribes, or confederations of tribes, spread over a vast amount of land.

The Roman invasion of Transalpine Gaul was known as the Gallic Wars (58-50 BC). The Celtic tribes fought a good battle, but the Roman armies were much too strong, and too well equipped to be defeated by the Celtic tribes who lacked strong leadership from a central government. They were bound mainly by speech, religion, traditions, and customs. The Celtic tribes within the Cisalpine Gaul location suffered defeat in 225 BC at the city of Telamon in Tuscany, Italy.

In general, the Celtic people were a subsequent, fragmented civilization having possessed intelligence, tenacity, good fortune, ability, and the admiration of people up through our current time. However, like the Greek civilization of which their ancestors played an important role in their development, the Celtic people were a late arrival to the continent of Europe. It also can be argued, and probably successfully, that the Celtic influence on the development of forming the civilizations of Europe was a grand accomplishment, which has not been equaled. In all though, the Celts cannot be listed as an original ancient tribe, from deep antiquity, whose presence was responsible for any initial events or actions which shaped the European continent, and its pre-historical civilizations.

The deep prehistory of Europe is beginning to make itself visible for public analysis, and inquiry. The information found in this chapter is merely an overview of the European experience. We know, deep down, there is more history to be uncovered, identified, and explained. Modern science, along with many current day researchers, is working to make that missing portion of the world's history understandable, and believable. Fortunately, we are beginning to visualize what once occurred in deep antiquity, and to explore the unexplained using education, and current divisions of contemporary cross-discipline sciences. As long as truth and fact play a major role in the search process modern man will discover the real prehistory of our world.

Pre-History's Chronology Enigma

Geological Period and Era Dating:

Era	Period	Dates (Millions of Years)
Cenozoic	Holocene Pleistocene Pliocene Miocene Oligocene Eocene Paleocene	Present-11,700 B.C. 11,700-2.5 M B.C. 2.5M-5.3M B.C. 5.3M-23M B.C. 23M-34M B.C. 33.9M-55.8M B.C. 55.8-65M B.C.
Mesozoic	Cretaceous Jurassic Triassic	65M-144M B.C. 144M-213M B.C. 213M-248M B.C.
Paleozoic	Permian Carboniferous Devonian Silurian Ordovician Cambrian	248M-286M B.C. 286M-360M B.C. 360M-408M B.C. 408M-438M B.C. 438M-505M B.C. 505M-590M B.C.

Table 1   Table by Terrance F. Johnson, 2014

Fig. 1   Figure by Terrance F. Johnson, 2014

If there is one thing that we should learn from the modern history of archaeology, it is that we have consistently underestimated the level of sophistication, and antiquity, of our forebears.
~~ Dr. Robert Schoch, Author
~~ Forgotten Civilization

Chapter 6

Ancient People of Central America

The belief in a "flat earth" was mainly a concept held by Europeans around the early to mid 1400s. The majority of the world civilizations knew, and accepted the fact that the world was round. They knew this fact from experience while sailing the seas for trade, minerals, jewels, and for general exploration. This was not a new experience to many of these ancient civilizations, for a majority of those people had ancestors who pioneered the oceans in makeshift rafts and boats, and ultimately in seaworthy sailing vessels. Most of these civilizations did not need Pythagoras, an Ionian mathematician and philosopher, to tell them the world was round. It was the Egyptian civilization who once placed the meridian at the center of Egypt, and from there mapped the world, and plotted precession for many centuries long before Pythagoras was born. For the Europeans to have believed in a 'Flat Earth' concept is just ludicrous. How could they have really believed this with access to so many people coming and going throughout their country engaging in trade and other forms of business? Was this a way to discourage business competition? Surely, they could not have been that ignorant. It has been hypothesized by some that the Catholic Church played a dominant role in what the people of that time would have and should have believed.

The discovery, by Columbus, of a new world was not really met with surprise by many. Probably what really surprised them was the possibility they found for new business enterprises. It has been suspected that Columbus had opportunities to study ancient maps of his predecessors who once sailed to the west, and returned safely. He also was aware of stories told about past voyages to the west. So it was not creation of his own independent thought that he could sail west, and possibly produce great wealth for himself, and the Spanish Royal family who bankrolled his voyage.

In reality, Columbus was not even close to being the first to discover America. In Chapter 8, we will discuss a number of early immigrants to the North American continent. One other very early explorer was Leif Eriksson, son of Erik the Red — a Norwegian who escaped to Greenland after killing an individual back in Norway. Leif, his second son, is credited with the discovery of a place on the coast of North America named, *Vinland* by Leif, who first arrived there. This incident happened around AD 1000, which is almost 500 years before Columbus set sail to go west from Spain on his first expedition. The Vinland discovery is not just old Norse myth. The discovery had been documented by an Icelander in Norway sometime close to around AD 1300.

The work was derived from earlier documents from various, well respected, writers who were considered honest and learned. The writing is called *The Frissbók*, which once belonged to an individual named Otto Friis. The book tells the story, in detail, of Leifr Eiriksson (Leif Eriksson), and his crew of 160 men who sailed west from Greenland, and in the process founded Vinland the Good. What is even more amazing about this tale is that Leif, and his crew saved another group of sailors during their expedition. It must have been another expedition sailing west in search of something thought necessary. From that time Leif Eriksson was also known as, Leif the Lucky. Now, if that is not enough of a surprise, during this trip while sailing along the coastline down toward where they discovered Vinland, Leif and his crew found the keel of a wooden ship, which meant that others had made it to that location before Leif and his crew. So we must ask ourselves — what happened to the survivors of that expedition? It is believed that this work is, perhaps, the oldest extant manuscript, which depicts the entire story of Leif's expedition.

The story of Leif Eriksson is unusual in the sense that we have a written account. Other chronicles of world prehistory probably have not yet been discovered. During the time that Leif Eriksson, and his crew were conducting this mission there were numerous indigenous peoples in both North and South America. We have touched upon the Chinese, and possibly the Japanese having made contact with both North and South America. However, we now must include the Scandinavians in that group as well. It might be that the Norse was also instrumental in leaving their mark on the southern hemisphere in deep prehistory. There seems to be good evidence of Scandinavian visits long before any Viking ships arrived on southern American shores. Belief of Norse, or proto-Norse, having visited Central and South America in deep antiquity supports the 'Experimental Hypothesis' laid out in *Our Missing Ancestors.* My last book attempted to connect a Norse seaman with some, or most, of the white gods named by the indigenous people of both Central and South America. Now it appears that my interpretations might have been correct. A scholar of Swedish heritage who lives in Mexico, Gustavo Nelin, believes that a Norse explorer named, Marson might have sailed to Mexico, and became the Aztec god Quetzalcoatl prior to Leif Eriksson's famous voyage. Nelin points to Ari Marson as a possible Christian who brought the fruits of Civilization to the indigenous people. Nelin also added a possible connection to a place called Tula, which is a place in Mexico where possibly Quetzalcoatl, and his entourage resided. He equates the spelling and pronouncing of the name Tula to the Scandinavian spelling "Tule." Tule is an ancient name for Scandinavia. Also, noting from my knowledge of German, and Norse is derived from the Germanic language, the 'e' in Tule can be pronounced as 'a'. So therefore, the words, though not spelled the same may be pronounced the same. One other reason for Nelin's reasoning is that Marson was white, and the Aztecs claimed Quetzalcoatl was white, redheaded, and approximately middle aged. Finally, Nelin concludes that the crowning touch to his theory is the Norse ship, which is called a "flying Serpent," and Nelin espouses that Quetzalcoatl was known to the Aztecs as the "Flying Serpent." Although, it has been the understanding of this author that Quetzalcoatl was known as, "The Feathered Serpent" — perhaps both.

Huyghe takes Scandinavian exploration of the southern Americas further back than the Marson theory. In his book *Columbus Was Last,* Huyghe tells of Alice Kehoe, a Marquette University anthropologist who defends a theory which states, Scandinavians could have crossed the Atlantic Ocean, possibly during one of the glacial stages, when sea levels were much lower than today's, and they accomplished this feat by using small boats made of wooden frames with sewn skin covers. Kehoe also claims these boats were so sturdy that some modern day versions are still used today in areas of Ireland. She believes the boats performed so well on the open sea that a voyage across the Atlantic Ocean would be possible providing the trip was broken into short segments. Kehoe points out that at the time of lower sea levels, there was much less water to cross. Hence, there was only a few of hundred miles from Scandinavia to the Faeroe Islands, then a span of a couple hundred miles to Iceland, another few hundred miles to Greenland, and finally, about an equal distance to Labrador– the northern portion of Newfoundland, Canada. From there, just as Leif Eriksson had done, they could have sailed south following the coastline. Kehoe's theory might not be too far fetched since today's researchers have located a number of Rune stones in America, which were used extensively by Norse seafarers during their expeditions. In addition a sea voyage theory, such as Kehoe presented, might also explain how people (from the Out of Africa hypothesis) paddled small handmade boats from their location in Southeast Asia to Australia around 40,000 years ago. The sea levels must have been at a lower level than we know them to be currently. It has been estimated that the distance from Asia to Australia — across the Timor Straits at the time of the crossing, was about 50 miles (80 km).

One main question, which needs to be answered by researchers, is — how far back can we trace human existence to Central and South America? Most archaeologists say that it is not as ancient as the continent of Africa, where mostly all scholars support the Out of Africa theory. However, there is one piece of new eye-opening evidence from the mid-1970s, which should cause science to rethink the time-line of human existence, and the Out of Africa hypothesis.

The new evidence surfaced at Hueyatlaco (spoken as, *way-at-la-co*), which is located about 70 miles (112 km) southeast of Mexico City. During the 1970s Virginia Steen-McIntyre, a PhD candidate at the time, was conducting research for her PhD dissertation when she uncovered the remains of a man-made fire, which dated back to about 250,000 years ago. Once word got out about her analysis of the finding, immediately the site was shut down, all artifacts were confiscated by the local government, and her hypothesis was instantly discredited. After all, how could such a finding be accurate, since most scholars abide by the Out of Africa paradigm? Discreditation of McIntyre's findings was based on dating procedures used. Scholars pointed to the dating method of Aspartic Acid Racemization (AAR), as being an inaccurate procedure because it must be based on accurately dated material in order to compare the two types of materials. In short, AAR dating is deemed inaccurate because carbon dating is also considered inaccurate. Catch 22, anyone? Could her findings be true? We probably will never know unless politicians, scientists, and researchers all take a pledge to seek out honesty and truth.

> *For a long period it was believed that Central America, with the exception of the Mayan city of Copán, had no ruins to speak of, nor lost cities. Says the French archaeologist Claude Baudez, "In general, with one or two exceptions, scholars tended until about 1950 to deny the existence in Central America of any historical dimension: their writings implicitly assumed that all the archaeological remains belonged to the tribes found in the area at the time of the conquest.*
> ~ ~ *David Childress, Lost Cities of North & Central America*

It is common thought among researchers that the Olmec cultures were the first people to have established a civilization in Central America. Most scholars place their date of arrival to Mesoamerica at around 1200 BC. In addition, evidence might indicate that the Olmecs were black people from Africa. This speculation is based on large heads carved into stones that have African features, and wearing what might appear to be an African style helmet. The gigantic carved stone heads were discovered near Tres Capotes, La Venta, and San Lorenzo, Veracruz, which made up the Olmec stronghold of their empire. These heads were placed by the Olmec facing east across the Atlantic Ocean towards

Africa. Some experts place the Olmec arrival to Mesoamerica farther back to around 1775 BC, and refer to this time as the *initial Formative*, with an ending date placed around 1500 BC.

Evidence for black people in Mesoamerica have been produced from a site determined to be an ancient Olmec cemetery dating prior to AD 100 containing skulls with African facial features, and skeletons exhibiting Negroid attributes. Some later site findings produced skeletal evidence showing an interbreeding with other local peoples, which resulted into an absorption process of the Olmec culture.

A somewhat new and interesting presumption about the Olmec arrival to the new world comes from *Ivan Van Sertima* in his book, *They Came before Columbus*. Mr. Sertima brings a different thought about the Aztec god Quetzalcoatl. As most writings indicate Quetzalcoatl, as well as all of the other gods of Central and South America were described as white, bearded, and red-headed. However, Sertima negated this image of the Aztec god when he wrote:

> They saw him standing like a king under a canopy that had been mounted on a stepped dais in the center of the boat. He was clothed from head to foot in long, flowing white robes. He looked like a true child of the sun burned dark by its rays. His black hair and beard stood out against the whiteness of his vestment. [1]

This new and different Quetzalcoatl is said to have arrived in Mesoamerica in AD 1311. Although we have already been informed that the arrival date of the Olmecs has been estimated to be at around 1200 BC. This new model of Quetzalcoatl, according to Sertima, is based on a Mali king named Abubakari the Second who, as acknowledged by Mali courts and recorded Cairo forms, set out on an expedition from the coast of Senegambia with a fleet of well-supplied ships of men and cargo. These ships sailed west using the *Canaries Current* — an Atlantic clockwise ocean current system, which bends south from the North Atlantic current, and flows along the coast of Africa and turns west near Senegal, where it continues over to the Gulf of Mexico. It is this African king's arrival into Mexico, which inspired native people to worship this black king as a god — they called Quetzalcoatl, the Feathered Serpent. Sertima further enlightens us that the connotation *Feathered Serpent* was drawn from a symbol of a large golden bird — eagle, emblazoned on the back of a canopy where the king stood on board his ship. The eagle represented the serpent-slayer to local natives. Sertima justifies the observation based on contact between Mexicans and West Africans found in Mesoamerican strata. He further supports his findings by indicating:

A black-haired, black-bearded figure in white robes, one of the representations of Quetzalcoatl, modeled on a dark-skinned outsider, appears in paintings in the valley of Mexico... [2]

Some other thoughts about how the Olmec arrived in Central America originally includes the possibility of African sailors, maybe from Mali, Africa, were caught in an accidental drift voyage, which brought them to the New World. This would be similar to what Pedro Alvarez Cabral, a Portuguese explorer / navigator, might have experienced when his ship was caught in a strong natural current, which carried him and his crew in AD 1500 to what is today the country of Brazil, South America. Because of this accidental drift voyage, Cabral is credited as the discoverer of Brazil.

The Olmec culture presents numerous questions and puzzles to be solved. First, most researchers believe the Olmecs are the people to have created civilization in Mesoamerica, but there is another situation, which presents itself to dispel this notion. It seems there might have been another culture in Mesoamerica, which may have proceeded them. These people, once again, point to the Chinese who probably came from the Pacific side of Central America. What makes this possibility so very interesting is that it includes paper making. In the book *Columbus Was Last,* Patrick Huyghe talks about Paul Tolstoy, an anthropology professor at the University of Montreal who has studied papermaking technologies. One particular portion of papermaking involves making paper using tree bark. Tolstoy credits the Chinese with inventing, and developing the process. Research knows that the Mayas made and used bark paper for their extensive writings. So now it appears that the Olmec also had use of this material and knowledge of how to produce it, gained from Chinese immigrants who arrived in Mesoamerica before 2,500 years ago. If this fact and dating are correct, this might mean that Olmec civilization is not the first since papermaking, and use of paper for writing suggest the establishment of a rather complex culture already located in Central America by time the Olmec arrived.

A second enigma produced by the Olmec is the possible connection with Phoenicians and Egyptians. There are strong symbolism, and similarities especially between the Olmec, and ancient Egyptians. For example, we discussed earlier the eagle that slew snakes became the *Feathered Serpent*, Quetzalcoatl. It seems that the symbolism of that snake slaying bird has its origins in ancient Egypt. The bird stories developed from Egyptian priests, and seamen traveling to the ancient city of Punt (The Republic of Somaliland today). Stories of a great bird, were told that had long legs, webbed feet, long sharp talons, and strongly resembled an eagle. Modern day scholars named this bird the *Secretary Bird.* The bird's feet were its main weapons against the serpent. Stories from Punt gave rise to a connection with Horus, son of Osiris and Isis, and the one-eyed Egyptian hawk-headed god who avenged the death of Osiris by attacking, and imprisoning Set — his uncle — the evil Egyptian deity who turned himself into an ocean serpent while in captivity. The circle in the image represented the sun; this too can represent Horus because he was also known as the "splendid young sun of morning and spring." The two serpents entwined on the disc, represent Uazit, a virgin earth deity who raised Horus, and Nekhebet, sister of Uazit — sometimes also portrayed as the vulture goddess of Upper Egypt. Sertima sees this symbol as representing the unity of both upper Egypt and lower Egypt. Thus, with the landing of the Mali King, the winged disc was brought to the Americas. The winged disc symbol is visible at Tiahuanaco's *Gateway of the Sun* in South America, as well as in other locations of Central, and South America.

Pyramids in the Americas are the next objects of similarity between Egypt and Olmecs. As most everyone knows, pyramids on both sides of the Atlantic Ocean have been a big mystery for scholars, and researchers alike for many years. One observation to be noted about the pyramids is the similarities, and differences between the two groups. The Mesoamerican type pyramids are usually designed and built in a landscaped-step type shape, and commonly called Ziggurats. The ziggurat pyramid design is also common in Mid-Eastern locations, such as in the ancient city of Ur. This type of pyramid is different than the Egyptian Giza type design, which extends in a straight line from the base to the peak. The step-type pyramid may also be traced back to China, India, and around the Mediterranean Sea area. Of course, there are a number of these type of pyramid designs in Egypt. The ziggurat design, in this author's opinion, is not the original design or the basis for all pyramid designs. These type of pyramids were constructed by cultures that followed the great builders of the Giza plateau megalithic structures.

The first pyramid to be built in the Americas, according to archaeologists, was a ziggurat type at La Venta, Mexico, in the State of Tabasco, which is the heartland of the Olmec empire. La Venta is also the location for the giant stone head carvings, which seem to depict an African race of people. Dating for this pyramid is placed somewhere around 800 BC. Sertima mentions in his book, that the Egyptians stopped building the ziggurat style of pyramids sometime around 1600 BC. The La Venta pyramid, just as the pyramids on the Giza plateau, is aliened to a north-south axis. Unlike pyramids in Egypt, and like most pyramids in the Americas, it is not as tall as ones found in Egypt. However, there are some pyramids in the Americas which are larger in area than those in Egypt, such as, the Pyramid at Choula, central Mexico, which covers about forty acres, and stands 203 feet (62 m) tall. This places the base of the Choula pyramid at about three times larger than the Great Pyramid at Giza.

One other aspect of the American pyramids are most were built to serve an astronomical and religious function. These functions combined, cannot be related to the Giza pyramids. We know that the pyramids at Giza serve some kind of astronomical function, but there is no recognizable evidence to indicate the pyramids served a religious function. Unlike the Egyptian Giza type pyramids, and other later pyramids, no interior chambers have been found.

Still one more sign of Egyptian influence on the Olmec culture comes in the form of art, or more precisely, statuettes found in 1914 by archaeologist M.A. Gonzales. Gonzales was excavating a Mayan site in El Salvador when he discovered two statuettes one male, and one female. The statuettes wore Egyptian style clothing, and each possessed a cartouche, which is an oblong scroll bearing a name of an imperator that would protect them from evil in both life and death. Since that time, there have been additional objects recovered from around El Salvador, which possess Egyptian attributes.

One explanation for the close tie-ins with Egyptians and the Olmec people, is that at one time as Egypt was experiencing an economical decline, and all of the grandness of ancient Egypt had long since passed, the Egyptians combined forces with the Phoenician empire to number one, have access to cedar trees to build ships, and secondly, the Egyptians needed qualified seamen to help man their ships, and Phoenicians were already sailing the Mediterranean Sea trading with other nations. Further, the Nubian people of the upper Egypt locations were more independent, and unattached from Egypt. Many of those people were most anxious to join seafaring expeditions since a number of these people were already qualified sailors resulting from Egypt's once far reaching commercial voyages. Therefore, it is suspected that an expedition, or a number of voyages, sailed to the New World in ships of Egyptian design, built using Lebanon cedar, and operated by a crew of Egyptians, Phoenicians and Nubian seamen. This observation might account for the diversity of artifacts, and similarities between those three ancient cultures, represented in the Americas.

The Maya was the next great Mesoamerican civilization to gain prominence, stemming from the Olmec demesne. On the Mesoamerican time line (see Fig. 1), the Maya began their development by interacting with the Olmec culture starting at around 1000 BC. As a dominant culture in Central America, they flourished until about AD 250. Just as the Olmec, the Maya used paper for writing, and they received their calendar knowledge also from the Olmec, which was determined to be more accurate than the Gregorian calendar of the sixteenth century. As it appears, the Maya seemed to have excelled ahead of the Olmec in scholarly pursuits. They not only developed the calendar to a more advanced level, but they also revealed their superiority in the field of written works with the creation of the *Popol Vuh* (meaning 'Book of Advice'). The work was a sacred text of the K'iche' people, a subgroup of the Maya, who resided in the Midwestern highlands of Guatemala. The Popol Vuh written in the language of the K'iche' people (similar to the Kaqchikel language of Central Guatemala) contained their full history, and mythologies. One unfortunate circumstance for archaeology is that the conquering Spaniards decided to destroy all written works of any civilization, which came into their possession labeling them evil or falsehoods created by *the evil one*.

Mathematics was another area where the Maya excelled; as indicated by their detailed calendar, their well designed architecture — exhibiting intricate carved stone work, and their ability to calculate time, and dates deep into antiquity as displayed on an ancient stele. Author, Graham Hancock offers an explanation of the stele in *Fingerprints of the Gods* :

> On a stele at Quiriga in Guatemala a date over 90 million years ago is computed; on another a date over 300 million years before that is given. These are actual computations, stating correctly day and month positions, and are comparable to calculations in our calendar giving the month positions on which Easter would have fallen at equivalent distances in the past.[3]

The architecture of the Maya is best exemplified by *Chichen Itza,* largest of all Mayan cities, and archaeological sites. It is home to the *El Castillo* pyramid (in Spanish, "The Castle"), also called 'Pyramid of Kukulcán', the Mayan Quetzalcoatl. This site was started in about the 5th century AD when the original founders built two stone stairways down to two cenotes, which are underground water holes accessible only through a small opening. Then at around AD 987, the Itzá culture occupied the area, and added another cenote just north of the first two. The original cenotes were still used for drawing water, but the northern cenote was left for religious rituals of sacrifices to *Chac* , the rain god. This site is also noted for Temple of the Warriors, the Great Ball Court, and over eighty *sacbeobs* (paved causeways), which cris-cross the entire site, and extend in all directions. Just as in Egypt and at other ancient sites on the opposite side of the Atlantic, this pyramid was built over an existing temple; however, this site contained a statue of the god Chac Mool and a Jaguar shaped throne painted red.

Although, the most unique feature of this pyramid is that on every Spring and Autumn equinoxes, late in the afternoon from the northwest corner of the pyramid, the sun casts a series of shadows along the western balustrade on the north side allowing an animation of a serpent wriggling its way down the staircase, representing the feathered-serpent — Kukulcán. A design of this nature certainly did not just develop from an ordinary everyday tribe of people who worked their land to provide a living for their families.

The next, and final great culture to exemplify the magnitude of Central America are the Aztec cultures. The Aztec name derives from "Azteca," meaning someone who comes from Aztzán considered by some to be a mythical place in northern Mexico. The Aztecs were looked upon as wanderers coming from the north, perhaps as far north as the North American Southwest region. Along those same lines, there might be some faint connection to an archaeological site in Wisconsin called, Aztalan. Alexander von Humboldt, a German researcher wrote that the Aztec, who he helped to name, came originally from a land of flowing water far to the north of Central Mexico. The now Aztalan State Park sits on the banks of the Crawfish River near Lake Mills, in the State of Wisconsin, U.S.A. At the Aztalan site there are a number of earthen mounds, a central plaza, man-made wooden fortifications along with two reworked flat-topped pyramid mounds (also see Appendix). We will discuss mounds later on, but for now it is necessary to mention these structures as it relates to the Aztec mythology. David Hatcher Childress wrote about his visit to the Aztalan site and made this observation in his book, *Lost Cities of North & Central America* :

> I was immediately impressed by the two main pyramids facing each other across a broad plaza. It was like a miniature version of Teotihuacan in Mexican, a pyramid of the Sun facing a pyramid of the moon.[4]

Tenochtitlán became the great capital city of the Aztec; but the name Aztec is not correct for these people. This term was placed upon them by Alexander von Humboldt to indicate where these people might have originated from in the north. The correct name should be *Mexica*, and they explained to the Spanish chronicler they originated from a womblike cavern of Chicomoztoc north of Teotihuacan. Chicomoztoc (pronounced, chee-co-moz-toch) was where seven caves were located, and each one of those caves corresponded to one of the *Nahuatl* tribes. The Nahuatl (Nawatlahtolli) people also migrated south nearly at the same time as the Mexica. In the broadest case, they were part of the Mexica people, and their language was Uto-Aztecan. This family of languages ranges from North and Central American Indian languages, which include Shoshone, Pima, Hopi, Comanche and Ute. All of these Indian Nations once occupied locations from Montana, Wyoming, eastern Idaho, across the Colorado Plateau, and down through southern Arizona into northern Mexico.

The Aztec/Mexica tell of their patron sun and war god named *Huitzilopochtli*, who led them during their migration to Central Mexico. Huitzilopochtli (spoken, weetz-ee-loh-POSHT-lee), toward the end of the journey appointed *Tenoch,* an Aztec patriarch to lead the migration under his direction. So when they arrived at their home city (today — Mexico City), it became known as Tenochtitlán, after the leader Tenoch. Although the Mexica still referred to themselves as, 'the people of the sun' because their patron god Huitzilopochtli fought to allow the sun to move across the sky during their journey into Central Mexico.

Aztec civilization thrived through trade with other surrounding cultures, including the remaining Olmec civilization. As population and business grew in the Valley of Mexico, two new centers were added one at Cuicuilco in the southwestern portion of the valley, and the other at Teotihuacan about 30 miles (48 km) northeast of Mexico City. Cuicuilco, sometime after, was destroyed by a volcanic eruption. The city of Teotihuacan had already been in existence by

100 BC. As to whom may have been the original builders of the city remains unanswered.

The Aztec believed, based on Nahuatl tribal myths, the city was in place long before the end of the Aztec's Fourth Sun. As some readers might recall, the Aztecs believed there were five suns, and we are now in the Fifth Sun, while all the others have ended by means of catastrophic occurrences. So this makes the city very ancient and no culture in or around Central Mexico has, as yet, taken credit for its construction. Most researchers place the city dating at about 100 BC. More recent studies of the ancient site have produced evidence of earlier works, possibly displaying construction work over an existing site, which seems to have been quite common among ancient builders. The new findings within the ruins, point farther back to around 4000 BC for construction on the original site. There are some signs of early Olmec knowledge of the site due to the presence of U-shaped drains, constructed to bring in water to a natural cave underneath the Pyramid of the Sun. However, there are no actual signs of extensive Olmec involvement with the building process of any of the structures. Due to the age and composition of the structures it is questioned if, perhaps, numerous civilizations have dominated the city, and at times many other cultures have lived there, and left their mark upon the archaic venue.

The Aztecs were so overwhelmed at the site of the timeworn city they named it 'The City of the Gods'; and proclaimed the city as — birthplace of the Fifth Sun, and the capital city of their god Quetzalcoatl.

Now what makes this site so unique when compared with other Mesoamerican sites is the fact that it exhibits a ground layout similar to ancient Egypt, and the pyramid placement at Giza. This might not be so shocking when we remember that scholars claim the Olmec were the first people to create civilization in Central America. If the ancient dating to around 4000 BC is correct, then that would pre-date the Olmecs by over 2,200 years. It is also quite obvious that time required to plan, and build these structures must be added to the time approximation of when an unknown civilization could have arrived, set up settlements in Central America, and to endeavor to create such a complex monumental site. As to whom these people might have been, it only seems plausible to suspect that they were either Egyptians or someone who had close contact with, or extensive knowledge of, Egyptian methods. In every respect this ancient layout is, so far, one of a kind in Mesoamerica since no other city or complex exhibits such detailed astronomical details. In fact, this site layout is far more extensive than the ground layout of Giza.

After examination of the site, researchers speculated about the star Sirius having an effect on the overall city layout. Another thought came from Stansbury Hagar of the Brooklyn Institute of the Arts and Sciences, who postulated that the Street of the Dead, which rested on an incline of 15° 30' east of north, could signify the Milky Way galaxy. Further study by Hagar, resulted in a hypothesis that Teotihuacan was a ground representation for a 'map of heaven'. He observed the pyramids, mounds and additional structures all symbolized heavenly bodies in relation to the Street of the Dead, which might symbolize the center of the Milky Way, as the Egyptians interpret the center of the galaxy as a river running through its midst. Another theory to support this idea might come from Alfred Schlemmer, an American engineer, who argues for a theory that The Street of the Dead was not meant as a street at all, but instead were rows of reflecting pools linked by a series of locks, which originated from the Pyramid of the Moon. This observation was reinforced by Professor Rene Millon, of the University of Rochester when he confirmed numerous waterway networks, which extended to Lake Texcoco ten miles away. Finally, just as in Egypt, the pyramids at Teotihuacan are all ground images of the three stars of Orion's Belt.

Graham Hancock in *Fingerprints of the Gods*, expounds on the layout of the Teotihuacan complex in some detail:

> Teotihuacan might originally have been designed as a precise scale-model of the solar system. At any rate, if the centre line of the Temple of Quetzalcoatl were taken as denoting the position of the sun, markers laid out northwards from it along the axis of the Street of the Dead seemed to indicate the correct orbital distances of the inner planets, the asteroid belt, Jupiter, Saturn (represented by the so-called 'Sun Pyramid'), Uranus (by the 'Moon Pyramid'), and Neptune and Pluto by as yet unexcavated mounds some kilometers farther north.[5]

Once again we find evidence of advanced astronomical knowledge presented by ancient peoples in deep prehistorical times. In my book *Our Missing Ancestors,* a number of examples were presented to highlight this knowledge among people in Earth's deep unknown past; for example, Zachariah Sitchen's interpretation of the Sumerian Enuma Elish or 'Cosmic War' epic. Another example is that of the Dogon's intricate knowledge of the Sirius star system. Knowledge of this technical nature, according to science, should not have existed that far back in time. Hancock concurs whole heartedly when he stated:

> No known civilization of that epoch, either in the Old World or in the New, is supposed to have had any knowledge at all of the outer planets – let alone to have possessed accurate information concerning their orbital distances from each other and from the sun.[6]

As for the people arriving here during pre-Columbian times or more precisely, in proto-historical times, one explanation comes from *John D. Baldwin* when he observed:

In Sahagun's history, it is stated that, according to the traditions of the people of Yucatan, the original civilizers came in ships from the East. A similar tradition was communicated to the Spaniards by Montezuma. The Abbe Brasseur de Bourbourg, speaking of the earliest civilization of the Mexicans and Central Americans, says : "The native traditions generally attribute it to bearded white men, who came across the ocean from the east." The native histories he has examined describe three classes of ancient inhabitants. First, the Chichimecs, who seem to have been the uncivilized aborigines of the country; second, the Colhuas, who were the first civilizers, and by whom the Chichimecs were taught to cultivate the earth, cook their food, and adopt the usages of civilized life; and third, the Nahuas or Toltec, who came much later as peaceable immigrants, but after a time united with uncivilized Chichimecs, caused a civil war, and secured power. The Colhuas were the bearded white men, who came in the earliest times across the Atlantic. They built Palenque and other cities, originated the oldest and finest monuments of the ancient civilization, and established the great kingdom of Xibalba...[7]

What makes the study of the Aztec so very valuable is the long range connection of this culture to North America, specifically with Ohio and Wisconsin, and with the same identical celestial knowledge as that of their descendant's, especially the Hopi of Arizona plus a possible relationship to the Anasazi of New Mexico, U.S.A. This topic will be discussed in more detail in Chapter 11. Knowledge, traditional actions and technical expertise all evident in, at least, three different cultures over a vast area of land, and many thousands of years must suggest an antiquity of an original culture, that arrived on the shores of North America possessing some form of higher education, and accompanied by a high level of technical skills. It does not seem possible that a culture practicing horrible rituals of torture, sacrifice, cannibalism, and fierce war-like conduct could have maintained a quest to teach, explore and to use advanced celestial awareness in addition to master building ingenuity all at the same time, while growing and expanding their civilization; and accomplishing all of these feats from paleo-Indian. Something just does not seem plausible with this observation.

Mesoamerican Time Line Graph

Olmec: Initial Formative ____1775-1500 B.C.
　　　　　Early Formative ____1450-1005 B.C.
　　　　　Middle Formative____1005-400 B.C.
　　　　　Late Formative ____400 B.C.
Peak of Civilization: 1350 B.C. _____Decline 400 B.C. Approximately

Zapotec:
　　　　Migrated from the north about 1000 B.C. ____Decline 200 B.C. Approximately

Maya:
　　　　About 1000 B.C. _____Decline A.D. 250 Approximately
　　　　Peak of ruling power — around 500 B.C.

Aztec:
　　　　Original name – Mexica — Migrated from the north about A.D. 1200
　　　　　　　　　　　　　　　　　　Decline A.D. 1521, Approximately

　　　　Their peak of reigning power around A.D. 1428 prior to the Spanish arrival in A.D. 1519

Chichmec:
　　　　Migrated from the north about A.D. 1100-1200
　　　　　　　　　　　　　　　　　　Decline A.D. 1590 Approximately

Toltec:
　　　　From around A.D. 900 _____Decline A.D. 1100 Approximately

Fig. 1　　　　　　　　　　　　　　Provided by Terrance F. Johnson, 2013

The Amazon and South America as a whole continue to reveal its history to us. If we ever assume that Southern American history is known, that is simply not the case. It was as recent as 1911 that Machu Picchu was discovered. The "Lost City of the Incas" is only 50 miles from the ancient capital Cusco, but apparently no one ever found it—

~ ~ Philip Coppens, Author
~ ~ The Lost Civilization Enigma

Chapter 7

Ancient People of South America

Just as we have found in Mesoamerica, written documentation of history and events are not available to us for a number of reasons. The main reason, perhaps, is the willful, and disdainful destruction of any and all written works once deemed to be evil-pagan works of the Devil by Jesuit Catholic priests accompanying the Spanish explorers on their gold hunting mission to the New World. The second reason might be that the Inca people had no known form of alphabet, script, glyphs, or clay cylinder forms of writing. What they used was a system known as *Khipu*, a complex form of knots consisting of colored cord, which were varied by an individual knot type, or a special form indicated by a twist to the left or to the right, some with dyed wool or cotton threads worked into the process. This form of communication was used in all Inca *suyus* (regions or provinces) for record keeping of government business, financial information, and personal data. There was one problem about this system, and that is — modern science cannot interpret how the Inca used these symbols and what they expressed. Back in 2005 a study at Harvard pronounced an initial breakthrough in understanding how the system worked; but since then no further update has been announced. This information exchange is very old, and there has been evidence uncovered at the ancient site of Caral, in Peru, which reveals the system was used as far back as 2600 BC. Caral is currently identified as the oldest settlement of the Americas; and Caral will be discussed later on in this chapter. The Khipu (or Quipu) system, once it had been identified as a communication method, was also destroyed by the Spaniards just as written sheets of paper were burned.

The early history, and origins of the Inca people are rather limited. We probably know more about their empire than we know about them personally. Some researchers suspect the Inca have their origins from an Andean civilization, which probably existed somewhere around 7500 BC. These people might be described as the "original mountain people." Archaeologists have submitted evidence of these people living at altitudes of 17,400 feet (5,300 m) above sea level in high altiplano temperature sectors. This unidentified civilization, just as the later Incas, produced no written forms of their past history or personal lives.

The Inca empire is rated as the largest during pre-Columbian times. The Inca empire at the high point of its existence covered almost the entire west coast of the South American continent, extending from the Ancasmayo River near Ecuador down to Santiago, Chile. The empire was divided into four suyus, or provinces. The first and most heavily populated, was Chinchaysuyu which covered the northern Andes. The second, Antisuyu, was located northwest of Cusco, the Incan capital — high in the Andes, and it became the root word for *Andes.* The third, was Collasuyu (or, Qollasuyu), extending from the Bolivian high plateau, and spreading over the greater portion of the southern Andes through Argentina projecting into Chile near Santiago. The fourth suyus, Cuntisuyu (or, Kuntisuyu) was located along Peru's southern coast stretching north up to around Cusco. The entire Incan Empire was known as *Tawantinsuyu* meaning, 'Four Regions' (four suyus), and they observed a national language called *Quechua*: although in many of the suyus different dialects, and local language forms were maintained.

Religion within the Incan empire mainly centered around *Inti* — the sun god, often depicted as a circle with a face in the middle, encircled with embellished flames. Although other forms of religion existed among locals in the form of *Huacas*, which was the worship of spirits who inhabited physical objects such as trees, mountains, lakes or stepped-pyramids. Then also, the Peruvians maintained the worship of *Pacamama* or 'Mother Earth'. Later on they also adopted worship of the sea or *Cochamama.*

When comparing Mesoamerica with South America, it might be quite correct to say that South America is much more mysterious than the Central American expanse. South America seems to possess many more unusual, more sophisticated architectural structures than found in the Mesoamerican regions. There is no doubt that the entire country is more mysterious than any of the others in the Americas. As Philip Coppens stated, South America keeps revealing itself. Even so, what has already been revealed is truly astonishing when it is understood that such unique archaeological sites have been created by such ancient, and unknown people prior to, or perhaps, even during the actuality of the Incan empirical age. What makes this even more inexplicable is the fact that the Inca people know little or nothing about any of these grand — highly technical megalithic and geographical sites. Of the complex at Puma Punku, Bolivia the Inca say gods built the structures in one night. One would think that with an empire the size of the Incan, surely one or more would have been credited to the Incan people. However, much like the city of Teotihuacan in the Valley of Mexico, most all of these mysterious structures were extant long before they were discovered, and possibly even prior to the Incan people themselves.

What legends that do exist today come mainly from verbal accounts of Incas who painstakingly produced painted pottery, and other artifacts to pass along their mythology after the Spanish destruction of what records they once possessed. One myth, which survived was that of *Viracocha* the Incan version of Aztec Quetzalcoatl. Viracocha, like Quetzalcoatl, was white and bearded. There are several variations of the Viracocha myth. One tells of Viracocha emerging from the bottom of Lake Titicaca and creating the sky, moon, stars, and men — by breathing life into stones. This endeavor failed because he created giants, which had to be destroyed. He then created people from pebbles, which were scattered throughout the world. Another version of the story is that Viracocha came out of the Pacific Ocean, perhaps from the Cochamama culture of Peru. Upon his arrival, Viracocha appeared at Tiahuanaco during a time of darkness bearing the gifts of light and civilization. Still, one other account of Viracocha comes from Graham Hancock in his book *Fingerprints of the Gods* :

> Viracocha himself, with his two assistants, journeyed north . . . He traveled up the cordillera, one assistant went along the coast, and the other up the edge of the eastern forests . . . The Creator proceeded to Urcos, near Cuzco, where he commanded the future population to emerge from a mountain. He visited Cuzco, and then continued north to Ecuador. There, in the coastal province of Manta, he took leave of his people and, walked on the waves, disappeared across the ocean.[1]

In one other version of this story it describes the pale Viracocha walking into the foam of the Pacific Ocean returning from whence he came. Viracocha, unlike Quetzalcoatl, left his people going west, whereas, Quetzalcoatl returned to his land going east. One answer for this might be that the Inca resided on the Pacific side of the South American continent, while the Aztec and Maya dwelled more on the Atlantic side of Central America.

> *And who could say just what civilizations might have existed in Peru in the unexplored regions of the past? Every year archaeologists come up with new finds which extend the horizons further and further back in time. So why shouldn't they one day discover evidence of the penetration into the Andes, in remote antiquity, of a race of civilizers who had come from overseas and gone away again after completing their work?*

Terrance F. Johnson

~ ~ *Graham Hancock, Author*
~ ~ *Fingerprints of the Gods*

Just as Quetzalcoatl had his great city capital of Teotihuacan in Mesoamerica, the god Viracocha laid claim to the great megalithic site of Tiahuanaco in the Andean mountains of Bolivia, South America. Once again this ancient site was probably extant many hundreds, if not thousands of years, prior to its discovery. The Inca claimed that they heard from their forefathers everything appeared in just one night. The indigenous native ethnic people, Aymara, are recognized for naming Tiahuanaco (also, Tiwanaku) because the name is based on the term *taypiqala,* which means 'stone in Center'. Tiahuanaco lies in Bolivia, South America at a height of approximately 13,000 feet (3962.4 m). Tiahuanaco is an important ancient city, since it is near this city that Lake Titicaca is located at a level of about 800 feet (244 m) lower than the city level, and it is in Lake Titicaca where myth stated Viracocha rose up from its bottom. At first these ruins were dated somewhere near 200 BC, but more recent astronomical dating placed it closer to 17,000 BC. Judging from the layout of the ruins, at the site, many believe it to have been an astronomical observatory. One structure, which has been excavated, provides some very interesting discoveries. A large appearing hill or mound standing about 59 feet (18 m) tall, and better known as the Akapana Pyramid Mound, was constructed with walls, and columns originating from its base with carved stones placed at the mounds summit. This structure, it is thought by archaeologists, was constructed using material from earlier buildings, which were torn down and salvaged for parts. The monolith was built with Ashlar stone shaped into rectangular forms, and stacked into courses complete with precise drainage systems. The Akapana, and one other edifice known as the Pumapunku Stepped Platforms, both contained conduits made of red sandstone joined together with a unique bronze alloy made of copper, arsenic and nickel. Depending at what age these monuments were created, the use of bronze would have been out of place 15,000 years ago. Remember, Egyptologists tell us that the Giza pyramids were built using only stone, wood, and copper tools. How then could a bronze alloy have appeared in the Andean mountains of Bolivia over 14,000 years before the Great Pyramid of Egypt was built? This point has been supported, somewhat, by studies conducted by Professor Arthur Posnansky, and others who have concluded from astronomical investigations of the ecliptic that the site might date to 12,000 BC or earlier. If they are correct, Tiahuanaco would be one of the oldest archaeological sites in the world.

The ancient site is also home to an immense archaeological structure known as the *Kalasasaya*. The structure is 390 feet by 426 feet (120 by 130 m) surrounded by high stone walls, and set to the cardinal points. The layout stands to the north of the Akapana, and just to the west of a Semi-Subterranean Temple. This temple's composition contains walls lined with carved heads, possibly representing (as David Hatcher believes) all of the races of the world. The wall material is sandstone pillars with Ashlar blocks. The largest stone weighs nearly 26.5735 tons (27 mt).

Also located inside of the Kalasasaya is the *Gate of the Sun,* which is carved from one megalith. It is disputed by many researchers that the large symbol was not located there originally. It may have been relocated to that spot during one of the renovation periods. The stone has carvings depicting the sun-god in the center with rays emitting out from his face in all directions. Other carvings show images of anthropomorphic beings with wings, and curled tails believed to represent astronomical references, thus, allowing some individuals to theorize that the large stone is a calendar (See site images at end of chapter).

Further efforts by Professor Posnansky dated the Kalasasaya (meaning, 'Place of the Up-right Standing Stones'— from the Aymara people) back even closer to the actual time of its layout through the use of solar alignments of certain structures at the site. This process resembles the using of stars or constellations for calculating where, and when they were positioned during a specific time in antiquity. Posnansky applied the Milankovitch Cycles in calculating the correct positioning of these structures to the time of sunrises and sunsets. This pertains to the axial tilt of the Earth — obliquity, and the angle of the tilt fluctuates with the plane of Earth's orbit. The fluctuations consistently slows by 2.4° obliquity variations — taking around 41,000 years to shift the tilt of the Earth from 22.1° to 24.5°, and back again. Currently scientists place the Earth's tilt to be at 23.44° from the orbital plane, and calculations show the lesser stage to occur about AD 11,800 with the last maximum stage to occur at about 8700 BCE. So therefore, by using a graph created by the International Conference of Ephemerids, he was able to plot a reading of 23° 8' 48" as the obliquity of the ecliptic during the time when Kalasasaya was staked out for building, and that time pointed to 15,000 BC. Posnansky also believed there were three building phases. The second building phase was plotted at 12,000 BC. These dates precede the Sumerians listed at around 6000 BC, and the Egyptians, according to many Egyptologists, are around 3200 BC. The third building phase, determined by Posnansky, was just before the last glacial period ended.

Posnansky's work at Tiahuanaco also included the discovery, and interpretation of an immense block of stone once carved into statue form. The stone (akin to the Gate of the Sun) was cut from one megalith, and dubbed 'The Great Idol'. The statue was shown wearing a type of hat with the hands placed across the chest appearing to be holding some type of object in each hand, while staring straight forward. On the entire surface of the body portion were designs very similar to the Gate of the Sun stone with winged beings, engraved faces, condor heads, a crown, scepter, and snakes. Posnansky's interpretation of the monument was that it represented a calendar dating back to around 15,000 years. Following Posnansky's death, Professor Hans Schindler Bellamy and Dr. Paul Allen continued the study of The Great Idol by calculating more than 1000 carvings on the stone. Finally, coming to the conclusion that Posnansky was correct, that the huge stone was a calendar only it did not go back to 15,000 years; instead it stretched beyond to about 27,000 years BC.

Posnansky also believed that Tiahuanaco was involved with the final melting of the last glacial maximum, ending at about 10,000 BC. In fact, it is suspected that Tiahuanaco was once submerged by glacial meltwaters. Further, Posnansky believed that the area may have suffered a number of floods, which might have pushed the Andes' region higher. This clearly indicated that the archaeological site was built prior to the end of the last glacial maximum. Proof of the flood waters was provided by stones in the complex covered with a thin layer of calcium deposits made by sea water at one time. In addition, sea shells have been found in strata by Augustus le Plongeon, a French anthropologist. The finding might have led to the theory that Tiahuanaco was once a seaport city located at a much lower altitude.

The concept of Tiahuanaco being submerged by meltwaters from the last glacial phase, probably gave credibility to the legend of the Incan creator god Viracocha rising up from the bottom of Lake Titicaca, and bringing light to end the darkness, and civilization for survival of the people. The ancient verbal accounts tell of Tiahuanaco being built by white strangers wearing beards. So we must ask ourselves — who were these white gods with beards? David Hatcher Childress offers one solution:

> Perhaps none other than those mysterious seafarers who mapped Antarctica before it was covered with ice, sailed the world spreading a megalithic culture, and wore red turbans over their blonde hair — the Atlantean League![2]

About one mile (1.6 km) north of Tiahuanaco stands another mysterious archaeological site even more perplexing than the capital of Viracocha. This site is actually a part of Tiahuanaco and it is named *Puma Pumku* ('Gateway of the Puma' or 'Door of the Puma'). A puma is also described as a cougar, panther or Mountain Lion in North America. Their habitat is from Canada in the north, to Patagonia in the south. Posnansky, after discovering this site questioned some of the native elders about the history of the place, and of course they new nothing other than verbal legend of white men — gods building the site; but they did remember that the original name was *Winay Marca,* meaning 'Eternal City'. Unfortunately, this name was ironic since the entire complex had been totally obliterated. By what force — no one knows. The first thing, which many authors write when addressing Puma Pumku is that, "...blocks are scattered...". Some, of course, offer an earthquake as the most obvious reason for the destruction. However, could raging flood waters have caused this great amount of damage to large stone objects? As seen by examples of water so powerful that it could change the course of mighty rivers — the answer to that question must be *yes*. Since this area is part of the Tiahuanaco site, it is quite obvious that if one area is submerged, then it is most likely this area would also suffer the same forces. This thought might be of some clarity as researchers explore theories of Puma Pumku once being a port city on the banks of Lake Titicaca. It is believed that at some time in the past, Lake Titicaca was much larger, and extended its banks very close to Tiahuanaco, and Puma Pumku. Some researchers have pointed out there once existed a canal at Puma Pumku, which was destroyed — possibly by an earthquake.

Whatever destroyed Puma Pumku had to be of a sizable magnitude. The blocks, always described as scattered, were of considerable thickness, weight, and locking design. Plus these blocks were cut from diorite stone with a grade of eight denoting hardness on the Moh's scale. It should be noted that the Moh's scale, according to some, is not the best measure to use when determining the hardness of diorite because of the amount of mineral substance make-up of the rock. Because of this variation, it is recommended to allow 2.5 to 7 points difference. Albeit, this stone was used by the ancient Egyptians to work granite blocks, so the hardness factor cannot be discarded. As an example of size, one stone is measured at 9 feet (2.7 m) long, by 5.2 feet (1.6 m) wide, and its weight was calculated at close to 18,500 pounds (8391.45 kg). David Childless, on one of his travel expeditions to Puma Pumku, expressed amazement at what he saw at the site when he arrived. He, too, used the word 'scattered' when describing the condition of stones, once part of some majestic monument. He mentioned sandstone and andosite blocks appearing as a child's building block set, scattered and tossed around, some weighing perhaps as much as 300 tons (272155.422 kg) each. The condition of the entire site leaves no doubt that some prodigious catastrophe caused this massive amount of damage.

In addition to the size and weight of the stone blocks, they also contained a very unique locking system, which joined them together, and was designed most likely to stabilize the structure from earthquakes; possibly another unfortunate irony, on their part. The locking system for the blocks was designed by cutting out spaces, which appeared as a capital 'I' only larger, deeper and wider, so as to accept the fit of either a solid object or to be filled with a metal liquid substance (See Figs.1 & 2). This locking system has never been discovered at any other site in the world other than at Ollantaytambo, located about 45 miles (72 km) from Cuzco. Once again from David Childress who wrote of the locking channel used in the megaliths during a stopover at the site of Ollantaytambo:

> Even more unusual is a stone in which a "keyway" has been carefully cut into the stone to hold a metal clamp, presumably to hold two colossal blocks together as earthquake protection. This unusual technique is found at Puma Pumku in Tiahuanaco and nowhere else.[3]

One possibility for the unknown catastrophe, which wreaked havoc on Puma Pumku, might connect to the sudden meltdown of the Wisconsinan glacial of North America around 17,000 BC. The mass acceleration of meltwaters entering the oceans of the world would most certainly have caused an equally increasing rate of sea levels along with colder sea temperatures, once considered as a cause for the commencement of the Younger Dryas glacial, which ended at around 11,500 BP. As the reader might recall, Graham Hancock expressed an image of what the North American landscape would have experienced starting at about 17,000 BC with volcanic eruptions, and earthquakes instigating a 350 foot (107 m) rise in global sea levels. It is quite possible that such a cataclysmic event could have triggered immense tsunami type walls of water to come crashing inward on Puma Pumku — perhaps not once but many times, resulting in giant blocks of stone initiating an image of a child's set of wooden blocks 'scattered' in every direction. (See Images of Puma Pumku at the end of the chapter)

The next question to be asked is — if Puma Pumku was totally annihilated by massive walls of water, then why were the structures at Tiahuanaco not in the same form of destruction? The area, and currently excavated structures are certainly in a state of wear and tear, but they do not exhibit the same considerable amount of collapse, and scattering as observed at the Puma Pumku site. As previously mentioned, Posnansky hypothesized that Tiahuanaco was built, at least, by 15,000 BC. If the estimate is correct, it might mean that Puma Pumku was built prior to Tiahuanaco, making it even older. Also consider Posnansky's observation that possibly Tiahuanaco went through three building stages. If correct, that might be a reason for Tiahuanaco to be in better condition than Puma Pumku. Perhaps, those ancient builders after yet another devastating blow to their complex started their repairs on Tiahuanaco first, and over time no longer completed work on the Puma Pumku complex for some unexplained reason.

One other view of the situation could be that Puma Pumku was built long before the Tiahuanaco structures. As suspected by archaeologists, the questionable canal, which many identify at Puma Pumku, did actually exist. If so, the canal could suggest that Lake Titicaca or the sea once provided a shore line for the Puma Pumku complex. Possibly once destroyed by rising seas, the builders might have decided not to pursue a rebuilding project or not to restore the precision work on Puma Pumku perhaps, from a generational phase out; much like the ancient pyramids of Giza giving way to lesser forms — such as, the stepped pyramids. The exactness of shape, the squareness of the blocks, the cookie cutter designs, the angular bored holes in some, the taper and angles involved in many operations, and the highly polished surfaces with edges still maintaining sharp skillful cuts exhibits the craftsmanship, and knowledge of a much higher level of mathematics than could be expected of people, perhaps living in 17,000 BC. The intricacy and nature of the cuts evoke images of modern day laser template processes. These specimens are so very well made that they give an impression of being prefabricated in a well-manufactured mold. How is it that we can find such detailed, precise objects tossed about on an Andean high plateau, which might date far older than 15,000 BC? These blocks are far more ornate, and technically designed, and manufactured than ones found on any other megalithic site in the world.

We have not yet completed our investigation of the Tiahuanaco site. Other mysteries call for our attention only this time we need to look at Lake Titicaca located near by Tiahuanaco, just north past Puma Pumku. Once again, in ancient times, Lake Titicaca was much larger than it is today, and it was once the shore line of Tiahuanaco. So what makes this lake so mysterious? First, in an area between Bolivia and Peru at the bottom of Lake Titicaca, evidence of possible ancient ruins has been discovered. Lake Titicaca is noted as the world's highest navigable lake. According to a team of international archaeologists who explored the underwater area, they think that it may be an ancient temple dating to 1000 to 1500 years old. The temple ruins appear to be about 650 feet (200 m) long by 164 feet (50 m) wide. They believe this temple ruins predates the Inca, and might possibly be connected to the Tiahuanaco builders.

Lake Titicaca is a sacred place to the Inca people. It is here where they say civilization first began with Viracocha rising out of its depths — creating the sun, and the stars. It was also at Lake Titicaca where the first Incan king, Manco Capac was born; recognized as the son of Viracocha.

Currently Lake Titicaca lies at 12,500 feet (3810 m) above sea level in the Andes Mountains straddling the borders of Peru on the west and Bolivia on the east. It is the second largest, and second deepest lake in South America after Lake Maracaibo, covering approximately 3200 square miles (8300 km²), and extending northwest-to-southeast for about 120 miles (190 km).

The lake is divided into two portions by a narrow strait named Tiquina; the smallest section lies in the southeast sector of the lake in Bolivia, and is known as Lake Huiñaymarca; while the large sector is in the northwest of Lake Titicaca, and called Lake Chucuito by the Bolivians. These two sections of the lake have different names by the Peruvians. The smaller lake is called Lake Pequeño; while the larger lake is known as Lake Grande. The name Titicaca is unclear in its meaning — possibly "Rock of the Puma," or "Crag of Lead."

Rumors of sunken ruins have persisted for years originating from local fishermen telling of sightings of buildings visible when water levels drop during drought conditions. Also there are numerous reports from local people, who after diving down into the lake tell of actually touching rooftops of stone buildings. In 1967 the Bolivian government organized a search for these reported buildings, but not until proper agreements were reached with the locals who became concerned since they deemed Lake Titicaca sacred. Then in 1988 National Geographic formed a group to also search for any evidence of underwater ruins. It wasn't until 2000 when the international expedition reported the discovery of these puzzling ruins. More than 200 dives were made to levels of 100 feet

(30 m) in order to record findings of high walls covered in mud, while in a state of erosion from saltwater. Their initial search followed paved pathways from the shore to the lake where these stones went down into the waters of the lake and met-up with a gigantic crescent-shaped base. The pathways consisted of finely cut stones, meticulously placed to produce thirty pathways altogether. The pathways ultimately served as underwater highways for the divers to follow, which led them to the ruin's location.

Divers were also able to find ruins buried under, at least, 6 feet (1.5 m) of sediment, on the bottom of the lake, which they estimated as far older than the causeway leading up to them. Dating obtained from fossilized sea shells found there, show the ruins date back prior to 12,000 BC. The mud layer on top of the roofs, it is believed, was not placed there from any soil seeping down from the natural shoreline; rather the soil was a result from sediment piled up from waters placed there after the 'Biblical Flood' indicating that Lake Titicaca did not exist prior to the Great Deluge, and that it was located at sea level prior to the flood. Additional proof of location is based on discoveries of terraced levels of earth used to grow crops, such as maize. The terraces were above Lake Titicaca demonstrating that maize could be grown above the lake area, and that people were farming the region long before any cataclysmic incident demolished the site, thus, ultimately causing a geological uplift of the Andes to a higher altitude where maize could no longer be grown due to inappropriate temperatures for that particular crop. If this is actually the case, then it must be obvious that not all people were killed off when the massive flooding occurred. As the Inca tell it — one man and one woman escaped death by climbing to the top of a mountain, and eventually repopulating the world after the great flood destroyed everything.

Lake Titicaca contains a large island named Isla del Sol (meaning, Island of the Sun). The island has no roads for automobiles, but it contains more than 180 ruins of the Incan period of c. 15th century AD. The island also has a labyrinth-like structure (the Sacred Rock) which the Aymara people call, Chicana, Kasa Pata, and Pilco Kaima. It is this location where the Aymara believe the Incan sun god Inti (often thought to be the father of Manco Capac) was born.

Another important feature appearing on Lake Titicaca is the reed boats used by the fishermen, which are made from Totora reeds. Many of these crafts are built as a houseboat, and support everyday family life, along side of everyday work requirements. The indigenous people occupying these boats will often form them into a man-made island by hitching the boats together. This creates a floating city, and protects the people from danger for they can simply disconnect the individual boats, and simply sail away from any threat. One other unique feature of these reed boats is that they resemble, very closely, reed boats built and used by the ancient Egyptians, and peoples of the middle east. The boat design is based on the upward curving prow, along with an upward curving stern analogous to the ancient German Saxon ships, which developed into the Scandinavian Viking ship design, and at some point was adapted to the Egyptian ships.

Many of these reed boats even possessed an image of a puma on the upward curving prow and stern, once again similar to the Scandinavian Viking ships. The Egyptian reed boat was built using papyrus reeds bundled, and then lashed together.

Once again we witness a possible connection between the Egyptians and the people of South America, only that connection does not end here. We spoke earlier of the large megalith which Posnansky discovered, studied, and was named the Great Idol. The surface was covered with numerous glyptic symbols suggesting to Posnansky that the stone was an ancient calendar. It seemed that most all of these symbols resemble the same type used as Egyptian hieroglyphs, but stretched further back into prehistorical times — back to 27,000 years before Christ. Von Däniken picked up on this enigma when he referred to Professor Bellamy in his book, *Twilight of the Gods*. Von Däniken wrote:

> Professor Schindler Bellamy argued for a rise and fall of pre-historic cultures. There must have been, he argued, other high cultures before the Egyptian culture that had foundered and disappeared for whatever reasons.[4]

The statement by Professor Bellamy offers support of my *Experimental Hypothesis* from my first book, which attempted to identify a very advanced prehistorical civilization, having a European origin, which sailed the globe during glacial periods leaving their mark on countries, and cultures wherever they went. There seems to be no other explanation for the ancient ruins, the amazing megaliths with archaeological sites serving the same purposes, the astronomical knowledge, the physical descriptions of white gods, the appearance of ancient maps extending back to 10,000 BC or earlier, and the number of ancient sites located all over the globe dating back to a period in prehistory, which we cannot identify. The closer modern day science, and independent researchers look, the more 35,000 plus years in the past seem to attract significant attention. Current standards of dating are still somewhat inaccurate, experimental, or based on artifacts found in layers of earth strata, which cannot be accepted as totally correct. All of these analogous archaeological locations could not have occurred simultaneously or within a few thousand years of each other. Intelligently speaking, centuries upon centuries had to have passed.

> *We call it the New World, because we believe it was discovered as recently as 1492 and because the civilizations that lived there appear to be far more recent than those of the Old World. But what if this were yet another illusion, projected by historians?*
> ~ ~ *Philip Coppens, Author*
> ~ ~ *The Lost Civilization Enigma*

The site of Caral, on the Pacific coastline of Peru — approximately fourteen miles inland, was mentioned earlier as one city where artifacts of Khipu (Quipu) had been uncovered by archaeologists. These samples of khipu are noted as the oldest known examples of the early Incan form of mass communication among the people of the empire. These artifacts reach back to 2600 BC.

However, it is not because of the samples of khipu which sets Caral apart from the rest of the Incan empire, but rather it has been designated as the 'First Civilization in the New World' by many archaeologists. The site was discovered in 1905, but not excavated. The first archaeological inspection took place in 1941 when investigators found a multi-roomed building, a clay floor with maize cobs underneath, and a large trash heap — always an asset to archaeologists.

The site would later produce the existence of platform temple-type mounds. As many as seventeen mounds were found in that particular area, and date to around 3000 BC, while dating at a nearby site dates even further back to around 4900 BC. In total, there are some eighteen urban settlements situated around the Supe River Valley. There are many more examples of earthen type pyramids located at Caral-Supe. Some investigators speculate these earthen mounds could connect with the earthen mounds found in North America, which will be discussed later.

The main emphasis here, in regard to the ancient site, is *urban* civilization without signs of warfare, human sacrifice, cannibalism or any other atrocity produced by mankind. In fact, the site indicated peace, harmony, and respect for the dead by ritualistic burials containing manmade artifacts with the body. This site also produced no evidence of pottery, metallurgy, written documents, or evidence of social stratification. These are all factors necessary for creating a political structure, which can produce public work's projects, and to build gigantic earthen pyramids. These urban people did possess a full scale agricultural system, which also is necessary for a social or even a political stratification to exist. Whoever these Caral-Supe people were, it appears evident they lived in a civilized environment without the standard materialistic elements.

The term *urban* signifies a densely populated city environment. In this context the word urban, might also suggest the presence of a social, and / or political stratification. It seems almost a necessary requirement for a large group of people to organize, create, design, and to build large to small type earthen pyramids. Social and political stratification would also be necessary for an abundance of food to feed the workers, and subordinates of these building parties. Some form of authority would definitely be required to maintain the peace, care for the sick or injured, to protect the established religious beliefs of the community, and to provide for the overall well being of all of its citizens. We, as urban dwellers today, understand quite clearly that within any group formed for a specific purpose or simply drawn together haphazardly, there will always be at least one leader to emerge who will seek control. Therefore, the absence of social or political stratification within that community must simply be overlooked by the archaeologists. Perhaps a little assistance from the anthropology field would be of some value.

As one observation about the Caral-Supe archaeological site is that the whole area is built using dirt, clay, and stone; but it bears no signs of megalithic structures, no obvious sign of advanced astronomical knowledge or awareness by these urban people. It exhibits no beliefs in the Incan sun god. The people of this river valley appear to have been totally independent. Perhaps they might have been from a part of North America, and had migrated to that location for some reason not yet understood.

Secondly, when Caral-Supe is compared to Tiahuanaco, Puma Pumku, and the more recent discoveries under the waters of Lake Titicaca, the site seems rather young and modern. As noted earlier in the chapter, the megalithic sites are being recalculated to place their existence to back around 15,000 to 17,000 BC. Furthermore, it is suspected that some of these structures, if not all, had been constructed prior to the end of last glacial maximum, thus forcing the terrain upward from their once sea level location to create the high plateau (altiplano) locations on the Andes' Mountains. This observation is not meant as criticism of Caral-Supe, rather it is meant to point out that such highly technical workmanship of megaliths, accompanied by advanced solar, and astronomical awareness cannot be overlooked or thought of as being planned, and constructed by a civilization without social/political stratification. Further, to build such elaborate, and complex structures it would be necessary to have knowledge of metallurgy, mathematics, some form of writing, and of course advanced knowledge of many divisions of science. Therefore, the designation as "the earliest civilization in the New World," might be highly incorrect. It is suspected that this civilized urban population is, perhaps, descendants of some previous culture long since vanished. Or, as we will discover later on in the book, they once were the forebears or a subgroup of a one-time prominent civilization from North America.

Sacsayhuamán is another mystifying South American location constructed using large stones brought in from a distant location. The design of the structure forms the head-shape of the Puma, which might give some kind of indication that there was a connection between the people of Tiahuanaco and the builders of Sacsayhuamán. The site was designated as an Incan fortress, which is probably not accurate. Archaeologists, and even historians, have attempted to date this site without much success. Many have determined that the stones are more than 3000 years old, but rocks are difficult to date with great accuracy. Dating for the site seems to place construction prior to the Incan empire, as with the site of Tiahuanaco, and the others. This site possibly could have been built by the same culture as the other megalithic sites.

The site of Sacsayhuamán is about 1 mile (2 km) from the Incan capital at Cuzco, at an altitude of around 11,663 feet (3555 m) above sea level. The so-called fortress was designed employing a layered wall system — as the landscape rises, each wall of stone is built higher than the previous one, and the incline of the hill gradually gets steeper. The Spaniards learned very quickly how difficult it was to attack, and fight the people behind these steep walls. One might say, "it is literally fighting an uphill battle!" Who would have designed, and built an elaborate defensive structure such as this — and from whom? It wasn't the Inca, even though they utilized the site for rituals and defense against the Spanish soldiers. One alternate thought for a reason of building a structure in this manner could have been as a defense against rising water. If this site was built by a civilization that suffered massive flooding, in their past history, resulting from meltwaters caused by glacial deterioration, this might have been a possible solution for surviving one of those horrific events. Another consideration might be, that this site is at a higher elevation than the Machu Picchu site, which could also have been built for the same purpose.

One more South American conundrum involves a land area named Patagonia, which covers about 300,000 sq. miles (777,000 km^2), and is located at the far southern section of the South American continent. Patagonia comprises the southern division of the Andes mountains moving southwest over to the Pacific Ocean; on the eastern side of the mountains it borders the Colorado River going south, ending on the Atlantic Ocean at Carmen de Patagones. Over all, the region of Patagonia covers about one-third of southern South America. What makes this region so special is this is where Ferdinand Magellan, on his AD 1519 voyage to the Spice Islands, encountered a race of *giants* waving at him from the shoreline. Magellan then named the place *patagón* (or *Pathagoni*) referring to the people as being giants, but the name ultimately developed into *Patagonia* meaning, "Land of the Bigfeet."

This story was recorded by Magellan's personal voyage chronicler Antonio Pigafetta, who was only one of seventeen survivors of that sailing expedition. Magellan did not complete the voyage, being killed by a chief of an island nation while trying to convert the chief to Christianity. Pigafetta's written description of the incident depicts a man of considerable height, stating that the heads of the crew members would only reach to the waist of the tall native. This tall native specimen did not seem to be an exception since others of his tribe arrived on the beach, and also were described as "taller and bulkier" than any of the Spanish sailors. News of this race of giants created a great deal of wonder and speculation once it reached Europe.

Later in AD 1578, Sir Francis Drake undertook a sea voyage to circumnavigate the globe, and he too witnessed the giants reported by the story of Magellan's chronicler. A full report of Drake's encounter with the giant natives was later made public by Drake's nephew.

According to Drake's account he also agreed with Magellan that the natives were larger than normal people, of the time, and that they did have voices which were of a hideous nature, but he did not consider them to be so large that they deserved the title of *Giants*. Drake's overall assessment of these people was that they stood at around 7½ feet (2.3 m) tall; this reduced their original recorded heights from 10 feet (3 m) tall.

Commodore John Byron, then Captain of the HMS Dolphin while on a circumnavigation voyage, also encountered these reported giants of Patagonia. Since he was there, he thought it would be an excellent opportunity to correct any inaccurate accounts of these giants of South America. However, to his amazement he learned these giants had accounts of their own about other ancient giants.

So who were these mysterious giants of Patagonia? According to some, they were members of the *Tehuelche* natives who once resided in the Patagonia region many years prior to the arrival of any white explorers. These people consisted of a northern and a southern group each with their own dialect. The northern people were known as the horse people, while the southern group was called the foot people. Together both groups exhibited stalwartness, and tall physique. Little is known of these indigenous people prior to their discovery by Magellan's expedition. Also, not much has been uncovered about their disappearance. The main reason for their disappearance, as determined by scientists, is that most died of diseases brought over from the European explores, much like what happened to the Aztec, and other Mesoamerican peoples.

There might be one example of a possible connection stemming from a more recent archaeological finding, and that is the discovery of larger than normal size bones in Peru, South America during a 1997-1999 investigation, funded by the National Geographic. Tombs in Peru having been excavated, produced the skeletal remains of five males considered to be of a more than average height. Archaeologists have dated the skeletons to be around 1,500 years old. The remains are believed to be members of the Moche culture, which inhabited that area around AD 100 to AD 800. As with many cultures of South America the origins of the Moche people are not known. Some suspect there might be a possibility of Scandinavian influence for the height variation. The skeletons uncovered at this site ranged from 5 feet 9 inches to 6 feet (175 to 182 cm) tall, in relation to the normal height range of the Moche people at 4 feet 10 inches to 5 feet 6 inches (147 to 168 cm) tall. The height difference does not seem all that strange in today's world. However, that height variation in the ancient world could have been quite shocking. As one example of individual tallness in modern times, during the creation of the Nazi SS (Schutzstaffel) a paramilitary branch in April of 1925, they only accepted men with a height of 5 feet 6 inches (167 cm) or taller. Even back in the 1920s of the twentieth century, 5 feet 6 inches was deemed to be tall by some cultures. Since that was the case, it seems some of the normal Moche people could have met that height requirement.

Perhaps one other explanation for the height differential could be caused from a physical distortion as a result of a condition called *Marfan Syndrome*. Marfan syndrome is found in all cultures, and it is an inherited condition. This condition effects the connective tissue in the body whose main function is to keep the body together. It effects the skeleton, lungs, blood vessels, heart, eyes, and more. If this condition attacks the skeleton, it usually effects the skeletal long bones making the individual taller, and more slender than usual. If the skeletal system is elongated it might cause skin stretching, eventually leading to unsightly marks on skin surfaces. This process would not just stop there, because it would also have an effect of the heart, lungs, eyes, etc. Of course, the Peruvian tomb excavation only allowed for skeletal remains to be studied, so we might not gain an answer for any of the other bodily effects. Possibly though, there may be some slim chance of a connection between the Patagonian giants, and the taller Moche people.

As an additional side note, and once again a possible Egyptian connection with South America, is the possibility that Pharaoh Akhenaten who ruled Egypt from 1353 to 1336 BC is suspected, by modern day archaeologists, of having suffered from Marfan syndrome. Akhenaten drew his name from the sun god *Aten*, and established a cult worship of the sun. Akhenaten, once known as Amenhotep IV until the fifth year of his reign, is the most enigmatic Pharaoh of Egypt for many other reasons, namely he was the father of Tutankhamun, and the creator of the monotheistic Sun cult.

One other person most well-known by many, is Abraham Lincoln 16th President of the United States. Because Lincoln was 6 feet 4 inches (193 cm) tall — taller than most men of that time, and because he was lean and thin, a number of physicians and scientists believe that he was afflicted with Marfan syndrome. The only way to confirm if any of the dead people had Marfan syndrome is to obtain DNA samples.

Images of Tiahauanaco

Gate of the Sun
Carved from one stone

Either the Sun God Inti
or Viracocha on Gate of the Sun

Wall of Heads

Wall of Faces

Calendar Stone

All Images courtesy of Peter & Jackie Main, 2014

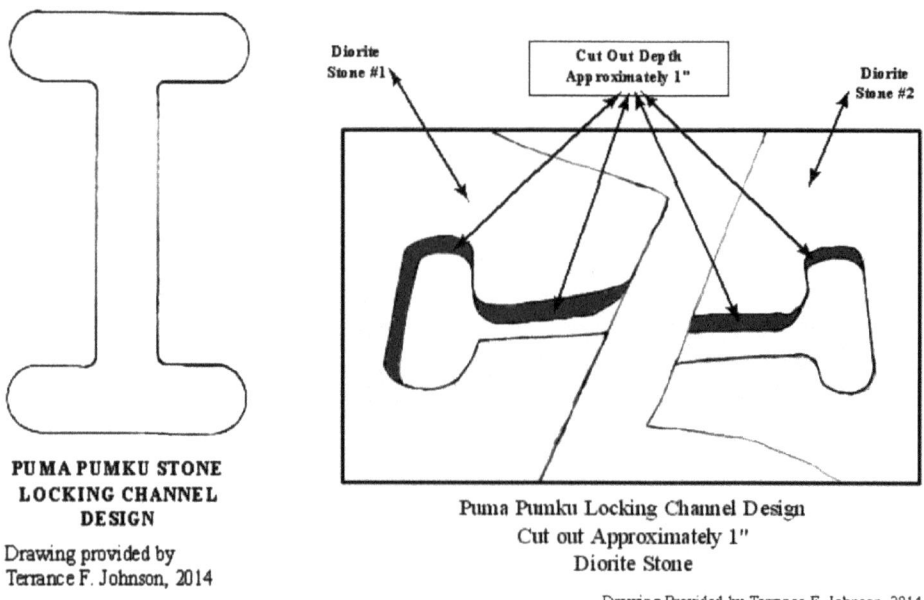

Fig. 1

PUMA PUMKU STONE LOCKING CHANNEL DESIGN

Drawing provided by Terrance F. Johnson, 2014

Fig. 2

Puma Pumku Locking Channel Design
Cut out Approximately 1"
Diorite Stone

Drawing Provided by Terrance F. Johnson, 2014

Pre-History's Chronology Enigma

Images of Puma Pumku
All images by Herbert Eisengruber of Paleoseti magazine

Immense volumes have been written to expound our knowledge, and conceal our ignorance, of primitive man... Primitive cultures were not necessarily the ancestors of our own; for all we know they may be the degenerate remnants of higher cultures that decayed when human leadership moved in the wake of the ice.

~ ~ *Will Durant*
~ ~ *Story of Civilization*

Chapter 8

Ancient People of the Americas

Ancient people of the Americas brings to mind many unanswered questions, along with many misconceptions about such people. Our current understanding, based on old school text books, is completely wrong and out of date. Many individuals in this day and age, when questioned, still believe that Columbus discovered America. When questioned further, they believe that Columbus was greeted by Indians from North America. In some cases, many people also believe humans did not reside in North America prior to Spanish exploration. This limited knowledge or misunderstanding, is usually the result of inaccurate information, which the individual has encountered in the past, and also a disinterest in the subject altogether. Just to set the record straight, and to enlighten those uninformed individuals, it is not correct that Columbus discovered America, nor is it correct that his expedition was greeted by American Indians. In the first place, ancient civilizations around the globe were very aware of the world being round; and that seafaring cultures had explored in far off locations for thousands of years prior to the voyage of Christopher Columbus. Secondly, North American Indians could not have met the ship of Columbus since popular agreement among historians, is that Columbus first landed at the island of San Salvador (which he named) in the Bahamas. The Bahamas, of course, is off the east coast of North America out into the Atlantic Ocean. Nonetheless, we can still celebrate the day each October 12th (1492).

As we have learned, over the past few decades there has been an upsurge of information, which attempts to clarify and correct the misinformation found in those old text books. Much of this new information is based on modern scientific techniques, such as, new ways to date rocks, newly discovered artifactual evidence, and more areas of science joining together to answer the questions which we, as a modern people, are seeking. Along with today's scientists, there are many amateur researchers around, who are contributing a great deal of important facts and ideas.

Speculation of human existence in North America comes from an internet web site — *resurrectisis.org*. This web site postulates that human civilization is a consequence of Ice Age meltdown. It covers both the European and American continents. Further, it presumes existence of humans in North America at the time of the last glacial period. For example, the writer states: "North America is a continent surrounded by oceans. During the Ice Age, there were very few people living on the North American continent." [1] The article offers no clues or points to any specific nationality for these people, but it does portray them as a hunter-gatherer people. Referring to the meltdown phase of the glacial Wisconsinan, the author described:

> The effect on humans was only minimal. They had to work a little harder to survive. They had to hunt larger numbers of smaller animals. The smaller animals and the smaller species of bison were able to survive the change. The humans were able to maintain their hunting and gathering way of life. [2]

The article goes on to point out that following the horrific meltdown phase, the North American continent could still provide sufficient flora to maintain herds for food and clothing needed by the surviving populations. The time period, which the article referred to, is not given. However, this time can be determined as being between 17,000 to 10,000 BCE, based on the information contained in Chapter 2 of this book.

The observation outlined in the article might be considered as total conjecture, if it were not for one piece of artifactual evidence produced at an archaeological site in the State of Oregon. The piece of artifactual evidence found at the Paisley Cave site, located in south-central Oregon, United States, is a sample of *coprolite*, which is simply human excrement, now fossilized. The coprolite is determined to be the oldest sample of human DNA found, thus far, in the United States. The age for the coprolite sample is placed between 10,750 and 12,290 BC. Along with the sample of coprolite, archaeologists discovered bones of large mammals, fish, waterfowl, and the remains of an American camel, now extinct.

One other artifact uncovered at the cave site was a tool made from a camel bone. It was shaped into a jagged-edged scraper, probably used for making clothing from hides produced from their hunts. The camel, surprisingly perhaps, was native to North America. Its origin goes back to around 40-50 million years ago. At first they were about the size of a rabbit, and as they grew in size they migrated south (about 3 million years ago) into South America where they had a determining effect on creating the llamas. Today the camel is only known to exist naturally in the middle-east, becoming extinct in North America around 8000 BC. Therefore, this phenomenon leads researchers to conclude that camels were taken out of North America, and introduced to Asia via the Bering Land Bridge. Of course, it is speculated that the people providing the fossilized sample of coprolite in Oregon, actually walked across the land bridge, and were most likely, determined to be Asians.

Still one other piece of evidence mentioned in my book, *Our Missing Ancestors,* is that of a Solutrean stone-spearhead found near the remains of a dead Mammoth in eastern Virginia of the United States. The hunting tool was said to be about 24,000 years old, and it was the unique work of the Solutrean culture of eastern France about 19,000-15,000 years ago. No other culture could have produced the effects on the stone like the Solutrean tool industry. This dating makes the time frame for the coprolite sample seem almost insignificant. However, they both attest to theories of human beings living in North America at the time of the last glacial period prior to its maximum extent and final meltdown recession phase.

Current understanding of North American colonization seems to lie with the formation of a dry solid piece of ground which was created, at some point, during the last glacial period — the glacial *Late* Wisconsinan (23,000-10,000 BP). It is thought by many historians, anthropologists, archaeologists, and some others, that when the so called "Ice Age" was in full process, enormous amounts of water from the sea were drawn up into the glacier, which aided in constructing the glacier. This glacial sponging action caused sea levels to drop significantly, and consequently it exposed land hidden beneath its surface waters. Then over time vegetation appeared attracting small game and animal herds, which in turn attracted groups of hunter-gatherers from Siberia, and Asia. This area of dry land is called, *Beringia* by scholars and researchers, but it is better known as the *Bering Strait* to most. This area of dry land has been estimated to have been home to many generations of Asian nomadic hunters, and as the waters began to rise as a result of the glacial melting, the people moved eastward into Alaska to higher ground following the herds. At this point in time these nomads seem to have settled in the Alaskan interior for some time, based on stone artifacts found in numerous areas. Then supposedly after the ice receded, the nomadic hunters followed an open corridor south into the lower forty-eight states region to where New Mexico now exists, and from there became the Clovis people. Eventually these people trekked southward through Mexico, and on into South America completing their journey, about a millennium later, in modern-day Chile. All of this might be true. However, some modern-day archaeologists and researchers are questioning the validity of this scenario.

First of all, many researchers today question if Beringia existed at all. Secondly, if this land bridge did exist, the researchers speculate that it was not the lush-green habitable hunting expanse that had been believed. Thirdly, modern thought about Beringia is that it might not have opened earlier than 14,000 years ago, if it did actually open. Fourth, if people arrived in Alaska from the land bridge, a movement south through an ice-free corridor might not have been possible since large ice sheets stretched all across Canada. Furthermore, had the ice sheets melted, the nomads would have encountered massive flooding from glacial meltwaters, as was discussed in Chapter 2, causing them insurmountable topographic difficulties.

If Beringia did exist, researchers estimate its size to be immense. Some scientists place the land-bridge stretching from the Lena River in Siberia over to Canada's Yukon territory, and then going southward nearly 1,000 miles (1,600 km-see Fig. A). Recent studies seem to indicate that Beringia was nothing more than a dry, bleak, dusty plain, incapable of producing vegetation rich enough to entice large animals to graze there. A place as inhospitable as this would most likely not have attracted the nomadic hunter if game was not abundant for survival. Further, no evidence has ever been presented to prove Beringia did exist.

The time for opening of the land passage is another sticking point. Most scientists tend to agree that huge ice sheets covered most of what is now considered to be the Beringia location, up until around 14,000 years ago. If this is the case, it could explain the coprolite sample found at the Paisley Cave site in Oregon, which is dated at 10,000-12,000 years old, and placed there by a person who had crossed Beringia. Of course, other theories prevail, which believe a land-bridge between Siberia and Alaska could have been created by more than one glacial period in North America. There were the two major glacials — Illinoian and Wisconsinan, and the Pre-Illinoian group, which also must have had effects to create a land-bridge at certain stages in their development. Then again, conflicting views about Beringia leave doubts about any type of land-bridge, between the two continents, ever having occurred.

One attempt at a solution for this question comes from *Patrick Huyghe* in his book, *Columbus Was Last.* Huyghe is quick to point out that archaeological sites do not get progressively younger as we move south from Alaska (Beringia). He also clearly stated, "The very earliest sites in the New World are not found in eastern Beringia." [3] Huyghe offers an explanation that it might have been possible for the Asian ancestors to have come to the North American continent by boat and not have crossed over any solid land mass. Huyghe also informs us that there is a 'coastal-entry model' developed by archaeologist, Knut Fladmark, which argues that Asian people came here by small boats, and followed the coast line southward, and established settlements as they went along. The Asian people commonly referred to are the Chinese. In some instances

Mongolians are included. However, it seems in most cases the Japanese are excluded as possible ancestors who might have arrived on North American shores during prehistorical times. Many people overlook the fact that the Japanese also possessed some type of ship or boat building skills. Just as a simple, unsubstantiated observation — their boat and ship construction knowledge can be correlated to those of the Polynesian culture. This thought is based on knowledge that the Polynesian civilization is very old, perhaps stemming from those Out of Africa cultures that sailed off to populate the south sea islands. Nevertheless, the Japanese sailor would have had the natural wind currents, as well as the Chinese, to complete a round trip voyage to the west coast of North America, and sail down the coast for a short distance, then turning back west toward home (see Fig. B). In addition to the northern currents they would have had an option of using a more southerly current, which would have brought them almost directly into Colombia, South America or more precisely, into southern Mesoamerica (see Fig. C). More recently in South America, there has been evidence produced of a unique pottery style found only in southern Japan, along with a human genetic illness trait, leukemia, common to that area of Southern Japan indicating similarities between some cultures in South America, and the Japanese people. If the findings are accurate, it would clearly establish an ancient contact period between the two countries.

One possibility to suggest the reality of an ancient land bridge from Siberia to Canada may be the discovery of stone implements (dated at 25,000 BC) found at the Old Crow Basin in the Yukon Territory, in the State of Alaska, U.S.A. These implements could not have been from the time estimated for the Bering Strait. As previously cited, Beringia is estimated to have ensued sometime during the last glacial. The time for the last glacial stage would have been the *Late Wisconsinan* dated at 23,000 to 10,000 BP. These implements are older than the last glacial phase, which would place them into a possible interstadial period when the surface temperature was warmer and wetter allowing for the possibility of higher sea levels. Perhaps if sea levels were higher, developed by meltwaters from the prior glacial, they would have covered any dry land between Siberia and Alaska. Once again, modern archaeology might want to consider boats as a logical explanation for these ancient artifacts.

Another interesting case in point is put forth by *David Hatcher Childress* in his book, *Lost Cities of North & Central America*. Childress spoke of samples of pottery located on Cobb Seamount near Seattle, Washington, U.S.A., dated at 18,000 BP. Again this date is prior to the time researcher's point to as Beringia being open to human foot travel. In addition, nearby is an archaeological site near Puget Sound outside of Seattle, containing thousands of earthen mounds named, "The Mima Mounds" for the Mima Prairie on which they stand. These mounds vary from 6 feet (1.8 m) to 70 feet (21 m) in diameter. They were first thought to be burial mounds, but no bones or artifacts have ever been found in any one of the mounds, which have been excavated. Many of the larger mounds measured out to about 7 feet (2 m) high. Hatcher clearly conveyed to us that there are no known Native American legends which might account for these numerous mounds. Therefore, it is a strong possibility that these mounds were built long before any established Native American cultures entered the area. Further, it is understood that these mounds were submerged by waters from the Pacific Ocean. This situation was probably due to glacial meltwaters toward the end of the last glacial period. Hatcher also speculated that the waters drained away only about 6,000 years ago.

Childress goes on to enlighten us that he equates these types of mounds to similar ones, which he had encountered on the Island of Bahrain in the Persian Gulf, and again in the Petén jungles of Guatemala, once the territory of the great Mayan civilization. In this case, the mounds were built there as foundations for houses, which allowed for elevation of the structure. Could there be a connection with all three locations? Maybe so. We will explore more later on about mounds, and those who built them.

In conclusion, an observation from Graham Hancock might offer some insight to more progressive thinking when contemplating archaeological issues. Hancock quotes from another work *Human Evolution*:

> With this and other evidence taken into account, 'a very reasonable conclusion on the peopling of Americas is that it began at least 35,000 years ago, but may well have included waves of immigrants at later dates too.' [4]

This statement might be very insightful, and very correct. Science and researchers have recently been producing realistic analysis, which indicates that such a conclusion cannot be discarded or scoffed at insultingly. In my book, *Our Missing Ancestors,* a call for a new, and accurate chronology was expressed in order to address more recent, as well as, the archaic dogmatic findings from scholars of old. We know from more current dating, resulting from more modern techniques that archaeological sites in South America and across the Atlantic Ocean, date back much farther than 10,000 -14,000 years. The only problem, which seems to be plaguing scholars are those times related to North America. Author Patrick Huyghe from his book, *Columbus Was Last,* referred to North America as the 'Berlin Wall', "The 11,500-year barrier for peopling of the New World... ." [5] This so called barrier seems to be facing destruction, much as did the old Berlin Wall of the 1970s, 80s and 90s. Can we really believe that the North American continent was prime virgin territory; and that no one other than now extinct animal species walked on this ancient 'prime real estate'? Must we only believe the Asians were the first exclusive people to populate the North American continent and only at the end of the last glacial period?

We have seen that the section of land commonly referred to as the *lower forty-eight* was capable of sustaining human life during glacial period times.

Why not? It supported vegetation to feed animals, and quite possibly berries, nuts, and roots for human beings. In addition, those humans living here had use of weapons, and tools to hunt and prepare their quarry. It is not outlandish to also believe that these people knew how to build shelters, and create fire. Of course, many groups probably migrated south as the weather turned colder or when waters began to rise up around them. After all, those individuals living here had to be a survivalist. These people were born into a harsh environment where they were forced to adjust, create, and to learn fast. We will look at other cultures later on that also played a significant role in North America.

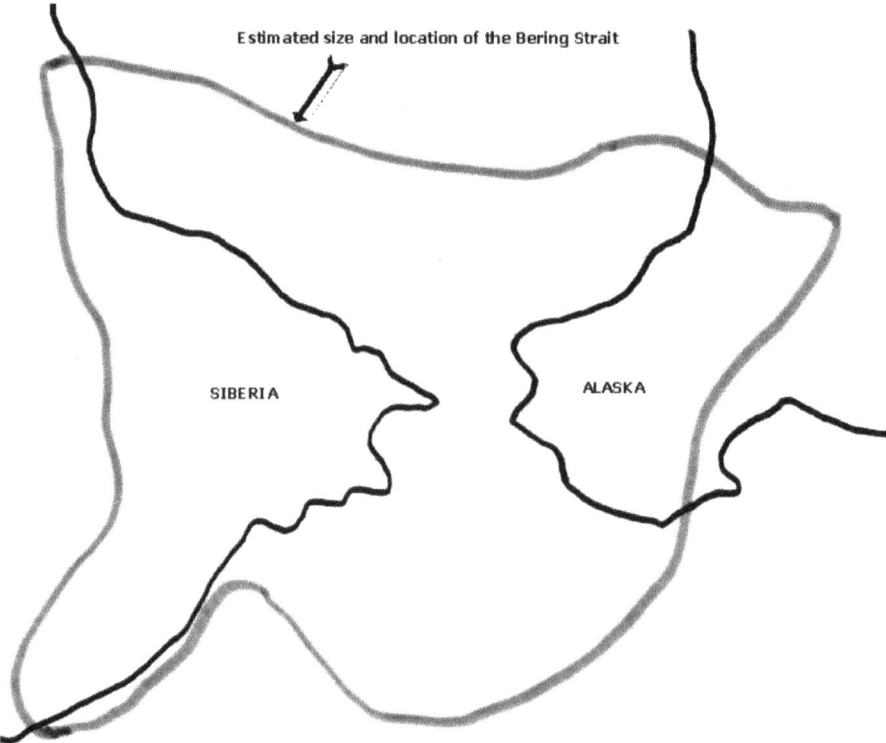

Possible location and size of Beringia at the close of the last glacial period.

Figure provided by Terrance F. Johnson, 2013

Fig. A

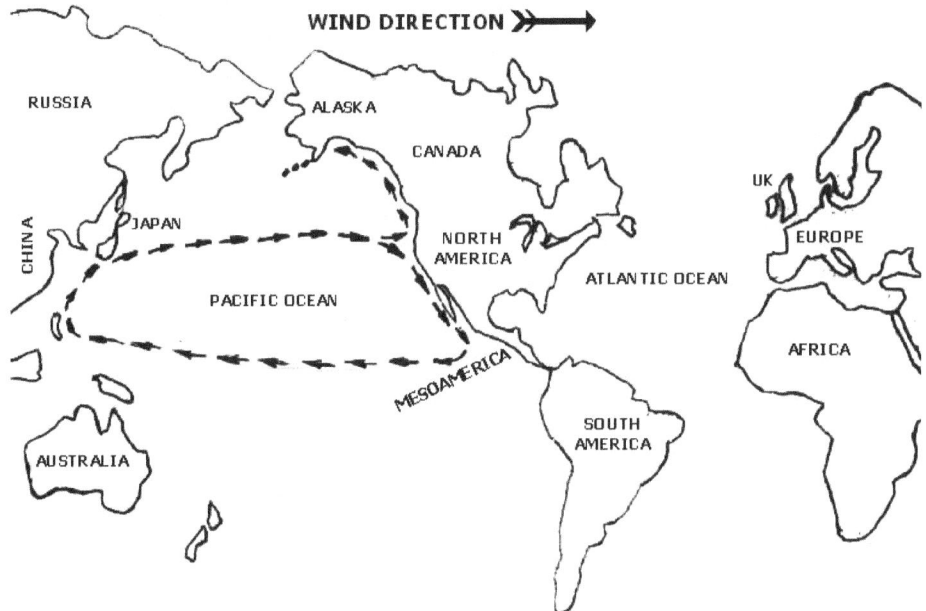

Asian Northern Pacific Ocean Currents to North America and Return.

Figure provided by Terrance F. Johnson, 2013

Fig. B

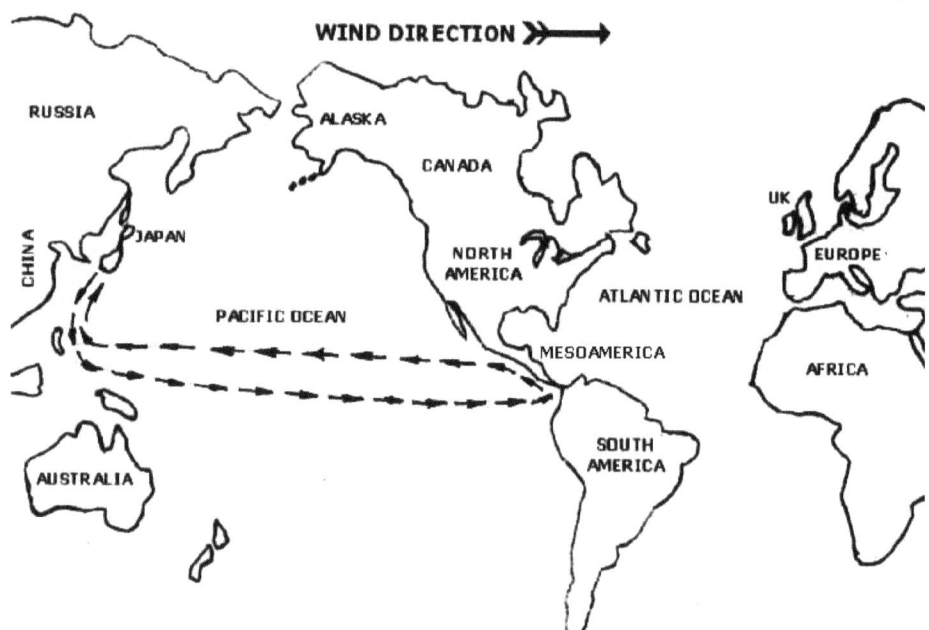

Asian Southern Pacific Ocean Currents to Mesoamerica and Return Route.

Figure Provided by Terrance F. Johnson, 2013

Fig. C

The United States was then busy fighting an undeclared war against the Indians, who blocked their path to expansion: the Indians were being pushed out of their territory, imprisoned, forced to migrate, or simply massacred; and as this century long campaign of genocide proceeded, it may have been comforting for the conquerors to imagine that there once had been another race that these Indians had pushed out in the same way. Consciences might ache a bit over the uprooting of the Indians, but not if it could be shown that the Indians, far from being long-established settlers in the land, were themselves mere intruders who had brutally shattered the glorious old Mound Builder civilization.

~~ *Robert Silverberg*
~~ *The Mound Builders*

Chapter 9

The Mound Builders of North America

The quote above is in reference to wars among Native American tribes long before the Europeans arrived in the 1600s. These combat actions are based on verbal accounts from tribal members of various nations during the 1700s when missionaries interacted with some of the local tribes to learn their ways, but more often to convert the people to Christianity. While carrying out this task missionaries would learn old stories from the tribal elders, about where they came from, who their enemies were, what ancient history could be remembered, plus any additional accounts of their past history, which could help to explain certain visual peculiarities like large earthen mounds or parallel earth embankments, which runs along for some great distances. In the case above, Silverberg's statement was in regard to a war between the Lenni-Lenape, their partner tribe the Mengwe (the Delaware and Iroquois tribes) against an old nation of territorial dominant builders of large and numerous cities in the ancient past, the Alligewi or Tallegewi. These cities had mounds built of earth towering many feet in the air, while encompassing many acres of circumference of the ground. As with the Giza pyramids of Egypt these earthen structures of North America were extant in the 1700s when they were first recognized by settlers spreading out, claiming land, and building new towns in the American wilderness. At first many of these structures were ignored, torn down, or plowed under to make way for new homes and public buildings. Without knowledge of, or interest in, these oversized massive configurations, sites such as those of Cincinnati, Circleville, and Chillicothe, Ohio, were willfully and systematically destroyed. Any thought of who may have built the formations, and for what reason or purposes they were constructed, was carried out by the local antiquarian. The main question of Silverberg's observation was what or who caused the decline, fall, and disappearance of these ancient unknown builders of earthen mounds and embankments? Silverberg offers speculation that it might be a possibility for another tribe or confederation of tribes to have forced their way into the areas of the Mound Builders, and for some unexplained reason made war upon them, and causing their extinction or widespread dispersion.

Reverting back to the conflict between the Lenni-Lenape, Mengwe, and the Alligewi, the story originated from British missionary John Heckewelder, who in 1772 began to live among the Lenape (Delaware), and published an account of this war along with some background history of the area and the Lenape in his work, *Account of the History, Manners, and Customs of the Indian Nations who once inhabited Pennsylvania and the Neighboring States.* In this account, Heckewelder stated that the Lenape tell that they made a long journey from the West to where the Mississippi River now flows. Once there, the Lenape sent scouts across the mighty river to find a trail and report what they observed. The scouts returned with stories of a powerful nation on the east side of the river who constructed fortifications, entrenchments, and many large towns. They were described as remarkably tall and stout with a tradition that stated there were giants among them. These strange people were called the Alligewi or Tallegewi; today we call them the *Mound Builders.* Stories of many battles among the Lenape, Mengwe, and Alligewi were told ending with the victory of the Lenape and Mengwe at a battle, which took place on the Huron River near Lake Erie where the Alligewi had built two earthen walls with a deep ditch on one side, and a number of flat mounds close by. The Lenape described the battle as gruesome claiming the lives of many warriors. Once observing that their fortifications would not stop the attacking tribes, the Alligewi abandoned their location, and fled back down the Mississippi River from where they originated, and never again returned.

During this era of young American expansion, theories were abundant regarding the local Native Americans as the European white settlers encountered the tribes and earthen structures. To the Spanish, in Europe, there must have been some knowledge of these types of structures, and possibly some forms of explanations by local tribes when Hernando de Soto landed in Florida in 1539 seeking gold. De Soto's expedition covered much of the Southeast and encountered many tribes along the way. Accounts, from three of de Soto's men, were recorded by, Garcilaso de la Vega — chronicler for de Soto, and published in 1605 on their observations of mound construction by a Florida tribe of Native Americans. However, this information had not been of use to the later period American settlers of North America.

A beginning to understanding what the North American continent was like prior to Columbus must include a discussion about an ancient civilization called the *Mound Builders*. No one can definitely state who they were or from where they originated, which is quite common when speaking about prehistorical people. These prehistorical people are credited with building different types of structures using only the local earth from near the structure being built; unlike the megalithic construction techniques used by the Egyptians to build pyramids on the Giza plateau. Nevertheless, many of these earthen structures are larger in size than the Great Pyramid in Egypt. Much research has been conducted over the decades and centuries, which have passed since the pioneers first spread-out over the North American landscape to discover the identities of these creative, tenacious individuals.

We have in Chapter 8, discussed a number of people who may have touched upon North American shores in deep prehistory, which in all reality are probably the people responsible for the tribal nations of Native Americans whom we today call, the American Indian. The real question surrounding this dilemma is the chronology attached to the existence of these ancient prehistorical people. When did they arrive? Who were they? Why did they come? Where did they go? In most cases, scholars point to the Asian cultures as the basis for the Native Americans. In part, it is highly probable they are correct. Still many artifacts, physical attributes, locations, and most recently language and writing evidence, which have been analyzed seemed to produce support for other cultures, from other worldly locations to have also contributed to the population of the North American continent. We have discussed the possibility of Solutrean presence on the North American continent perhaps as far back as 24,000 BC. From the artifactual evidence of the Clovis and Folsom spear point similarities to the original Solutrean *Biface* production method, it gives great likelihood to the hypothesis that they were all the result of the same form of workmanship and design; and that they were not the product of an Asian culture, but that they were the product of an ancient people who once lived in Northeastern France. Could it possibly be that people from Europe arrived in North America at such an early date? It seems that today, evidence of Paleo-Indian (Early-Indian) can be traced back to the Clovis culture at about 13,000 years ago, with the Folsom culture dated somewhat later, both stemming from the original Solutrean design. An explanation of these findings can be found in the literary work, *Native American Tribes: The History and Culture of The Mound Builders*:

Radiocarbon dating estimates the Clovis, the earlier of the two, occupied North America between 11,050 B.C. and 10,800 B.C. Although pre-Clovis finds indicate human occupation of North America as early as 13,000 B.C., with the earliest occupation speculated to be as early as 50,000 B.C., most physical evidence was erased from the landscape by glacial movement during the Ice Age.[1]

With dates and evidentiary facts offering potential for a much deeper antiquity for North America, it would be sensible to conclude that many people came to this northern location at many different times, for many different purposes, and arriving by means from many different ways. Once here, as today, North America became a melting-pot for cultures to interact, learn, gain support, and in some cases do battle with each other for some material or conceptual reason. With this thought in mind, an exploration of the Mound Builders archaeological findings might advance our understanding of antiquity of the North American landscape.

The Mound Builders are essential when speaking of chronology and prehistory at the same time. The reason for this is simply that these mounds of enormous size, in some cases, date well back into North American prehistory of ancient unidentified cultures. Archaeologists when speaking of the Mound Builders usually refer to them in terms of cultures, rather than tribes. Tribes generally stipulate sociopolitical groups, which might consist of families, clans, or other confederations who share a common ancestry, and dwell under non-formal types of leadership, which are usually not of a permanent makeup. A culture, on the other hand, is a distinct way of life or a specific social group, with or without common ancestry. For example, an individual can be adopted into a specific culture, but that individual cannot be adopted into a specific ancestry. In addition, more than one tribe can make up a particular culture.

Today's archaeologists prefer to use the term *Hopewell Tradition* in place of Hopewell Culture when speaking of the Mound Builders. The term Tradition replaces Culture, once coined by archaeologist Caleb Atwater in 1820 to refer to the Ohio Mound Builders. A Tradition can be defined as a way of life — practiced by a specific culture or a number of different cultures who are implementing the same social practices in almost the same manner.

As with European tribes, cultures and nationalities, it becomes difficult when laboring to sort out times, locations, people, groups, etc., which might produce, and identify a certain ethnic culture and civilization. Archaeologists working with artifacts and locations have been able to say, with some sense of certainty, that North America has been the home for paleo-Indians since about 20,000 years ago. Of course, we know that 20,000 years ago the upper portion, mainly, of the North American continent was experiencing effects of glaciation because the final melting process of the Wisconsinan glacial had not yet commenced. This hypothesis for people in North America only seems to confirm that the Bering Strait concept of Asians crossing over into the "New World" around 10,000 years ago, and populating the continent, while establishing themselves as the Clovis tool culture, leaves much to be challenged. Nonetheless, there is evidence of people who are, very probably, a beginning influence for the American people of today.

One early culture, which can be glimpsed from deep antiquity, is the Adena culture who resided in the Ohio Valley at the time of their historical exposure. According to archaeological findings, this ancient culture can be traced back to around 2500 BC, placing them into the Archaeological Period of *Paleo-Indian,* which means that they had knowledge of fire, used and made stone weapons and tools, and lived by being skilled nomadic hunters. Eventually these people advanced into the Archaic Period, which allowed them to establish quasi-permanent villages, while still engaging in seasonal travel to follow herds, using improved weapons for hunting and fishing. Some scholars speculate that the Adena people descended from the Clovis culture of what is now, New Mexico. However, there might yet be another explanation of their ancestor's — that being they are more direct descendants of the Solutrean people, who we know lived on the East coast of the continent around 24,000 years ago. The Clovis, as it seems, were descendants of the Solutrean, as were the Folsom culture. So in any case, the Adena could have been related to any one of these cultures, but it is a stronger possibility for the Adena to have resulted from the Solutrean cultures residing on the east-side of the American continent. Adena was known to hunt with fluted spear heads, which is a design developed by the Clovis tool industry as a change to the original Solutrean tool creation, and was carried over, and modified by the Folsom tool industry. The Solutrean design was accomplished by knapping the flakes from both sides of the stone without a flute in the center. The Clovis added a flute on each side of the stone in the center; while the Folsom then extended the flute from the Clovis design. (Fig. 1- end of chapter). The Clovis tool industry had many locations in the east. (See Maps-end of chapter)

Scholars of prehistory seem to agree that around 9000 BC, during the recession phase of the Wisconsinan glacial, a number of people resided in, and around, the Ohio River Valley, which included Ohio, Pennsylvania, a portion of West Virginia, Kentucky, Indiana, and Illinois. States to the north of that region would have still been under ice and meltwater conditions.

Then at around 700 BC the Adena made an appearance in that area, and began building mounds of noticeable size. Credit for the first mounds built in North America goes to the Watson Brake culture of Ouachita Parish, Louisiana, back in 3500 BC. However, the new Adena style mounds were much larger and more creative in designs. The Adena culture consisted of many tribes or groups, which made-up the Adena culture. Very little is known about these groups of people in regard to their social, economical, and political structures, but scholars do understand that the Adena culture participated in the same religious beliefs because of their involvement in building the new style conical mounds. In most cases conical style mounds were discovered to be burial mounds when excavated by archaeologists of both amateur and professional status. Although many were similar in design but what was discovered inside was, to some extent, quite different. When early archaeologists in the 1800s began to open these mounds in search of answers they found, in some mounds, evidence of cremation with signs of charcoal and ash, but no bones. Further, there were no signs of logs or grave-goods inside the mound. Some other mounds nearby, when excavated, produced skeletons with no signs of cremation. These discoveries then led to the question — were the differences in burial procedures a way to indicate separation of family members, royalty, or religious leaders? These questions have not yet been answered. It was also noted, at the time, that the mounds within the same location varied from conical to a circular form, which might suggest that these mounds were built at different times or that they were built by different cultures.

During the early 1800s Henry Brackenridge, a Lawyer and amateur Historian, noted a much more complex form of mound burial within some of the conical mounds. One such mound he described as about 12 – 15 feet (3.6 to 4.5 m) high, and about 100 feet (30.48 m) in diameter. Inside of this mound he described the bodies as being placed on their backs with the head facing inward toward the center of the mound, and each corpse was spaced in a circular pattern about 2 feet to 3 feet (0.5 to 0.9 m) apart. When this circle of bodies was complete, another outside row of bodies were placed in the same manner as those on the inner circle. What determined the circumference of the mound is unknown, but Brackenridge speculated that the mound could have contained as many as hundreds or thousands of corpses. Brackenridge also noted that pottery was buried with the body, consisting of two jugs of water placed on each side of the head, a container of food resting near the side of the chest, and held in place by one of the arms, which were folded ritually across the chest. Brackenridge further stated that these pottery vessels were always placed in the exact same location for each corpse.

Conical mounds, as well as the other type of mounds created by these indigenous people range in age from the more modern (later period) to the more ancient type, perhaps extending back in time as far as hundreds or thousands of years. Even so, all of these mounds have been found to have been created by one people, based on common beliefs and characteristics of each. It must be obvious to modern civilization that these ancient people possessed a respect for their dead, and engaged in a well organized and well structured form of religious beliefs to have dedicated so much thought, time, and energy into creating elaborate forms of cemeteries to honor their loved ones, leaders, and heroes. This respect along with their beliefs carries forward to today's modern Native Americans, and to some extent to current modern worldly cultures, by signifying that the dead occupy "sacred ground." As time progressed, generations and circumstances changed, thus, allowing for new ways to express respect for the dead. Some Native Americans would simply place the corpse into a shallow pit, and cover it with rock and stone. Others would place the dead body on stretched animal hide, and raise it up on stilted poles to deteriorate back to the "Sky Spirit," from where all had originated. Still other tribes would hang the corpse from trees until there was nothing left but bone, and then those would be gathered up and buried in some ritualistic manner. In any case, the dead would have a place in 'Sacred Ground'.

The concept of sacred ground extends to another mound form called "Effigy Mounds." An effigy is an image, in one sense to burn, which represents a hated person or thing; or still in one other capacity it can be an image representing a deity, what can be placed into a field or village to dispel evil. In one broad sense of the matter that probably is what the effigy mounds were meant to signify. It was an appeal to the "Sky World" for help to produce good crops, to protect the village and people from harm, and to guarantee fertility for the future of the group. Effigy mounds took on different forms and sizes; some depicted turtles, bears, otters, lizards, and other animals. Their sizes varied as well, with those around the Great Lakes being lower, usually no more than 3 – 4 feet (0.9 to 1.2 m) high, and more representative of birds, reptiles and men. Of course, there is the great "Serpent Mound" of Adams County, Ohio, which is listed as the largest effigy mound in North America with a length of about 1,330 feet (405.38 m), and around 4.5 feet (1.3716 m) high at the highest point.

In another sense, these effigy mounds might also have represented 'Tribal Clans', which could be described as a large family group or an extended family who are a part, or a subset, of a tribe or nation. The clan, in many cases, derives its structure from the women, especially within the Seven American, and two Canadian Nations of the Potawatomi. In other nations, the clan is structured by the men of the clan, and also there are tribes, and nations which do not recognize clans at all.

Clans within the various nations have specific duties, and responsibilities to their own clan members, the tribe, and to the nation. It is the duty of the clan elders to teach and guide the younger members of the clan in understanding, and performance of obligation to others. These individual clans also identified a 'Spiritual Person' who would oversee the religious needs of the clan members and assist those members who required special attention, even those who were not from a clan or those who were from different clans.

An individual becomes a clan member from birth, and it is said that the clan walks with, and looks after that individual always. It must be presumed from this possessive nature of the clan that this particular obligation to the person would also carry over into death. Therefore, if along with burial mounds nearby effigy mounds, could it be the effigy mounds were placed there to protect the deceased clan member in death? As a rule it has been observed that effigy mounds were not used as burial mounds. Usually conical shaped mounds were built to serve as the final resting place for the dead. However, if both types of mounds were located in the same area, the effigy images might have served as grave markers or 'Sacred Geography' for a specific clan, in addition to its function as a protector of deceased clan members. This observation is quite reasonable when it is acknowledged that clans identify themselves with living animals who exhibit physical attributes, or traits, which the clan members believe distinguishes them best. For example, the Bear clan very prominent in America's southwest, signifies protection. Because of the bear's size, strength, and its fierce nature when defending its young cubs, they are considered *guardians* who are capable of protecting all clan, tribe and nation members. In fact, the Bear clan is considered to be the most sacred clan of all of the clans by many nations.

This animal connection, and use of its image expanded into clan members painting these symbols on the sides of their teepees (tents), stamping them into pottery, making pendants called totems, which they wore around their neck, and in some instances decorated the shields of their warriors with those images to protect them during battle. Possibly the depictions of animals, serpents, birds, and reptiles in effigy mounds might have been an early beginning of the clan, as a prominent group within tribal units. It is also possible that clans existed much longer in deep antiquity then known because clans used images of local life, and what we may be viewing are only the images available to those people at that point in time; perhaps they left others elsewhere.

Since the early excavations of the mounds discovered in the Ohio River Valley during the initial American expansion period, archaeologists have been unsure how to identify one culture from the other who were involved with the mound building and mortuary rituals exhibited by the individual "type sites," which means features *typifying* a particular culture. It seems the problem involved with this dilemma is that both the Adena and Hopewell groups exhibited the same types of behavior, and blended together. This observation has led some archaeologists to believe the two groups co-existed over an extended period of time, with both groups sharing a common Tradition. As an example, there have been reports that both tall people and shorter people were placed in the same mound. Also, some archaeologists have observed skeletons described as long-headed with narrow skulls in the same locations as skeletons which exhibited a more ponderous appearance featuring large mandibles, broad faces, and flattened skulls potentially caused by the use of unpadded cradleboards, which were used to bind infants so the mother could carry her child while she performed her daily chores. As a side note, these unpadded cradleboards have been on record as far back as AD 750, and were used by the *Anasazi* or *Ancient-Ones* of the American Southwest. Even today there is no one conclusion stating which group was first to settle in the Ohio River Valley. An earlier theory argued for the Adena as being the original settlers, and they were described as the ones with long-heads, lanky in stature, with lean bodies. Then at about AD 700, the

Hopewell culture made an appearance in the Ohio River Valley, and was described as shorter, muscular, with a rounder face. Then some 120 years later, many archaeologists were describing the Adena as those with large round skulls, protuberant foreheads displaying a heavy brow-ridge, and a jutting chin. In addition, these skeletons were listed as being unusually tall with women over 6 feet (1.8 m), and men standing near 7 feet (2.1 m) tall. Researchers also concluded that these people arrived into the area somewhere around 1000 BC.

One study of the Drake Mound in Kentucky, listed as the latest Adena site, places a range for Adena at about 800 BC to AD 900, and a Hopewell mound offered artifacts which show a range from about 600 BC to AD 1500. Robert Silverberg, in his book *The Mound Builders* addressed this issue when he stated:

> New tests left the early range more or less unchanged, showing the start of Adena between 1000 and 800 B.C. and of Hopewell about 400 B.C. But a second reading for Drake Mound sample showed that it was about a thousand years older than had previously been thought. Similarly, the most recent Hopewell dates now proved to be about A.D. 500, except for one questionable date of A.D. 900. From the revised carbon-14 evidence, the Ohio Valley flourished for about fifteen centuries, overlapping during most of that time, and that both were fading out by the fifth century A.D.[2]

Perhaps a few observations might assist with determining one group of people from the other. First, we have previously been made aware that the Adena were thought to be connected to the New Mexico Clovis culture, who were probably the descendants of the Solutrean people of ancient Europe. This connection would offer a strong probability that Adena might have a body type resembling those body forms of Europe, rather than an Asian body type. Secondly, it has been observed by researchers that large circular areas with a ditch dug into it on the inside, were found at various sites. Archaeologists dubbed these "Sacred Circles." Readers who have read *Our Missing Ancestors* might recall a discussion about similar circles found in ancient Great Britain around 3500 BC, only those were called *henges*. Knight and Butler, in their book *Before the Pyramids* addressed these henges in great detail, concluding that these henges were used for astronomical calculations. They further speculated that the henges might have been used as meeting places for large groups of people for ceremonies or other important gatherings, similar to the 'ting' once used by ancient German and Scandinavian people who occupied Britain at one point in early history. In short, the Adena might have used these large circles with a ditch attached in much the same way as they were used in Britain. We know the Adena were aware of solar movements by placing the corpse in an east-west position inside of their burial mounds. So therefore there is no reason to believe they knew nothing about astronomy. As we shall see later, the Mississippian culture built and used log astronomical sites, and it is common knowledge that the Hopewell Tradition was spread over a large area, which included the Mississippi River Valley. Third, the significance of the long-headed, narrow skulls found in the conical mounds might be an indicator of still another group of people who have their roots in northern Europe. Those people could have possibly been the Scandinavian explorer population who made numerous expeditions to the American continent prior to the appearance of either the Adena or the Hopewell. In fact, some researchers have theorized that the Adena, and in some cases, the Hopewell came from the northwest around the Great Lakes region, where huge amounts of copper had been mined in early antiquity by some unknown civilization. This might be the case since most Native American groups are not known to have developed metallurgy interests. However, found in a great many burial mounds in the Ohio River Valley, were beads and other items made of copper. So where, did these people come by copper items? As most archaeologists believe, they came from around the copper mining area of the Great Lakes, from either trading or from people bringing such items with them when they moved into the location.

There is strong evidence to indicate that the Scandinavian explorers might have been one of these cultures who came to North America and mined copper, and returned back to Europe. If so, this was long before the famous voyage of Leif Eriksson in AD 1000. As the reader might recall, Eriksson's expedition found the wreckage of a boat while sailing along the coast to where Vinland had been founded. Could these have been some of the crew members from that wrecked ship? And, could there have been other explorers who could not have returned to Europe for the same reason? If so, perhaps what the researchers are looking at are the remains of a people with dolichocephalism, a condition where the head is long and narrow, which is notable to the Swedish race.

Fourth, archaeologists both past and present have mentioned some of the corpses were covered with *Red Ochre,* which is an iron oxide, and exists in several different forms. Red Ochre is known to have been used in burial rituals for thousands of years by many different cultures. This finding might indicate that these people could have had a possible connection with some of the ancient worldly civilizations. A closer examination of red ochre, and its uses will be covered in the following chapter.

Fifth, according to the story related to missionary Heckewelder by the Lenni-Lenape (Delaware), the scouts returning from a reconnaissance venture across the Mississippi returned with news of a people who built many great cities, and who were described as tall, stout (possibly meaning muscular), and telling of stories about giants among them. It is feasible to entertain the idea that if there were people of Scandinavian, even Phoenician or perhaps Egyptian representatives among them they surely would have appeared as giants. This concept is not so outrageous when one takes into consideration numerous reports of archaeological finds of skeletons reaching 7 feet (2.1 m) tall or more. For example, a site in Tennessee listed skeletons averaging 7 feet, which explains there were other skeletons at that location measuring at a taller height. In 1879 a 9 foot 6 inch (2.3 m) skeleton was exhumed from a mound near Brewersville, Indiana. Also in 1884, at a West Virginia mound location, a skeleton listed at 7 feet 6 inches (2.3 m) tall was excavated. There are many other examples found in Ohio, Minnesota, Wisconsin, and in locations west, such as, Nevada, Kansas City, and Utah. This can only mean that skeletons of those proportions are not merely freaks or exceptions to the rule: nor can they be explained away as having been misinterpreted by those doing the excavating, because there were more than just a few specimens, which have been placed in the archaeological record. There must be an explanation for individuals of that size residing among shorter people of that time. Probably during the Archaic, Woodland, and Mississippian phases, the maximum height for a male would have been around 5 feet 6 inches (1.7 m). Women would probably have been around 5 feet (1.5 m) tall or shorter. One explanation to this dilemma is that there were people from Europe, and the Mediterranean Sea area who had arrived and settled in North America during prehistorical times, and eventually were absorbed into the populations.

Sixth, is support for the people of the tall skeletons as discussed in the preceding paragraph. One example for early "Old World" cultures being part of paleo-Indian through the Late Mississippian Tradition might be explained by a grave site opened in 1874 by Reverend M. Gass and two of his students, near what is today Davenport, Iowa. While exploring a small burial mound containing the remains of a Native American, the amateur archaeologists discovered additional skeletons underneath the first, consisting of two adults, and a child lying between them. Nearby they also discovered a tablet, which contained engravings of an unknown origin. Today this tablet is identified as the Davenport Calendar Stele. The strange markings on the stele were at first considered a fraud because no one was capable of translating the markings to anything understandable. Fortunately the stele was preserved, and Professor Barry Fell of Harvard gained the opportunity to examine the stone, and what he discovered was that the engravings depicted an Egyptian celebration of the New Year beginning on the morning of the equinox, which was later than our current date, based on the ancient calculations. In the center of the stele appeared an illustrated scene surrounded by inscriptions of three different languages, which were identified by Fell as Egyptian, Iberian Punic, and Libyan. Fell, also, confirmed that all three of these languages were written in their appropriate alphabet and heiroglyphic characters. Fell speculated that the Egyptian text could have been a copy of an original, dated as far back as 1400 BC. Fell further noted that the Priests of Osiris might have provided the stone as a means to regulate a calendar for explorers in far off places, such as Iowa on the banks of the Mississippi River in the center of the North American continent.

At the time when the stone was found neither the Iberian Punic nor the Libyan scripts had been deciphered, which made it impossible to translate the inscriptions. Fell after much research, decided that the Libyan language was very similar to Egyptian, only they used an alphabet developed from Carthage instead of using the hieroglyphic system of Egypt. Punic, as Fell pointed out was the *Semitic* tongue of Carthage, and Iberian Punic was made up of distinctive letters created by the Basque people. With this knowledge, Fell was able to decipher the stone engraving, plus, dating its creation at around 800 to 700 BC. As the reader might recall, sea trade and exploration conducted by crews made up of various cultures was mentioned in Chapter 4. The discovery of the Davenport Stele is probably an excellent example of proof for such an observation; besides the support for giants among the Alligewi. Once again there are numerous other examples of deep prehistorical contact with people from Europe, and from Mediterranean Sea locations. This book will touch on some of those examples as we move along.

This knowledge of Egyptian presence along the Mississippi River around 700 BC might assist in understanding the Mound Builders (Alligewi) of the Mississippian Period (about 3400 BC to AD 1500s), which extended from the mouth of the Mississippi River in the Gulf of Mexico, north into where Wisconsin sits today. Many researchers include the Mississippian people in with those of the Ohio River Valley, suggesting that they are an extension of the Adena, and Hopewellians. If these people are all connected, then the east-west range of the Mississippian locations would extend from Ohio westward to around Kansas City, Kansas.

It is current understanding, by archaeologists, that the style of pyramids and burial rituals began to change along the upper Mississippi River around AD 700. The conical and circular style mounds were being upgraded or replaced with larger flat-topped truncated style mounds, which were designed and built to serve a different function from the conical burial mounds of the Ohio River Valley. The people of the Mississippian Period were, once again, made up of many independent cultures who joined together forming a Mississippian Tradition, once referred to as the Mississippian Culture. Archaeologists still consider these Mississippian location sites as part of the Hopewell groups found further east. However, it might be that the people who left the Davenport Calendar Stele could have had an altering effect on the groups along the Mississippi River in contrast to the groups of the Ohio River Valley. As we learned earlier, the scouting report from the Lenape described the Alligewi differently than what they considered normal Native American body types, of that time period, to be. If it is possible that the Alligewi had absorbed members of Mediterranean explorers into their groups, could it not also be that they were informed of pyramids from those Egyptian crew members? Furthermore, discovery of other artifactual forms of evidence extending from the banks of the Mississippi River west into

Oklahoma and New Mexico, which also point to foreign explorers from across the Atlantic Ocean, leaving signs of their prehistoric arrival.

This speculation can be taken forward even further when we compare the style of these truncated (terraced) pyramids with those of the Egyptian stepp-pyramids, and the Mayan stone type pyramids of Mesoamerica. Their appearance is unquestionably similar. In fact, they are so similar that researchers must give serious thought of how they might be connected. It is not out of the question to suspect the groups along the Mississippi River could have had a trade connection with the Mayan culture from Central America, directly across the Gulf of Mexico. It is now accepted by archaeologists that the Mayans had use of reed boats, much like the ones developed in South America, which they utilized for trade along the coastal areas of the Caribbean Sea, and in the Gulf of Mexico. That being the case, from Tulum, a prominent port city in Quintana Roo, Mexico, to the mouth of the Mississippi River across the Gulf of Mexico is about 690 plus miles (1110 km). To a civilization like the Maya, 700 miles would probably not be of any great achievement.

It is well documented in the archaeological record that the Hopewell Tradition carried on extensive long range trade arrangements with groups south, west and north of them from the Ohio River Valley. They procured mica from Appalachia, copper from the Great Lakes region, sea shells from the Atlantic Ocean coastal area, conch shells from Louisiana, and maize from Mexico, which is where the crop originated as a tall grass. It probably is very likely that the people along the Mississippi also had extensive trade with people from the American Southwest and those nations of the upper Northwest of the American continent. We know today these groups along the Mississippi used dugout canoes for travel along the rivers, tributaries, lakes, and new canals, which they built much like the Maya. Most of these canals were built by nations located in what today is, Missouri. In fact, the name for Missouri was taken from the local tribe called *Missouri* meaning, "Town of the Large Canoes." Similar style dugouts were also used by the nations in the Southwest around the same time. The more popular birch-bark canoes, as seen in movies, were a product of nations in the northern part of North America, in what are now Wisconsin, Minnesota, Michigan, and others including Canada. This northern area supported a strong supply of birch trees from which to obtain the necessary bark. Bark from the birch tree was also used by French explorers and businessmen, and later by early Americans for map making, and document writing material. In many grave mounds silver was found, which could only mean that it came from the American Southwest. Also, a certain amount of sea shells native to the Pacific coastal region had been unearthed at various sites, again suggesting southwestern trading contact.

One further observation for an inclusion of foreign people into the local cultures along the Mississippi River Valley comes from a study conducted by Dr. J.W. Foster while studying site locations along the Mississippi River during the later 1800s. Dr. Foster wrote:

The results of my observations have led me to infer that the mound-builders' crania were characterized by a general conformation of parts, which clearly separated them from the existing races of man, and particularly from the Indians of North America.[3]

This observation by Dr. Foster might be quite typical for that time, since there were many theories put forward by various people possessing varying interests. A number of those theories revolved around Biblical stories, including the Ten Lost Tribes of Israel. Perhaps one example in support of that theory might be the Los Lunas, New Mexico, stone containing what has been described as the Ten Commandments written in Hebrew. According to the local scholars of Los Lunas, knowledge of this stone located on private ranch land has been around since, at least, the 1880s. A number of scholars have examined the stone and, of course, have determined the markings to be fakes: although in 1949 Robert Pfeiffer, of Harvard's Semite Museum, stated that the inscriptions were a mixture of Moabite, Greek, and ancient Phoenician — Paleo-Hebrew or Jewish script before their exile to Babylon around 586 BC — traditionally dated at 597 BC. In any event, if the stone dating and Hebrew script is accurate, it would simply be one more ancient artifact to support Old World influence on early American cultures. It would not be prudent to believe that foreign expeditions or immigrants arriving in North America did not have contact or knowledge of Native American people.

A change in burial customs along the Mississippi River groups also might point to outside Egyptian influence. With the Mississippian mounds, it was documented that burials including cremation had ended. This seemed to be true all along the villages of the Mississippi, and it was also shown that burials of leaders became more elaborate and ceremonial as indicated from an excavation carried out of a huge mound, perhaps larger than Monk's Mound at Cahokia, in St. Louis, Missouri. The mound was located on the corner of Broadway and Mound Street in St. Louis, and completely removed in 1869. This large mound was one of many in and around the St. Louis area, which is almost directly across the Mississippi River from the Cahokia site. The location of the two gigantic mounds has led to speculation that these high mounds might have been used also as signaling towers — for warnings of danger or perhaps to indicate ceremonies in progress. The height of these mounds made it possible for fires to be seen from numerous site mounds, miles away, in the surrounding areas.

The mound was discovered by French explores as they moved along the waterway of the mighty river. It is not quite clear who named the mound, but it came to be known as the *Big Mound.* Once the mound was opened, it became clear that the interior was very different from any already excavated in either the Ohio River Valley, the upper Mississippi region, Indiana or West Missouri. Inside of this mound were chambers for burial with bodies of what might have been a chief, and his wife laid out on their backs and bedecked with beaded necklaces strung along pieces of common hand-twisted twine. Around the bodies was an array of grave-goods consisting of conch shells from the Louisiana bayou, ivory beads, an ivory spool — described as having been turned on a lathe, two unidentifiable items of copper, and pieces of cloth. In order to enter into this burial chamber it was necessary to move through elaborate passageways, which were described as having level solid floors with solid raised walls inclining outward, and covered over with a form of plaster made of moist clay. The ceilings of these passageways were covered with heavy timbers with earth stacked on top of the wood. It was estimated that the tunnel extended for about 72 feet (22.9 m). The burial vault itself was described as also having ceilings of timber with a solid floor on which the bodies were placed on their backs equidistant from each other, about a few feet apart, with their feet facing towards the west — very comparable to Egyptian, Scandinavian, and Anglo-Saxon burial rituals. At the peak of this mound was, discovered buried at a shallow depth of about 18 inches (45.72 cm), bodies believed to be those of some local Indians of a later period. All Mound Builder bodies were buried ritualistically in deeper areas of the mound. What is evident about this structure is simply that it seems to copy the burial pyramids of Egypt. It possesses archaeological design, an abundance of passageways with chambers, a great size, with bodies inside — laid out in a ritualistic manner, surrounded by material items to sustain them in their afterlife, and placed in an east-west reclining position honoring the great sun-god.

The sun during Egypt's Old Kingdom (2686-2181 BC) became the central religious figure of their kingdom. The religion revolved around the sun-god *Ra*, associated with *Heliopolis* (the City of the Sun), which was located during Pre-dynastic times, about 5 miles (8 km) east of the Nile River across from the Giza Plateau. Within this region of mound builders the existence of terraced (truncated) mounds, accompanied by an interest in solar movements, seemed almost too intentional to be considered coincidental. When the Maya are brought into the picture, the connection becomes even more structured and planned. Even the amount and type of mounds are clearly seen to be different along the Mississippi River. They are larger, more concentrated, more selective for purpose, of grander design, and contain constructed additions on top of some of the various types. Although, many of the Mississippian sites still used the Ohio type conical, and in some instances, circular type mounds for burials; but in these locations they appear to be of more compact design and sizing. The Cahokia mound site, near Collinsville, Illinois, is an excellent example of the different mound types, and the actual layout of the prehistorical towns. The word town is probably much more accurate and descriptive, than village. The site, during ancient times consisted of more than 120 mounds extending over more than six square miles (9.6 km^2). This area was actually smaller than the area of St. Louis where hundreds, if not thousands, of mounds were placed directly across the Mississippi River. At one point, St. Louis was known as *Mound City;* however, most of the mounds were destroyed by white settlers, and urban-sprawl. Today Cahokia is a State Historic Site, and maintains about eighty of the mounds (See pictures at end of Chapter). Approximately in 2013, a new bridge was constructed across the Mississippi River near St. Louis, and Collinsville, Illinois, where Cahokia is located. During excavation on the Illinois side, they discovered another settlement, which researchers believe was once part of the Cahokia site, and they referred to it as *Little Cahokia.* All of the artifacts were gathered up, and moved to the Illinois State Museum at Springfield, Illinois. Unfortunately there is still not a lot of information available about this site.

The Cahokia site offers a view of some of the different mound types, along with a view of what the ancient site might have been like during ancient times. Some of the mounds, and their functions, are as follows:

- Burial Mounds: Usually constructed as conical shape, with varying diameters and height.
- Circular Mounds: Also used as a burial mound-possibly created by a different culture.
- Funerary Edifice: A burial mound shaped more like a pyramid-one contained about 900 bodies with grave goods.
- Temple or Sacrificial Mounds: Used primarily for religious purposes — Sacrifice was a main ritual of their religious practices. Both men and women were sacrificed — some buried alive and women in their early twenties subjected to mass sacrifices.
- Garden Mounds: Used to grow edible plants — elevated gardens.
- Pottery Mounds: Contained pottery works, and pieces of broken pottery items.
- Crania Mounds: Filled with only bone fragments from the skulls of many humans — the purpose is unknown, but probably for religious reasons.
- Residence Mounds: Filled only with broken pottery, and house ware items.
- Effigy Mounds: Representations or images of animals, birds, reptiles, and humans.
- Battle Mounds: Used for defensive purposes, usually shaped like a tortoise — hard shell, sometimes containing the ashes of as many as 500 or more dead warriors.
- Festival Mounds: Built in a triangular form with 3 embankments-not enclosed, containing a central low mound, and 3 small circles near the openings. Thought to be used for marriage ceremonies or other ritualistic functions.
- Truncated Mounds: Described as terraced, step-type pyramid, similar to the *teocallis* — a stone pyramid of Mexico once built by the Maya and

Aztec — Spanish translation *Gods House*. Monk's Mound is the best preserved example — 22 million cubic feet of earth, covering 14 acres at the base, extending to a height of 100 feet. Once, possibly, contained a temple built of wood and stone on the rear of the flat top. Also, a house for the chief and his family, along with a ceremonial space to build large fires. Other unknown types of buildings and gardens with trees were placed along the first terrace. Stairs led up to each terrace level, and were made of wood; in some cases a winding walkway was used.

As one might observe from the individual functions of these various type of mounds, aspects of Mayan, and possibly Aztec, influence is very prevalent; such as the style and design of the truncated mounds, their purpose, the ritual of sacrifice, trade good items, and food all point to a strong connection between Mexico, and the Mississippian culture.

On the east side of Monk's Mound (named for French Trappist monks who once resided there from AD 1809-1813) archaeologists recovered a sandstone tablet dated at around AD 1300, which depicted a man wearing a winged costume and a bird-like mask possibly caught in a dance type movement. On the back side of this tablet was a design of simple crosshatching — possibly meant to represent snake skin. The interpretation of the symbol found in one of the Cahokia site pamphlets explains that the symbol probably represents, "upper or sky world (bird), this world (man), and the underworld (snake)." Coincidentally the Egyptians also recognized three worlds with Horus (the Hawk-headed, one-eyed god) representing the sky above, the Pharaoh — who represented mankind-the earthly-being, and Osiris god of death — representing the underworld, resurrection, wine, and agriculture — and all which comes from the earth. Perhaps with the symbolic relationship of snake and bird figures, there might be a Quetzalcoatl-god connection from the Aztecs, and Kukulcán from the Maya.

One other symbolic association with the Aztecs and Maya may lie with their beliefs in *duality*, embodied by the god Ometeotl. This belief was based on opposites, such as, day and night, up and down, feminine and masculine, etc. This concept of duality might have been represented by the flat-topped truncated earthen pyramid, which in its original state could have symbolized the flat earth. The meaning of the duality for 'flat earth' is described in *The Complete Illustrated History, Aztec & Maya*:

> The level of the flat earth or Tlalticpac was the first plane of the nine underworld realms and also the first plane of the thirteen celestial realms. It was both terrestrial and infernal.[4]

As may be seen by the pyramids of Mesoamerica, many contain nine layer levels leading up the pyramid, representing the nine underworld realms. It is very possible that when the large earthen structure (Monk's Mound) was built, that it was based on a representation of the nine layers; but over the many years and numerous attempts at reconstruction, that symbolism was destroyed. Furthermore, it is very possible that Monk's Mound is far older than what archaeologists have dated it to be. Remember, when the French arrived at Cahokia there was only a tribe of local Indians who they called the Cahokia. However, it is highly unlikely that those Native Americans were the people who had originally built the pyramid type mound, which now stands in that location. In fact, these earthen mounds probably date further back to around 8000 BC.

Evidence of more ancient dating for Mississippi River Valley sites comes from an ancient site just north of Cahokia along the Illinois River at today's town of Kampsville, Illinois. The site once located there was called The Koster Site, and it was dated from around 8500 to 8000 years ago, or about 6500 BC. This site, when excavated, indicated human habitation for a period of more than 7,000 years extending back into the Early Archaic period. This date may predate the Adena and Hopewell. The kind lady at the local Historical Society in 2013, informed this author that the Koster site had been closed for about thirty years. The only information available was from a display, which was set-up in their showroom. The entire area of the Mississippi River Valley down to the Gulf Coast flourished about 600 years longer than the Adena and Hopewell.

Another mound site nearby, along the Illinois River is called the Rockwell Mound, and it is located in Havana, Illinois, (named for the Havana Hopewell Tradition), which is around 45 miles (73 km) southwest of Peoria, Illinois. The Havana Hopewell covered an area from just across the Wisconsin State line — bordering Lake Michigan, over into Iowa close to central Iowa near Des Moines, then moving southwards into the State of Missouri just east of Jefferson City — the State Capital, and crossing over into Illinois at just south of the East St. Louis area. There were many mound sites located within this Havana Hopewell boundary, but today many of the mounds have been destroyed. The area at Havana, Illinois, was once a cluster of mounds, but today only one mound exists (see photos at end of chapter). The Rockwell Park where the mound now stands was once the site for campaign speeches by Stephen A. Douglas and Abraham Lincoln in 1858. Douglas spoke first on August 13th in Rockwell Park, and Lincoln spoke the next day. The Rockwell Mound unfortunately offers very little in the way of artifactual evidence for accurate dating due to "civilization." It is quite possible that the entire area might have existed at the same time as did the Koster Site, which is only about 75 miles (120 km) away on the Illinois River. It is unknown if the area around Rockwell Mound has ever been thoroughly excavated due to farming and business interests, or how much of the artifacts uncovered were haphazardly destroyed by people who considered them a nuisance while building or plowing, but it might be that the grounds still have much to tell about the ancient civilization that once inhabited the region.

Just across the Illinois River from Havana, Illinois, are the Dickson Mounds in Lewiston, Illinois, just one of 60,000 locations in Illinois, which have produced Native American artifacts. This particular location traces Native American Culture from post-glacial age hunters of about 12,000 years ago, to those cultures dated at AD 1250. The mound was excavated by Dr. Don F. Dickson, a chiropractor and amateur archaeologist. The excavations produced over 3000 burials at this location with the earliest burials found in mounds dating to be near AD 800. Later burials were found to be in cemeteries as communities began to focus on the village as a place of everyday living, rather than resting places for the dead. Sacrifice was also found to be part of this culture's activities when four bodies were unearthed missing their heads, which were replaced by pots. Archaeologists have determined that this was an example of later ritual practices. All of the human skeletons were placed on display from the 1930s until 1992 when the museum complied with the *Native American Graves Protection and Repatriation Act,* which was signed into law on 16 November 1990. The law was designed to protect graves, and to return to Native Americans all "cultural items" retrieved during archaeological site excavations: from that time forward the mound display has been sealed.

A nearby mound called Tampico Mound, one of a number in the area, was opened by the owner Robert Gooden. The mound produced 70 human burials, and it was the only mound to be excavated in the region. This provided extended knowledge of cultural awareness of the people who resided in the region.

Some other sites, which became known was one on an Illinois River bluff top close to East Peoria, Illinois, exposing a mass grave; another site was near Washburn, Illinois, which exposed a layer of human bones in a farm field — later uncovering four ossuaries containing more than several hundred human remains: finally at Quincy, Illinois, on the Mississippi River a site was found, which produced more than two dozen human burials along with bone bundles suggestive of the Late Woodland Adams Tradition — this Tradition disappeared from the Illinois cultural record around 12,000 years ago. Up until 1969 when the site finally closed Eagle Scouts, and scouts working on their Order of the Arrow projects, operated the museum and worked as tour guides — this author is a proud recipient of both scouting achievements.

This creation, of which the Mound Builders belonged to, was of a rather large populace of cultures. These individual cultures stretched from up-state New York, sweeping southwards into the western tip of Virginia across into Indiana, Illinois, Missouri, Iowa, Kansas, and north up to Wisconsin, Michigan, parts of Minnesota; then south as far as Florida, Georgia, Alabama, Mississippi, Louisiana, Arkansas, and into the eastern sections of Oklahoma and Texas. These various cultures were known by many different names; for example, the Trempeleau Hopewell of Wisconsin, the New York Hopewell, the Crab Orchard culture of Southern Illinois, Indiana, Kentucky, Tennessee, and a section of Missouri; the Swift Creek culture of Florida, Georgia, and Alabama, and the

Plaquemine culture of the lower Mississippi River Valley, who were descendants of the Troyville-Coles Creek cultures. The Plaquemine culture occupied almost all of Louisiana except for areas occupied by the Caddoan culture of western Louisiana, Arkansas, eastern Oklahoma, and Texas. As can easily be observed by their various locations, these cultures covered most of the central and eastern portions of the North American continent; yet all, or most, engaged in activities, which placed them into the Hopewell Tradition.

According to many archaeologists the Plaquemine culture was one of the last of the Mississippian Tradition cultures. Similar to the Cahokia people, they built flat-topped mounds, only with a few exceptions. On top of their mounds, they built smaller mounds, sometimes on top of old temple ruins or houses. Further, unlike at Cahokia they built these structures using a method called, "wattle and daub," which consisted of strips of wood — the *wattle,* covered by a mixture of sand, dirt, clay, and animal feces — the *daub*, which when dried resembled a type of plaster. Their burial rituals also differed from many of the other cultures since they used oval and rectangular grave shapes inside the mounds, and quite often filled with items of pottery, pipes, stone hunting points, and axes. In some instances a grave would contain only one skull, while another grave was found to contain sixty-six (66) skulls. Samples of their earthworks may be found at sites in Medora (West Baton Rouge), Emerald Mound (Winterville), and at Holly Bluff (Lake George) in Mississippi. One thing all of these sites had in common were larger Grand Plaza areas than at Cahokia, which is listed at 40 acres (16 hectares).

What caused the decline and fall of the Mound Builders is yet unknown. In comparison to other archaeological endeavors, the Mound Builder phenomenon is relatively a new challenge for the modern day researcher. Some point to the commonalities between the Maya, and the Mound Builders of the Mississippi River Valley. Some even speculate that the Mound Builders, in those locations, were a branch from the Mesoamerican Maya population; still other scholars point to an Aztec connection between the two peoples. So it might be of some benefit for researchers to seek out specific causes for the Mayan collapse, which allowed for the rise of the Aztec civilization. We know the Maya became prominent due to the decline of the Olmec civilization — but causes for that are also yet unknown. We also know that the entire Mound Builder Tradition engaged in long range trade relations with other cultures from as far as the American Southwest, and on over to the Atlantic Ocean, north probably into modern day Canada, and along the Gulf Coast. It would be quite natural for a portion of these cultures to have blended-in or to be absorbed by other cultures. It also would be a normal practice for civilizations to simply drift to other interests as the younger generations matured and learned new ways from others who they had encountered through trading relations or from exploration expeditions into other continental locations.

Some researchers have speculated climate change as a possible reason for their disbandment. Perhaps a colder climate developed, causing agriculture to decline for the large population.

One other researcher suggested their disappearance might have been the result of disease caused by improper disposal of their own garbage and human waste. Perhaps this might have been in relation to their use of such particulars in agriculture production. Or perhaps, disease and illness brought on by insects or contact with individuals outside of the main culture.

Nonetheless, the size of their populations very well could have contributed to a decline by either sudden or long-term means. It has been established that at its height, Cahokia's population exceed that of London in Great Britain. In order to feed such a huge population, while conducting strenuous physical labor intensive activities of earthen mound building, would surely have taken a toll on needed nutrition. This need / requirement possibly could have intensified the religious practice of sacrifices. A further result of food shortage could have motivated some people within the culture to expand outward to other locations, seeking food, shelter, cleaner water, and opportunities for survival and growth. Once removed from the main cultural practices from, which they were once part, ideas and attitudes changed according to needs, and availability of assets. Thus, the 'Old Ways' were lost, and changed to suit the needs of the modern people.

Of course, there is the possibility of some other rouge nation, after having encroached on Mound Builder ground were the ones responsible for severe extended times of war and destruction, as questioned by the observation of Silverberg at the beginning of this chapter. This possibility is quite plausible since there is knowledge of other existing Nations of Native Americans that were roaming the North American continent during the high-point of the Mound Builder Tradition. A reference to such an occurrence is brought out in the book, *Mound Builders & Cliff Dwellers* by *Time-Life Books*, when they pointed out:

> Although some versions of the vanished-race notion had the mound builders migrating to Mexico to found advanced civilizations there, most depicted a livelier denouement. The mound builders were destroyed, many writers suggested, by barbarous American Indians. In his 1832 poem "The Prairies," William Cullen Bryant wrote, "The red man came — The roaming hunter tribes, warlike and fierce, And the Moundbuilders vanished from the earth...All is gone; All— save the piles of earth that hold their bones.[5]

It is possible such a scenario could have played out as that in Bryant's poem. However, this view point leaves much to piece together. There are too many missing possibilities, which go unexplained in order to accept such a theory. It might be more probable to accept a theory of mass distribution of the cultures into other locations, possessing more modern, less inhumane forms of religious beliefs, accompanied by different concepts what is necessary for survival as a group or nation.

Of course, there are always examples of powerful nations and governments who fall prey to 'hubris', and cause decline of their own empires. The powers controlling the empire often over-look the needs of their people, failing to provide necessary resources, happiness, good health, a chance for success, and much more. Instead selfish-greed and out of control power is the focal point for misguided tyrannical rulers — providing for a collapse from within.

Pre-History's Chronology Enigma

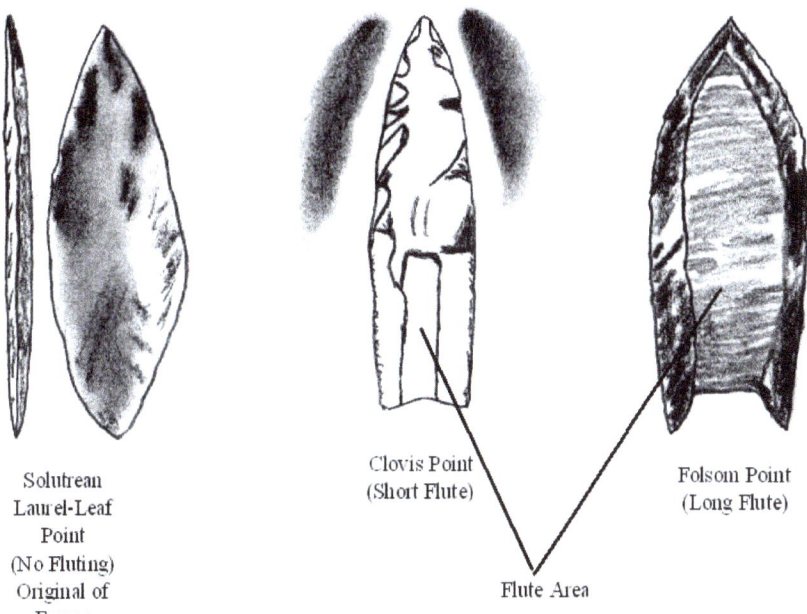

Drawings by Terrance F. Johnson, 2013

Solutrean tools 22,000-17,000 BCE
Attributed - Charnier Solutre
Pouilly Saone et Loire, France
Wiki Commons

Clovis Point
Public Domain
Wiki Commons

Folsom Point
Public Domain
Wiki Commons

Fig. 1

Terrance F. Johnson

Maps of Ancient Clovis Sites and Artifact Sample Locations

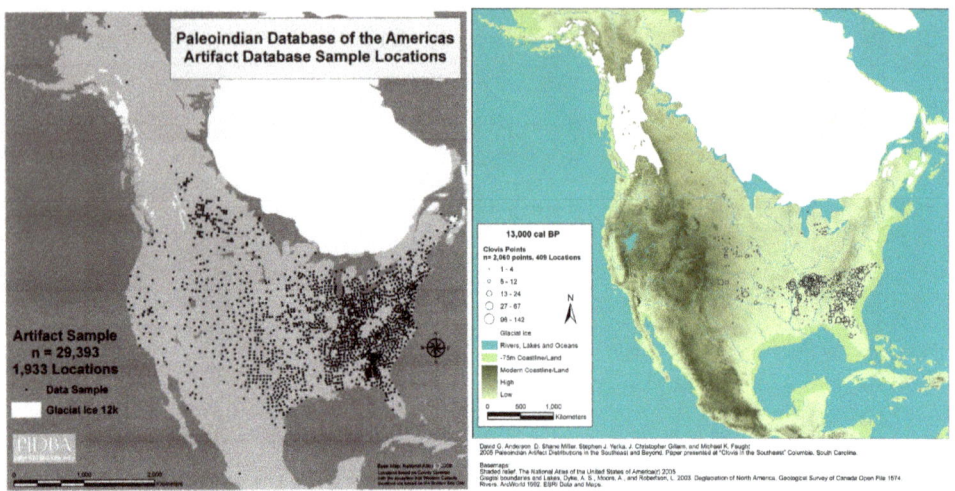

Artifact Location — 12,000 BP

Clovis — 13,000 BP

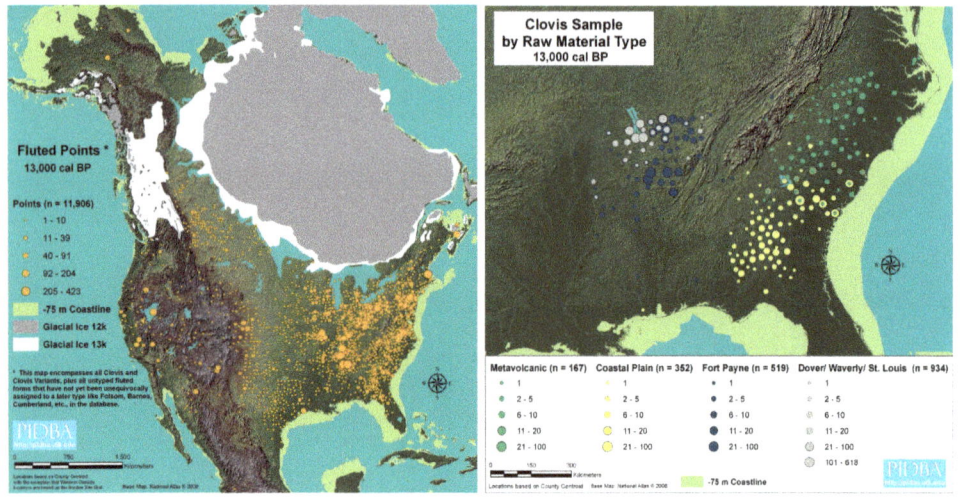

Fluted Points 13,000 BP

Clovis Raw Material Type 13,000 BP

All Images: Anderson, David G., D. Shane Miller, Stephen J. Yerka, J. Christopher Gillam, Erik N. Johanson, Derek T. Anderson, Albert C. Goodyear, and Ashley M. Smallwood. 2010 PIDBA (Paleoindian Database of the Americas) 2010 :Current Status and Findings. *Archaeology of Eastern North America* 38:63-90.

Cahokia
Author's photos, 2013

Monk's Mound Stairway from Grand Plaza

Monk's Mound from Grand Plaza #2

Grand Plaza from top of Monk's Mound Looking South

Facing West from top of Monk's Mound Mound #41- Woodhenge in background

Mound #56 in the Grand Plaza

Village Stockade Fence recreated

Woodhenge looking N. E.

Mound #72—Chief's burial

Terrance F. Johnson

Rockwell Mound- Havana, Illinois
Author's Photos, 2013

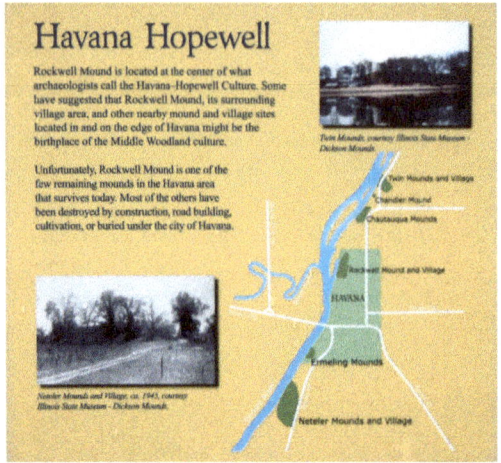
Information sign at base of mound

Location Map

Looking up to the top

The very top of the mound

Pathway down-front of mound

Top of mound

By whatever theory we may be pleased to adopt as to the manner in which was first peopled, we are carried back irresistibly to times so remote that we rise from our study of this subject with the conviction that the origin of the first inhabitants of this continent must ever remain hidden in the darkness of oblivion.

~ ~ *A. J. Conant*
~ ~ *Foot-Prints of Vanished Races*

Chapter 10

The Mystery of Red Ochre

In the last chapter we reviewed one of the oldest known organized civilizations of the North American continent. Archaeology of Native American people is somewhat of a challenge for the modern researcher due to legal restrictions placed on burial sites, and the great amount of thoughtless destruction of artifactual evidence by business and personal interests. Fortunately most of what we have learned from the ancient Mound Builders was acquired by early antiquarians, and both amateur and professional archaeologists in search of new answers for unexplained structures, which was hindering their settlement progress in the new wilderness. One small observation about Adena burials comes in the form of an iron oxide substance, which may help investigators to retrace the footsteps of the ancient Native Americans back from their early locations and even, perhaps, to an understanding of their formation into a cultural entity. This widely used substance is *red ochre,* which seemed to be of high value to a number of cultures in deep antiquity.

This chapter will attempt to identify some of the people that have been identified as users of red ochre, and explore a possible beginning for the use of red ocher in North America. The use of red ochre in burials was a mystery to the antiquarian doing research on the ancient mounds in the Ohio River Valley. Many of the bodies discovered during excavation were covered with the iron oxide pigment, and those doing the excavating did not arrive at any conclusion for what the ritual could have signified. One researcher, possibly Patrick Huyghe, mentioned it could have been used to give the corpse the "Blush of Life." The Adena culture, as discussed in Chapter 9, was a mysterious culture that seemed to simply arrive in the Ohio River Valley of North America in deep antiquity. The Adena, for many years were credited as the only culture to have used red ochre in burial rituals. It was known at the time of these early excavation, that many of the local tribes used red ochre for body painting and art work, but not for burials. It was not until 1882 near the mouth of the Penobscot River, not far from Bangor, Maine, that the mystery of red ochre began to unravel. A local farmer near there reported a red substance pooling on his land. After the initial investigation, it had been determined that red ochre, just below the surface, had been mixed with rain water after the farmer had plowed his field, and formed into blood red puddles of water. Ochre in its natural state is a clay substance colored by iron oxide found in deposits around the world. The investigation was conducted by Augustus Choate Hamlin, one time mayor of Bangor, Maine, geologist, physician, author and antiquarian. Hamlin also found large stone structures near the site, which he thought might have been ruins of the Vinland site of the early arriving Norwegians. Included in his discoveries, in the farmers field, were polished stone tools of very high quality. No tools exhibiting such elevated qualities of sharpness and fabrication had ever been uncovered in North America. This accidental discovery actually turned out to be the first evidence of a Maritime Archaic culture, which flourished in the northeastern part of the United States, and into the eastern regions of Canada over 7,500 years ago (5500 BC).

Ochre in its natural form is dark yellow or reddish brown, and is usually used as a pigment when making paint. What makes ochre so fascinating to archaeologists is the fact that this substance was used by cultures going back into prehistory more than 300,000 years. One of the earliest recorded uses of red ochre is listed at about 100,000 years ago at Blombos Cave, located in South Africa along the coast line on the Indian Ocean. The Blombos site was dated to be Middle Stone Age, and contained a number of types of stone tools and shells. When two of these shells had been pulled apart a fairly good portion of red ochre was found inside; possibly its use was a storage container for the valuable red substance. In addition, at the Blombos site archaeologists found two pieces of ochre, which were deliberately engraved with geometric patterns, dating to around 75,000 BC.

Another site known as GnJh-03 in Zambia, South Africa, and dated to be around 300,000 years old — predating Blombos Cave by 200,000 years, produced slabs of ochre with some containing patterns carved into their surfaces. A site at Klein Kliphuis, in the Western Cape of South Africa also produced pieces of ochre scored in a cross-hatching design. Since Klein Kliphuis is about

249 miles (400 km) from Blombos Cave, some researchers have argued that the geometric designs carved on the pieces of ochre were symbols used by the Middle Stone Age people to communicate with one another — or a form of original ancient writing.

Europe is also not without examples of red ochre usage by ancient peoples. Neanderthal sites located in Europe have generated red ochre use for burials (or religious) purposes. Most of the Neanderthal sites found dated to around 73,000 BC. Elsewhere, Cro-Magnon cave site wall paintings have disclosed artwork created with red ochre, dating to about 33,000 BC.

Recent studies of red ochre have brought forth findings from several other African locations of Middle Stone Age people, that indicated red ochre was blended with a starchy plant resin, which would assist tool makers with attaching stone spear points to wooden shafts, worked from tree limbs. This unique technology has also been found at a number of Paleolithic sites in France. Paleolithic dating is from 2.6 million BC — ending at 10,000 BC, which is prior to the Mesolithic period — determined by the use of flint, stone and bone tools created by early man.

The United Kingdom also provided another site called *Paviland Cave* where a burial was recorded, and referred to as the "Red Lady" because the body was soaked in red ochre. This site is estimated to be roughly 23,500 years old or 21,500 BC. One other site dating to around the same time period is *Arene Candide* a cave site in the Ligurian region of Italy on the Mediterranean Sea. This site revealed a skeleton dubbed, *The Prince* buried close to 23 feet (7 m) below the cave's floor, placed on a bed of red ochre, and surrounded by many other grave-goods.

In 1975, the Danish National Museum exhumed nineteen burials at Vedbaek, Denmark. One of the burials was of a woman adorned with a necklace of boar and deer teeth along with other assorted grave-goods, and beside her was placed the body of a child. Both bodies were covered with red ochre. The people of this burial were part of the Ertebølle culture that hunted marine animals, had a steady diet of shell fish, made pottery, domesticated dogs, but did not involve themselves with farming. Archaeologists believe, due to the extravagant burial arrangements of the woman and child that it exhibited the first signs of social stratification found in that region. The woman must have held a high rank of social status within her culture — a queen, perhaps, and the child of a king.

A burial on the island of Téviec, off the coast of Brittany in France, found in 1927 at the bottom of a shell heap (midden), were burials of bodies covered with red ochre while ritualistically placed into small stone structures buried under circular earthen mounds. In some cases other bodies were found in what was a partially dug pit covered over with midden debris. This burial phenomenon was also practiced by a Native American Nation of the Southwest known as the Anasazi or *The Ancient Ones*, and there remains a great deal of speculation for them having roots from the Solutrean culture of France. This burial site contained middens filled with shell-fish remains, squid, fish, birds, crustaceans, wild boar, and red deer. Some of the bodies at this site exhibited death by violence, and C-14 dating places the site at more than 7,000 years old.

Burial mounds on Téviec resembled burial mounds created at Bohuslän, Sweden, on the Norwegian border in the southwestern part of the country, which is also a maritime province. In the entire country of Sweden there are hundreds, if not thousands, of burial mounds very similar to those at Téviec, and in the Ohio River Valley, in now the continental United States. In just one area the Royal mounds of Gamla Uppsala, about 40 miles (64 km) from Stockholm, Sweden, 250 mounds remain standing, which at one time contained 2,000 to 3,000 burial mounds. Burial mounds of this type have also been identified in Germany. One such site with burial mounds is at Bomlitz located in a large nature reserve of Lower Saxony (Niedersachsen) in northwestern Germany known as, Lüneburg Heath. Along with menhirs (large standing stones) dated to be about 2000 BC, the area is home to about ten earthen burial mounds dating to at least 1500 BC. The ancient site lies between the cities of Hanover (south), and Hamburg (north) not far from the Elbe River leading out to the North Sea, which could indicate that these people were also from a maritime culture. These similarities among earthen burial mounds and the use of red ochre in Africa and Europe have led some scholars to endorse a theory of diffusion for this phenomenon. The diffusion theory believes that the European cultures crossed the Atlantic Ocean over to the American continent bringing with them the ritualistic practices of burial mound building, and the use of red ochre applied to the dead body. Much of this theory is based on maritime cultures of Europe; people with ship building skills, celestial navigation expertise, and deep sea fishing capabilities. Reasoning for this diffusion theory results in findings, which point to maritime cultures as the main users of red ochre, and the cultures most noted for building earthen burial mounds.

The diffusion theory is taken further in a NOVA documentary entitled *Secrets of the Lost Red Paint People*, which clearly shows there is a strong link between the megaliths of Europe, red paint burials of northeast America and Canada, and the Mound Builder civilizations of Midwest America.

A short time after Hamlin's research of the Penobscot, Maine, site Charles Willoby, an archaeologist for the Peabody Museum at Harvard, commenced scientific excavation activities at Hamlin's site. He detected that all of the artifacts had been placed in the mounds in a ritualistic pattern indicating formality of burials. However, he found no bones to actually validate an existence of burials with the artifacts; so his conclusion was that no bones were found along with artifacts because the burials were so old it caused the bones to deteriorate completely.

Later anthropologist, and self-trained archaeologist Warren K. Moorehead led an expedition along the rivers of Maine looking to find additional sites exhibiting the use of red ochre, and samples of the highly advanced tools. Moorehead by 1900, had excavated a number of mounds along the coast of Maine, but he never found any skeletal remains. The tool artifacts, which he found were described as highly worked, and produced by a highly evolved culture; but that some of the stone used in making various tools were made of stone not native to Maine or to the New England region. This observation led Moorehead to conclude that this was a sign of long distance trade with other cultures. Approximately 80 years later researchers were able to match the stone tools, found by Moorehead, to a stone type found at Ramah Bay, Labrador called *Ramha chert*. Ramah Bay is close to 115 miles (100 nautical miles) north from the coastline of Maine, U.S.A. Additional discoveries of the Ramha chert have been placed at locations in the states of New Jersey and Vermont.

In the 1930s at Blue Hill Bay, Maine, under a heap of sea shells (a midden) skeletons covered with red ochre were found by archaeologist Douglas Byers. The Niven Site, as it was known, also produced swordfish bills, barbed harpoons, needles, and moose bone daggers exhibiting carvings suspected to be the earliest prehistoric decorative tradition around the Maritime Peninsula. Tools found at this site, such as sharpened stone gouges used in ship building, along with remains of fish and birds alerted the researchers that these people were a seafaring culture.

The next major discovery came in the 1960s when, once again, from the bottom of a shell heap (midden) on North Haven Island in Penobscot Bay, Maine, five graves were exposed containing red ochre along with remains of cod and swordfish, both deep water species, plummets or fishing weights, stone gouges, and harpoons. A Carbon-14 test on the site placed it near 2500 BC. Archaeologists realized that this culture had the capabilities to sail out away from shore for many miles, to catch large game fish, deep water cod fish, and then return to their original base location, which also implied celestial navigation knowledge. It was clear that this culture was quite distinct from any of the local people in those areas.

The search for this sea-going culture resumed in 1968 when Dr. James Tuck of Memorial University at St. John's, Newfoundland, found skeletons covered with red ochre at Port au Chox, in northwest Newfoundland, dated to around 2000 BC. Once again artifacts at this burial site consisted of toggle harpoons, barbed harpoons, fishing spears called listers, with three or more prongs for piercing fish, and to hunt seal and walrus. One unusual finding at this location was a large number of bird images with some carved into bone-combs. Also a great many beaks were uncovered from a now extinct bird known as the Flightless Giant Auk. The Auk was very similar to penguins and they were native to cold water regions around Norway, the Faroe Islands, Greenland,

Iceland, and the coasts of Canada. It is suspected that the seafaring people might have followed the flocks of the flightless birds across the northern Atlantic Ocean from one of the northern countries over to the coast of Canada, and southward to the shores of the Carolinas, in now the U.S.A., for hunting purposes. The results of these new findings convinced Tuck to label this culture *Maritime Archaic*.

In 1980 another discovery by Dr. William Fitzhugh, of the Smithsonian National Museum of Natural History in Washington D.C. discovered what appear to be remains of houses on a desolate beach in northern Labrador's Nulliak Cove. What Fitzhugh found were foundations of twenty-six houses containing multiple rooms in each complex. This layout signified that these seafarers existed in an organized community structure. All earlier sites, which had been excavated showed no signs of social activities leaving an impression that these people were only of a nomadic extraction. Some of the multi-room structures measured 100 feet (90 m) in length, and contained the remains of fire scars, and tool making activities. Also located near the foundations was a small stone mound covered with red ochre linking this site with other previous archaeological assemblages from New England to northern Labrador in Canada.

Along with rectangular stone foundations the site contained conical pits usually clustered together in groups of four to five. Some of the pits had larger stones placed around them, possibly for hunting blinds, others are suspected of being storage pits while one was believed to be a burial pit.

In addition to the most common artifacts found at all of the other locations, a new stone tool was introduced at this site. They were small-stemmed projectile points (small arrowheads), probably created to hunt birds. This type of point also brings speculation that these people had adopted the use of the bow and arrow, in addition to listers and spears. A number of these projectile points have been found along age-old caribou paths in that area.

Another feature of this northern site were pinnacles placed along the shore line in positions visible from sea locations. Current understanding for these objects is that they might have been placed there for spiritual reasons or practical purposes. One practical purpose would be for pointing the direction to a settlement when returning from the sea. The Eskimos call these stones Inuksuk (a stone landmark) built by humans, and also used by other peoples of the Arctic regions such as, the Inupiat, Kalaallit, and the Yupik. One type of Inuksuk was a tall flat stone stood on end and propped up with smaller stones; while the second type was built by piling smaller stones into some form of recognizable heap with both forms placed on high portions of land easily seen from seagoing vessels. Inuksuks have also been located along the shores of Quebec, and Nova Scotia, as well as, Labrador.

At L'Anse Amour, the oldest site discovered and positioned on the coast of Labrador, a chamber mound built using flat upright stones, with one larger flat lentil stone placed across the top of the entrance was discovered at the center of a burial mound containing skeletons, and toggle harpoons. This type of chamber very closely resembled the type discovered at the French site of Téviec, and one other site on the Isle of Scilly — off the southwestern tip of the Cornish peninsula of Great Britain. This type of stone building procedure, according to many researchers, is typical of Maritime Cultures. Grahame Clarke, Professor of Archaeology at the University of Cambridge had determined, from years of study, that most megaliths when plotted on a map, are placed close to coastal waters indicating that these structures were the creation of cultures that based their survival on fishing, and not on farming (See Figure 1-end of chapter). In addition it was observed by researchers in 1952 at the Varangerfjord site in Norway, that the stone building techniques found at the Canadian locations were very similar to those employed at the Varangerfjord site. Residents at Kven of Varangerfjord are mainly descendants of northern Swedes and Finnish immigrants. At the burial site at L'Anse Amour red ochre was used on the body of a small child placed into the mound with the head facing west, along with two fires placed north and south of the body. Charcoal exhumed from the mound was determined to be more than 7,500 years old or at 5500 BC. Dating for the Téviec site in France was placed near 7,200 years old or 5200 BC. These types of stone structures also are very similar to the vast number of dolmens found in Europe and elsewhere.

As pointed out in Chapter 9, antiquarians noted their findings of grave-goods, fire-scares, body placement of the corpse, and the use of red ochre during burials in conical earthen mounds. From information gained in this chapter it is obvious there are many similarities between the Maritime Archaic culture and the Adena culture of Ohio. It probably is very unlikely that ritualistic practices, as had been noted, could have developed independently by two different and geographically located peoples. Many scholars hesitate to use the term 'diffusion' to account for the similarities among cultures; but if knowledge and ritualistic acts are not conveyed from one entity to another, then how can the same identical acts be explained when found to be used by one or more cultures separated from each other by time and space?

After all of the discoveries made in identifying this Maritime Archaic culture, the most common feature seemed to be the use of red ochre in their burial formalities. As discussed earlier in this chapter the use by ancients of red ochre goes back, at least, approximately 300,000 years. In more recent prehistory, of the North American hemisphere, archaeology once again records evidence of its usage among, what some would consider being, an unsophisticated, backward band of woodland people. To some extent exploration of the beginnings of the red ochre chronology, and its uses among cultures from deep prehistoric Africa to the continental United States seems to indicate that its uses, applications, and symbolism was brought to the location by descendants of those ancient cultures; and the Maritime Archaic culture of New England and Canada is the main contributor of its introduction to North America. The fact that the use of red ochre was so important to this seafaring culture, for use in their burials, that some researchers began referring to this culture as *The Red Paint People*. Red ochre usage among Native Americans still exists today for art work, ceremonies and crafts, but it is not used in rituals for burials.

Many modern day archaeologists are beginning to challenge the paradigm that Native Americans originated from a single origin. It is quite clear the evidence presented points to a very strong connection between sea-going cultures of northern Europe, and the Red Paint People of northeastern Canada and the New England area of the United States, and not with cultures from Asia. Current day chronology dates the Maritime Archaic culture beginning at 4,000 years ago; however from archaeological sites discovered in Canada and Europe, this date is pushed further back, at least, by three thousand years or perhaps closer to 7000 BC.

The end of this culture is placed somewhere between AD 1000 and AD 1500 with the formation of the Beothuk people of Canada who are considered a descendant of the Red Paint People. Their use of red ochre for art works on canoes, houses, tools, and body decorations earned them the name "Red Indians" by the incoming Europeans. The meaning of their name in the Beothuk language is "People." The entire nation was destroyed by diseases brought over by the Europeans, and by later battles between the European invaders and the Beothuk people. The last survivor of the Beothuk people was a woman named *Shanawdithit* who died of tuberculosis at St. John's, Newfoundland, in 1829. The Beothuk are considered a *First Nation*, and some scholars believe that it might have been the ancestors of the Beothuk (The Red Paint People) who were mentioned by the early Norwegian explorers of the AD 1000 expeditions from Greenland. Still today, some members of the Micmac (pronounced *Migmaw* in Canada) claim ancestry with the Beothuk.

Another people thought to be descendants of the Red Paint People are the Dorset culture, who is classified as the Dorset Tradition, a Paleo-Eskimo culture. This Tradition preceded the Inuit and received their name from Cape Dorset in Nunavut, Canada. By AD 1500 the Dorset Tradition was completely eliminated by the Medieval Warm Period, to which they could not adapt. The Tradition was replaced by the *Thule* who migrated eastward from Alaska around AD 1000. The name Thule is derived from the onetime location of Thule in Greenland where their remains were first discovered at Comer's Midden. From Alaska, the Thule moved across Canada over to Greenland where they were in contact with the Norse inhabitants who referred to them as *Skræling* (Barbarians). It just might be a possibility that the Norse expeditionary voyages could have encountered the Thule much earlier, and they traveled back to

Greenland with the Norse explorers. As the reader may recall, Thule in Swedish means North.

The Algonquian (Algonkian) are Canadian descendants of the Red Paint People; who also identify a league of separate Native American tribes that speak a related language. The sundry of nations, which make up the Algonquian have, at one point in time, branched off from the original Maritime Archaic culture probably during a declining period, and eventually formed into tribal groups, and migrated to distant locations. Evidence of Algonquian words can be traced to the American Southwest through the Zuni language. As anthropologists, historians, and archaeologists study this vast region of North America it is unmistakable that the original theories of populating North America was, and is, totally incorrect. Science cannot disregard the Maritime Archaic culture anymore then they can ignore or discount early Norse arrivals and ancient copper mining activities around the Great Lakes region by some unknown entities, most likely not of Asian heritage.

It probably is correct to believe that these people, making up the Maritime Archaic Tradition, were not the only nationalities from Europe and the Mediterranean Sea area to have landed on the shores of North America. As Professor Barry Fell has so professionally pointed out, North America has been inundated with all sorts of people, and cultures going farther back than most scholars care to believe. Early science did not give early man enough credit for tenacity, creativity, and their physical abilities to have accomplished world travel. It remains unclear if these ancient seafarers were of a circumpolar culture. Many scholars still question a theory, which believes a culture originating in Russia could have, and did make the Arctic Circle regions their home and highways for globe exploration. In any event, we know certain cultures did inhabit the Arctic regions in deep prehistory; we are simply unclear as to what extent.

Conceivably one other aspect, which might connect the Maritime Archaic Tradition with Norse seafarers, is the creation and use of slate in tool making industries. There is evidence that somewhere between 3000 BC and 2000 BC flint and bone tools were replaced by slate both in areas of Scandinavia, and in areas of the American and Canadian Northeast at approximately the same time. Nowhere else on the globe did these phenomena occur except at these two global locations, leading some experts to argue for a connection between these two civilizations. The first evidence of slate tools was recorded at Nulliak Cove in northern Labrador when they discovered a grinding slab suspected to be used for polishing ground-slate axes and gouges.

Slate is a fine-grained rock with a dark bluish dull-gray finish formed from clay, which is easily worked by splitting the rock along parallel cleaved planes. Slate, once split into pieces with sharp edges, is the best substitute for a metal cutting tool. Certain variations for the use of slate in the different cultures did exist, for example, in the American Northeast, slate was used in funerary rituals more often than in everyday activities, whereas, the Scandinavians used slate in their daily life activities, and the Canadian culture used slate for tools and weapons such as, axes and bayonets. Many slate tool items of similar design and use such as, a D-shaped knife resembling today's kitchen stainless steel scraper/chopper tool, have been found at each Maritime Archaic location.

The slate tool similarities obviously confirm some form of ancient contact between the two parallel cultures. With so many comparably shared traditions, which are most obvious to even the amateur archaeologist, it raises the question — how long contact between the cultures existed? Did the Maritime Archaic culture come from Scandinavia? Had they always been in contact with people of their homeland? Are they the people who brought red ochre awareness to North America from areas in Denmark, Sweden, and Norway? There is positive evidence this could be the case. Examples of Maritime Archaic Tradition have been uncovered, not only in Europe, and eastern regions of North America, but also along a sea pathway joining the two continents. For example Great Britain has produced sites exhibiting the use of red ochre and megalithic chambers, while megalithic dolmens appear frequently in Ireland along with artifacts made of ground-slate, while the same variety of ground-slate artifacts were found on the Orkney Islands north of Scotland. These individual locations seem to establish a sea route from one sea-faring culture to the other. It would be highly unlikely that all of these cultures developed the elements of the Maritime Archaic Tradition independently, and at almost the same time.

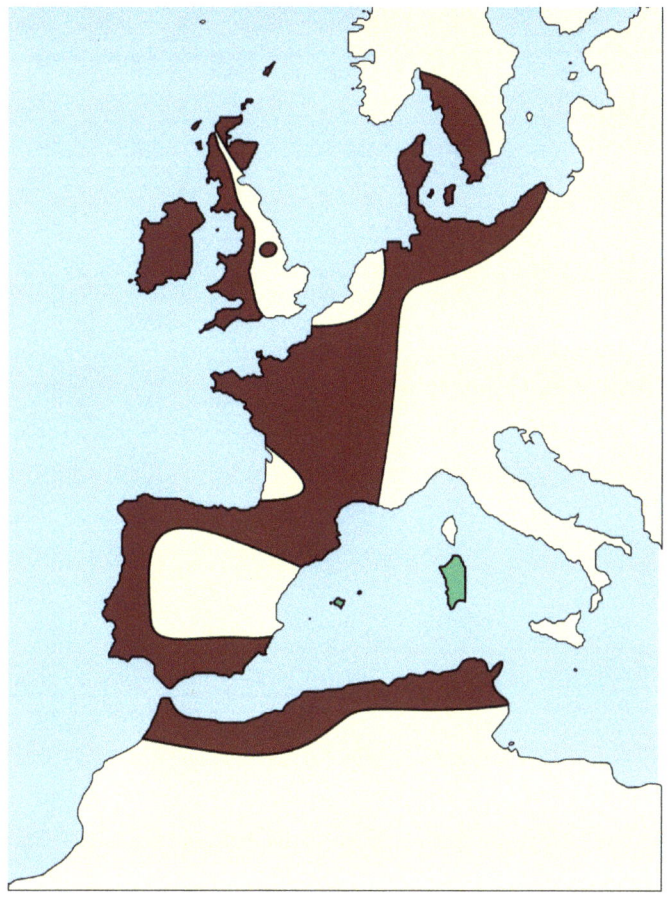

Map of Megalithic Cultures and Principle sites
of Europe in black.
Wikimedia Commons_ Public Domain

Fig. 1

Note: This map does not take into consideration the megalithic works on the east side of the Mediterranean Sea, such as the Giza Pyramids of Egypt, and the Baalbek site of Lebanon.

Everyone agrees that man did not originate in America. Other than this we can be reasonably certain that the first people to settle the Americas came here from Asia. But we have been wrong in assuming that because they came from Asia they were all of Mongoloid stock. Scholars, now more than ever, are expressing serious doubts over whether the people we call "Native Americans" had a single cultural origin.

~ ~ *Patrick Huyghe, Author*
~ ~ *Columbus Was Last*

Chapter 11

First Nations of North America

The idea of North America being populated by merely one group of people, is totally out of the question. The old concept of Asians crossing over Beringia around 10,000 years ago cannot stand-up against today's more modern findings; most carried out through scientific means. There are many challenges to the "Land Bridge" theory, which simply places all prehistoric inhabitants of North America into the Asian category. It probably is quite valid that many explorers and immigrants, of the continent's deep prehistory, were of Asian extraction. However, this theory fails to take into account the other various means and dates for which Asians, and yes, other nationalities might have arrived on the shores of the American continent. It is now known, or highly accepted, that adventurers from Asian countries, including Japan, and more recently, seafaring people from Polynesia have arrived in deep prehistorical times, in addition to Chinese sailors. Further, as we have observed in the last chapter America, as well as Canada, had been home to the very ancient *Red Paint People* probably long before any Asian culture created permanent settlements in northern America or Canada. These ancient people were a sea-going culture, and probably arrived by boat. However, it is quite possible that other cultures from Europe might have crossed over by way of the frozen ice packs on foot. It is becoming very clear that there were a number of cultures who inhabited areas of the Arctic Circle in deep antiquity such as, today's Lapps of Scandinavia, and Eskimos of North America.

One other possibility for mixed races of immigrants to the American continent might be, that during anyone of a number of crossings over the Bering Strait during glacial periods, both Caucasian and Asian cultures could have come across the land bridge either together or in separate groups. This likelihood might have occurred since archaeology already understands that people from Europe had arrived in Asia in deep antiquity from stone tool artifacts discovered there, and also in Siberia of northern Russia. Mentioned in *Our Missing Ancestors* Solutrean design spearheads from a northeastern France location were found as far east as Siberia: and items from Solutrean tool industries are unique and only attributed to the people of northeastern France. So this is a very clear sign of people from Europe crossing the massive land expanse over to Russia and possibly Asia, approximately a distance of 3,700 miles (5900 km). With this being known — would it be so outlandish to consider ancient cultures, prior to the Solutreans, to have migrated eastwards from Europe into the Americas, on foot, crossing any conceivable type of land-bridge?

Many will question the validity of this observation based on lack of evidence, and they might be correct in doing so. However when variations of body types, root language forms, clues of stone inscriptions, and obvious similarities in religion, architecture, and astronomical awareness, in relation to cultures of Central, and South America is brought to light this concept possesses verisimilitude. In the mid-1800s early archaeologists settled on forty (40) stock languages of the Native Americans: today that number has climbed to more than 200 linguistic roots, indicating many sources for early arrivals to the Americas by many diverse cultures. It is not feasible to believe that the entire northern population of America is due to Asian influence, and that white people arrived only after Columbus 'sailed the ocean blue'.

In the early to mid 1960s Stanford Linguist, Joseph Greenberg believed all languages could be condensed down to a handful of common roots, which would identify the language's origin. In 1963 he published *Languages of Africa,* which stated there are four groups (or *Phyla*) of African languages. This finding was accepted by many scholars. Greenberg then went on to define the Native American languages into three groups using the same process as with the African research; however this attempt failed. What Greenberg theorized was that all Native American languages were the result of only three major migrations from Asia, each being from a different location within Asia. Today science recognizes this theory as incorrect with the help of modern researchers like Barry Fell, once Professor Emeritus at Harvard University, who published numerous books on pre-Columbian history during the 1970s. Fell's work began by researching trans-Atlantic incursions of Old World civilizations into the Americas. His study ultimately produced evidence of hieroglyphs and petroglyphs, which pointed to the presence of ancient Scandinavians, Celts, Egyptians, Phoenicians, Africans, and many others who had arrived on the shores of North America long before anyone even considered any such early accomplishments.

There is no hard evidence, which archaeologists can point to in order to establish the various civilizations from Europe, the Middle East, or cultures from around the Mediterranean Sea to have made their way into Siberia, and blended in with Asian stock within those localities. Also, there is no evidence which indicates people living in that region during glacial and/or interglacial times actually walked across any type of land-bridge, which might have presented itself between the Russian continent and Alaska. Further, it seems few if any researchers have offered a theory about these people using water-craft to make a crossing between the two continents, instead of making the journey on foot. Crossings could have been made during a sea level rise when glaciations were in melting stages: after all, distance by sea was also only about 55 miles (88.5 km) or in some cases — even shorter depending on sea-level conditions. A boat crossing cannot be ruled out since we know ancient Stone Age people built, and used various types of water-crafts.

Scientists have been able to identify areas in Siberia, where humans had once resided for some extended period of time. Their excavations have produced hard surface floors, where once a house or public building stood. Such locations have been noted to be on and near the Lena, and Yenisei rivers in the northern latitudes of Russia, and dated to be approximately 200,000 and 300,000 years old. No skeletons have yet been produced, so archaeologists are still pondering if these inhabitants were *Homo sapiens sapiens* or a sub-species like *Homo erectus erectus.* After all according to archaeologists, modern man did not materialize until around 40,000 years ago out of their natural African continental homeland. If such inhabitants did build boats or even simply walk across from Russia to Alaska, some 200,000 to 300,000 years ago — what form of *man* would have been first to set foot in North America? However, if the crossings took place at later dates, say from 100,000 to 10,000 BC. it would then seem feasible to assume that it was modern man who first came to the North American shores, based on current information.

In addition to the findings listed above, in 2012 archaeologists released findings of a gigantic geoglyph in the shape of an elk or deer near Lake Zjuratkul in the Ural Mountains, which some say might pre-date the Nazca lines of South America. This stone structure is estimated to be, at least, the length of two American football fields or about 200 yards (188.8 m). The animal faces north and may be seen from a nearby ridge. Inside of the structure are built-in passageways with walls prepared with clay, and crushed stone while large stones are placed on the outside.

Archaeologists have informed us that hundreds of megalithic sites have been constructed in the Ural Mountains; but the most expansive geoglyph is to be found 35 miles (60 km) northeast of the elk structure on an island in a freshwater lake. Many of the tools excavated indicate a time from 300 to 200 BC : although researchers have identified a process called *lithic chipping* used, dates to Neolithic and Eneolithic (500 to 200 BC) periods. This new finding gives support for the civilizations discussed in Chapter 5, possibly civilizations inhabiting northern Russia in deep antiquity.

Patrick Huyghe, author of *Columbus Was Last* seems to also negate the premise that a purely Asian population is responsible for the Native American peoples. Huyghe stated:

> It seems that the people of the Americas were actually a hodgepodge of races. Scholars have erred in choosing but one category, "American Indians," to describe this great diversity of peoples. How this mixture came about, no one has yet been able to determine. Perhaps the original incoming populations was already mixed. Perhaps one people did settle here, but diverged over time in response to America's varied environments. But such dramatic changes could not occur over a period of just a few tens of thousands of years — maybe more.[1]

It seems our understanding of the population of America or the entire North American continent still rests with the Bering Strait theory. Although gradually, scientific efforts are discovering alternatives to the Beringia theory, which points to a more southern coastal entrance for the bulk of new immigrants coming into North America. These coastal locations suggest that people, probably of Asian descent, came across by some form of water-vessel, following the western shoreline of what is now California, and ultimately settled along the sea coast. Not much evidence has been produced to confirm any certain archaeological sites of these early settlements, possibly because of rising sea waters during glacial meltdowns. Even so, a number of sites which have been uncovered, most likely from more inland resettlements due to rising waters, are considered to be older than any sites found in Alaska, Canada, or the upper northwest of the United States. Still we cannot rule out exploration from cultures once located in Central and South America, who are known to be far older than any culture found in the northern hemisphere. We know that these southern civilizations built and used water-vessels made of reeds or balsa wood, and these crafts were quite capable of sailing in ocean waters; — what would hinder sailors from one of these ancient civilizations to have followed the coast north in search of new trading business or simply for curiosity? If these people did arrive at locations further north, trading with other people found there, and continuing this practice over an extended period of time this surely would have influenced language, customs, and possibly DNA of those in the northern locations.

A theory for southern Pacific coastal entries into the New World might be supported by languages of existing members of Native Americans. Linguist Richard Rogers of Des Moines, Iowa Origins Research Institute, discovered there were fewer original ancient languages in areas where glaciation occurred then there were from more southern areas of what is now the continental United States. The southern languages showed greater diversity than those farther north, indicating these regions as the more probable entry points for seafaring cultures.

Conversely southern port entries can also include the coast line on the Atlantic side of the continent, as well as with ports located along the Gulf of Mexico. This gives rise to exploration from Europe, Africa, and perhaps in some long range effort, to Mideastern and Asian civilizations. All in all, the North American continent was being inundated with explorers from all directions in America's ancient times. Barry Fell in his book *America B.C.* included a map of the eastern half of the United States, extending over to around Des Moines, Iowa, from the Atlantic coast, and from just above the Great Lakes down to the middle of the Gulf of Mexico. This map contains two legends showing *Monuments* and *Cultural traits* of civilizations that have their origin from across the Atlantic Ocean, those of Egyptian, Libyan, Iberian-Punic, Basque, and Celtic. Symbols from the legend are placed on the Map to show point-of-entry locations for these seafaring people, river routes they used, the purpose of their travel, such as mining, and certain visible clues, which they left behind such as, cultural scripts, temple observatories, calendar circles, burial urns, and earthen mounds. Fell's title and explanation for this map is *European and North African cultural interfaces and colonies, circa 800 B.C.* If the country was exposed to such forms of exploration by such diverse cultures, then there is a strong case for Native Americans being a part of some or all of these traveling cultures, and adopting some of their knowledge, which can be symbols to create written forms of communications, traditions and religious beliefs, words or structure of language, and astronomical knowledge. The prehistory of North America is far older than our text books allow. The fact being, if cultures from across the sea arrived here by 800 BC. there can be no other explanation than to believe these influences had an effect on those already here, and these effects had to have an interacting relationship with any Asian cultures. So it would be quite implausible to believe that the entire Native American population was derived strictly from Asian heritage.

As discussed in the last chapter the Red Paint People existed, according to Scholars, until around AD 1000. At this point the society simply appears to have vanished, and archaeologists offer no explanation for their disappearance. Unless these seafaring people just packed up and sailed away to another location or were overwhelmed by some major catastrophe, it seems quite unlikely that this ancient culture simply disappeared into thin air. The most probable explanation for their dissipation is an absorption into other tribes who might have come into their areas or who might have occupied those regions since time immemorial. Or perhaps, this culture decided to move inland, and apply their seafaring skills to America's mighty rivers and extensive lakes. This concept might account for the Ohio Mound Builders quandary where archaeologists debate about *who came first*, the Adena or the Hopewell cultures; and from where did they originate? It just could be that one of these cultures came from members of the Red Paint People who followed the rivers southwest into the Ohio River Valley, and established settlements. Still one other justification for such a suggestion would be that the Adena, as sourced from archaeologists, used red ochre in their burial rituals. Coincidence? Perhaps not.

Along this same line of conjecture there is another culture, known as *Micmacs,* who once inhabited a portion of the regions of the Red Paint People, and might have absorbed some of their members, thus, allowing for a departure of the Red Paint culture. The Micmacs, just as the Adena, used red ochre in their burial rituals. One must question if the use of red ochre developed independently among individual cultures or was it passed along from one culture to another from direct contact.

The Micmacs are a tribal member of the Algonquian culture that inhabited the Canadian region of Acadia. Today the Micmac web site states, that they are also related to the Maliseets, Passamaquoddy, Penobscot, and Abenaki tribes. This alliance forms the *Wabanaki (wabun* implying "light", and *aki-* denoting "earth"). They are also known as, *People of the Daybreak.* It could very well be that some or maybe all of these various tribes were at one time the Red Paint People.

The language of the Wabanaki confederation is Algonquian in structure, which made use of a form of hieroglyphics to create their writing system. For example, a five pointed star represented heaven, while a circle symbolized earth. The people would carve these, and other, symbols into tree trunks, stones, and onto pieces of tree bark, which they could send by messenger to leaders or people of other tribes much like our "snail mail" letters of today. The Micmac have a myth about a "culture hero" who in antiquity came to them, and told the Micmac people that their home was from the east — 'far across the great sea'. Dr. Barry Fell, from his studies, concluded that their language was taken from the Egyptians who had, at one time, passed through or settled near the Algonquian's homeland. This writing system of the Wabanaki is very old, and had been used for quite sometime long before the French explorers arrived in the region. It was first mentioned by Pierre Maillard, a French Missionary, who took some credit for inventing this writing while teaching religion to the tribal people. He noticed that when he would use certain terms or words as he spoke, the native children would scratch symbols into sections of tree bark. Later when he discovered what each symbol represented, he attempted to revise the system to suit his own needs, and ultimately claimed credit for the writing knowledge of the Algonquian. Fell's observation of Egyptians being the basis for the Algonquian language, might account for the large amount of mining activity, which took place around the Great Lakes region. It would be very understandable that the highly developed Egyptian sea-going, trade oriented culture could have easily encountered the Algonquian civilization as they entered the mouth of the now, St. Lawrence seaway, which would have provided a direct route into the Great Lakes area. As was stated earlier, the Egyptians were active — ancient sailors, and business people. There is no reason to suspect that this world exploring people could not have sailed across the Atlantic Ocean, through the waters of the St. Lawrence River, into Lake Superior, mined for copper, and then returned the way from which they entered. Once back at the mouth of the great future seaway, they would probably have rested, and made preparations for their Atlantic voyage back home. While there, much interaction between the Native peoples and Egyptians could have occurred, ultimately producing knowledge of writing, and language learning.

It might be reasonably comprehensible to believe that if the Algonquian language is derived from Egyptian, then these Native people would have been living in that location of the upper northeast into the subarctic regions of eastern Canada perhaps during Egypt's Pre-Dynastic period. If so, could they have been as old as the Egyptians themselves or could they have been a subgroup of the *Dynamic Civilization*? Today we realize that the Algonquian people, as a whole, were a wandering, expanding, exploring people, who in modern times encompass some twenty-nine (29) or more individual tribes, which represent groups originating from the subarctic regions of Canada, and who speak an Algonquian language. Some of the better known nations are the Blackfoot, Cheyenne, Cree, Delaware (Lenni-Lenapi), Fox, Kickapoo, Chippewa, Potawatomi, and Shawnee (a nation thought to be a remnant of the Hopewell cultures). The Algonquian language once spoken only in Canada around Labrador now stretches down to the Carolinas of the United States, and from the Atlantic coast over to the Rocky Mountains in America's west.

Furthermore, the Algonquian nation was a people mainly of fishermen, who built sea-going vessels in order to catch deep-sea type of fish, and mussels. A testimonial for a boat of this type was described in the work *Narrative and Critical History of America* by *Justin Winsor* an historian, librarian, and writer.

Winsor referenced a boat, which he called a canoe that was built for sea-going purposes. One other author *Marc Lescarbot,* in his work *Histoire de la Nouvelle-France* of 1609, commented that he had seen a Micmac boat, which contained a picture of a Moosehead painted on the sail; and still later on, John White an illustrator during the Sir Walter Raleigh voyage described the Micmac as "Picts" from Scotland. Perhaps this could explain the stories from many about red-skinned people washing up on European shores in early times, some wearing only loin cloths, and some with painted bodies. Winsor, based on his research of Acadia in 1606-1607, wrote about these Micmac boats sailing from the coast of Baccalaos, which is today Newfoundland, to Lubeck, Germany, in AD 1153 and that the voyages were repeated on a regular basis. It appears that the Algonquian groups were not simple people foraging for food, and hunting small game. In fact, French explorer Jacques Cartier arrived at the future city of Mount Royal (Montreal) in 1535, and found a large defined city with streets emanating out from the city's core like spokes on a wheel, while hills and fields of wheat surrounded the town. The Iroquoian name for the community was *Hochlaga* (meaning "Beaver Dam"). The Iroquois Nation was not part of the Algonquian Nation, in fact at times they were bitter enemies, but their upscale culture during prehistorical times indicates that probably other surrounding nations may have operated in much the way as the Iroquois, especially since we now know of the vast connections of the current Algonquian people. If stories of "red-skinned" people arriving in Europe during early times are true, then it is a good indication that they were the sea-going peoples of eastern Canada, and northeastern America. It could not have been the Inuit because the Europeans were already aware of the subarctic culture, and their seafaring excursions.

The Inuit or Eskimo are known as a sub-Arctic and Arctic culture, primarily inhabiting regions of Siberia and North America, although extending their realm of travel as far as Greenland, and beyond. Their name "Eskimo" was derived from the Algonquin people of eastern Canada, and they are descendants of whale hunters that migrated, following the whale flotes, over to Greenland. They live mostly in sub-Arctic latitudes, but travel into the Arctic Circle for food as required. The region, which they call home, is usually described as barren, frozen tundra, and their homes today are located on shorelines near to the sea, and are built of stone or igloos during the winter months, while they use tents of skin, at times, in summer months. Some communities located in Siberia along the shores, have been created using driftwood and earth. Today the Inuit hunt more walrus and seal than whales, and supplement their diet with fish, mussels, bread, and fresh fruit obtained from modern markets, since the land on which they occupy only thaws but a few inches during the warmer months, stifling any crop growing activity.

One interesting, and controversial story in support of Egyptian presence in North America comes from an article, which appeared in the Phoenix Gazette newspaper on 5 April 1909 about a discovery made by G.E. Kincaid, an explorer from Lewiston, Idaho, who made his way from Green River, Wyoming, down the Colorado River in a wooden boat to Yuma, Arizona. He, at that time, held the record for being the second man to accomplish that feat: he was also the first white man born in what is today, the State of Idaho. During this expedition it is reported, in the newspaper article, that Kincaid discovered what appeared to be an entrance located 1,486 feet (452.93 m) down the side of a sheer canyon wall. Kincaid found a way of reaching and entering into the cavern, and what was discovered was a long passageway, which led to a large chamber with numerous passageways branching off from there. It was noted that several hundred rooms were discovered with one room explored for a distance of 854 feet (260 m), while still one other room was investigated for a length of 634 feet (193 m). The article further stated, some items found were thought not to be native to this country such as, unidentified weapons of war, copper instruments, and items described as 'sharp-edged', and 'hard as steel'.

Kincaid described the main passageway as being about 12 feet wide (3.6 m) then narrowing down to around 9 feet (2.74 m) at a length of about 57 feet (17.34 m) from the main entrance. From this location, side-passageways split-off on each side exposing a number of rooms thought to be about the size of a living room near the 1900s; with some exceptions ranging in size to around 30 to 40 square feet (2.7-3.7 m^2) containing oval-shaped entry ways ventilated by spaces through the walls estimated to be about 3 feet (0.9m) thick. Kincaid also pointed out that from about 100 feet (30.48 m) from the entrance, is what he called a cross-hall about several hundred feet (61 m) long where he found an image or idol of what he thought was the people's god. The idol was placed in a sitting cross-legged position with a lotus flower or lily in each hand, and possessing oriental facial features, with Kincaid comparing it to Buddha. The article stated that the scientists could not identify what religion this idol might represent; however some point to ancient Tibet. The bulk of the excavation was conducted by the Smithsonian, under the direction of S.A. Jordon, according to the article. Surrounding the idol were many smaller images depicting distorted shapes along with two large cacti with protruding arms. In an opposite corner of the room were many different copper tools and a work room with a bench containing the remains of charcoal and other assorted minerals.

One of the largest chambers discovered contained tiers of mummies each resting on hand-hewn shelves with a bench in front of each one with pieces of broken swords, and a copper cup. Only some of the mummies were covered with clay, but all of them were wrapped in fabric made from tree bark; and all of the mummies were male.

Some researchers, including author David Childress, alludes to the possibility that what Kincaid discovered, and related to the newspaper, denoted Egyptian symbolism. Childress tells, in his book *Lost Cities of North & Central*

America that he phoned, and spoke to a person at the Smithsonian Institution about this article and about any artifacts, which might have been recovered at that mysterious archaeological site. The woman at the other end of the line possessed no knowledge of any artifacts or information regarding Egyptian presence in North America.

There are other challenges to a theory of Egyptian presence in North America, and to the discovery of a man-made cavern located in the Grand Canyon of Arizona. The archaeological site itself, which according to the newspaper article was excavated by the Smithsonian Institute [sic], is claiming no knowledge of any such prehistorical site. However, what is explained in the news article are a number of examples, which might tend to lend authenticity to such a discovery of ancient Egyptian presence in Arizona. When 1909, the date of the article is taken into consideration, the question must be asked about how much knowledge pranksters in 1900s Arizona would possess in regard to Egyptian traditions, religion, burial rituals, and symbols. Today we know Egyptians grew and cherished the Lotus flower, which the article points out, was placed in each hand of the idol. Secondly, copper items, some unidentified, were manufactured, and placed in the chamber of the idol; and we know that the Egyptians mined, and possessed the metallurgy skills necessary to create copper tools. Third, Kincaid noted the presence of grave-goods included in the idol chamber, which was similar to a number of Egyptian tombs of leaders discovered in more recent years. Fourth, Kincaid stated that mummies were found in a large chamber with walls which slanted back at an angle of about 35 degrees: the mummies, he described, were laid in a ritualistic manner, once again, symbolic of Egyptian practices. Finally, the article mentions that hieroglyphics were discovered on urns, walls, and over doorways, which the Smithsonian investigators could not identify, and in addition, similar hieroglyphics have been found further south in Arizona — no locations given.

If this article was merely a prank the reasoning for the prank is not obvious, the article appeared on April 5th not April 1st (April Fools Day). Further, Kincaid's descriptions are very meticulous, and seemed to present possible symbolic similarities between the cavern contents, and ancient Egypt. The mention of pottery as an important artifact, along with charcoal residue found there, would be something considered prominent by educated professionals working in a scientific field. However, at this time not much seems to be known about G.E. Kincaid. He is referred to as an explorer, but no other detailed information is available about his education level or professional qualifications. The scientific information seems to have been obtained from those doing the excavation work on the site; supposedly investigators from the Smithsonian "Institute" (should be Institution), that today claim no knowledge of this twentieth century excavation.

Still, some of the descriptions presented in the newspaper article reveal a similarity to the "Big Mound" excavation of 1869 in St. Louis, Missouri. As Brackenridge's comprehensive work exhibited, the man-made gigantic mound contained built-in passageways with solid floors, sloping walls, large chambers, which held the bodies of, what might be, a leader and his wife surrounded by, and bedecked with grave-goods. Knowledge of the archaeological excavation would have been available to the public by about 1879 when the book *Foot-Prints of Vanished Races in the Mississippi Valley* was published. However, there were more examples of Egyptian symbolism expressed in the newspaper article than what is listed during the Big Mound extrication, which would mean that either someone with archaeological training presented the story or the facts presented in the article are correct, and true. We might never know which statement is correct unless the Smithsonian staff comes forward with information or archaeologists are allowed to seek the location of this underground citadel on Government land.

One other answer to this mystery might lay with someone's knowledge of the Hopi people of Arizona. The Hopi reservation, located in northeastern Arizona, is near to the Grand Canyon, and the Hopi people have lived in that location for thousands of years. What is now their reservation land was at one time much larger in area, but is now reduced in size, and surrounded by the Navajo Nation reservation. The Hopi are in many respects a very private, but friendly, and peaceful people. In fact their name means "Peaceful Person" in the Hopi language, which is derived from Nahuatl — a Uto-Aztecan language, shared by the Pima, Comanche, Hopi, Ute and Shoeshone.

The connection might stem from an ancient Hopi legend, what states that their ancestors once resided in an underworld location of the Grand Canyon until a struggle erupted between the people of *one heart* (the good), and the people of *two hearts* (the evil). Escape from the underworld was not possible until the chief grew-up a tree, which penetrated the roof of the cavern, allowing the people of good to climb out, and settle next to the Red River (the Colorado). Here, these people grew beans and maize, and built homes — pueblos, also kivas for religious rituals. The structures were made of adobe, which is clay and straw sunbaked into a hard brick shape or made into a mortar — a workable form of plaster to hold stones in place. In order to enter into the kivas it was necessary to climb up a ladder usually adorned with the skins of the gray fox. At this point, it should be noted that not only are there symbolic, and mythological connections between the Egyptians and the Hopi people, but also with the Hopi, and the Dogon tribe from Mali, Africa — a people, in prehistory, that had a very close relationship with ancient Egypt.

First, we can relate the Hopi underworld as the underground cavern supposedly discovered by Kincaid. Secondly, it was stated that several granaries still with seeds were found, that could only be entered by ladders once suspended from copper hooks — the design of these granary chambers were compared to those in oriental temples. The granary design, which was described in the newspaper article also, can be compared with the type constructed in Egypt. The use of a ladder, might be extended further when attached to the gray fox symbolism of the Dogon people of Africa. The *Pale fox* is sacred to the Dogon; in fact they say it is the Pale fox's land.

The gray fox skins attached to the ladders of the Hopi kivas indicate still more symbolism by their observation, what states, after the sun rises it would "lay off the gray skin, and put on the yellow fox skin"[2], which would create the "yellow dawn" of the Hopi. The connection to yellow, in the news article, might tie in with the yellow stone, strewn everywhere on the floor, referred to as 'cats eyes', and listed as, of no great value. Still one other reference to yellow comes through the Hopi myth of the *First Journey Through Grand Canyon*, which is a story about the son of the Hopi chief, and generator of the Snake Clan who resided on the rim of the Grand Canyon. The young lad would spend hours sitting on the canyon's rim contemplating where the Colorado River ended. One day his father granted him permission to pursue his quest. After drifting in his boat, with the current over a period of time, he found himself in ocean water where he came upon an island, thus, meeting the *Spider Woman* who possessed supernatural powers. After informing the woman of his quest, she volunteered to help him achieve his goal. As they moved along toward the mysterious location they encountered many frightening beasts, but the Spider Woman gave the lad a lotion, which protected him. Ultimately, the pair met up with warriors; and their Chief invited them in. During the visit the warriors dressed in snake costumes, making hissing sounds while writhing on the dirt floor. The Chief of the snake people then turned his daughter into a yellow snake with rattles, ordering her to wriggle about on the floor with the other snakes. The chief then ordered the lad to choose which snake was his daughter. Spider Woman helped the lad to choose and he selected the chief's daughter earning him praise, precious beads, and the secrets of the Snake People, which he could take back to his father, and the Hopi people on the rim of the Grand Canyon, along with his new wife.

A symbolic relationship is also present with the *Spider Woman* in the Hopi story, and the Dogon Dada, which means "mother" in the Dogon language. Dada is also a spider who is sometimes compared to *Neith*, the Egyptian goddess who wove matter. In Dogon Tradition, Dada is the weaver of the primordial thread, which the Dogon believe is the source of all matter.

To the Hopi people, women are important assets to the Nation. The Hopi clans are matrilineal, where families trace their heritage through the mother's side of the family. The women, as well as the men, participate in music, art, and storytelling during ceremonies. The women of the Hopi Nation are also involved with medicine, and aid to tribal members. In short, from the story of the wise son, we see that he is guided by the powerful Spider Woman who gives him lotions, and advice so that he may achieve his quest.

The wise son story also brings into focus the importance of the snake to Hopi tradition. The Snake Clan, of the Hopi, is very powerful, and sacred. It was only a few decades ago where stories came out about certain sacred ceremonies performed by the Hopi, which told of Hopi men placing live rattlesnakes in their mouths while performing ritual dances. This movement shocked individuals outside of the Hopi Nation, and calls for this ritual practice to be stopped were heard clearly, especially in the Southwest. When this author resided in Arizona, the understanding, at that time, was that the Hopi no longer allowed outsiders to attend their ritual ceremonies. The belief in power of the snake creeps into the Kincaid story when the article speaks of one mysterious chamber, which cannot be lighted sufficiently in order to explore properly. The article stated this one chamber was not ventilated, and it smelled "snaky." The entire explanation of the area expresses mystery, fear, and potential danger — just as the wise son experienced while he was in the presence of the Snake warriors.

The snake symbol is found in many cultures, and it represents different things to different civilizations. In regard to the Egyptian and Hopi symbolic connection, it manifests itself clearly in the serpent and egg form, and helps to explain some prehistory of the Hopi people. In ancient Egypt the priests acknowledged *Cneph* as the Divine Eternal Spirit, who they proclaimed as the architect of the universe. Cneph was symbolized by a serpent with an egg in its mouth. The serpent represented his hieroglyphic image, while the egg represented the elements associated with chemical elements, which make up life and matter.

The Hopi relate to the Egyptian Cneph through the telling of their arrival into the New World. The Hopi tell of the true *Pahana* (the Lost *White Brother* of the Hopi) who was commander of a large fleet of reed boats (used in Egypt, Mesopotamia, and South America), which were filled with people and family members who escaped the Great Flood. This fleet landed on the shore of Turtle Island (North America), and Pahana led them to the Ohio River Valley where they built the effigy Serpent Mound, naming it *Tokchii* (a type of swift racer snake), and meaning "Guardian of the East," symbolizing the direction from which they escaped the Deluge. Much as the Aztec, which used "Suns" to explain great cycles, the Hopi (still today) uses the term *Worlds,* and currently the Hopi places us in the Fourth World. Following the Deluge, the Hopi entered the Fourth World led by the Spider Woman away from the Ohio River Valley location. Once the Fourth World had commenced Pahana left to return to the east across the great water, and the Hopi began their migration west. According to ancient legend, Pahana will return one day from across the sea, then the wicked will be destroyed, and a new age of peace will begin with the start of the Fifth

World. It is said, each evening the old men of the tribe can be seen looking east from their roof tops. Hopi burials always place the body with the head facing east so they might see Pahana upon his return, while members of the High Snake Clan adorn themselves with necklaces made from seashells to remember their transatlantic voyage, which brought them to Turtle Island (North America).

All of the past identifiable possible connections to Egyptians and Hopis might not explain the Phoenix Gazette news story, but it does offer some explanation for Egyptian/Libyan writings found in the western part of the United States. It might also help to account for people, other than Asians, having contributed to populating the North American continent. Still further, the Hopi people draw in the Aztec civilization which, in itself, creates numerous questions and speculation. The Hopi language is derived from the Aztec language, which brings up questions about the Aztec origin. Scholars tell us the Aztec came from the north of Central America in about AD 1200, but as to a specific location no information is given. Speculation, on the other hand, offers a location in southern Wisconsin called Aztalan. The area of Aztalan is part of the Mound Builder cultures along the Mississippi River Valley. The original name of the location will probably never be known, but the current name consists of two Mexican words: *atl* (meaning water), and *an* (meaning near). One other explanation for the meaning of this word might originate with the layout of Tenochtitlán, the one-time capital of the Aztec Empire which, according to an old myth, was founded by Aztec priests after they witnessed a sign from an eagle clutching a snake in its mouth while standing on a cactus. This symbolic experience prophesied the location for their new city. Then around AD 1350 the Aztecs began construction to build canals and causeways, which encircled the capital city — forming it into an island. Since the Wisconsin site was named much later, and scholars drew comparisons found at the site with the ancient Aztecs, it might be a reason for how the archaeological site was named by two Mexican words with a relationship to water. For additional information about Aztalan, refer to the Appendix section of the book.

Judging from the ruins at Aztalan it is believed, by some, that the site was intentionally burned, and abandoned for reasons unexplained. One theory for their disappearance might have been because of their cannibalistic lifestyle. It is thought that other cultures, such as the Chippewa (Ojibwe) in the area, did not accept that type of behavior, thus, banding together, and attacking the people living there, and driving them out of the area permanently.

In support of this theory the Hopi speak, through their myths and stories, about two peoples within their Nation in ancient times; namely the people of one heart (the good), and the people of two hearts (the evil). They tell of problems, which separated the two peoples, and resulted in their dissolution. There are two different stories of their origin; one, being the escape from the Grand

Canyon underground cavern, and two, their arrival at Turtle Island, and led into the Fourth World by Spider Woman, known as *Koyangwuti* (pronounced Koh-kyang-woo-tee) who, it is believed created humans from clay. Story telling among the Hopi people is not a word-for-word process, instead stories are told by individuals using their own words, and speaking from what each learned about an individual story. This brings up how the two factions separated in the story of the landing at Turtle Island. If they split prior to migrating west, perhaps the *evil* people were the ones who ended up at Aztalan in Wisconsin, and continued evil ways by practicing cannibalism, causing others to declare war on them.

If these unwelcome people were the *evil faction* of the ancient Hopi Nation, and moved south into Mesoamerica, it might be very likely that they became the people who we today call, the Aztec. Evidence of this connection might be observed through Aztec rituals involving cannibalism, and sacrifice. The Aztec, according to scholars, were classified as a war-like, dominate culture who controlled vast amounts of land, and ruled over their empire in a domineering manner. One practice in particular denoted their hostile methods quite clearly. Most of the time captives were immediately put to death, but in some instances captives were used as slaves because they were deemed useful for playing music, dancing or for some other talent, which they might have possessed. These captives were usually purchased by merchants to gain favor with other merchants who they did business with or with noblemen, and leaders within their communities. These captives were called 'bathed slaves' who after serving their master's purposes were bathed in a spring, deemed sacred to Huitzilopochtli (pronounced Weetz-ee-loh-POSHT-lee) deity of war, sun, and sacrifice — nine days before a religious festival. On festival day, the merchants owning the captives would walk the victims around the Great Temple four times, and then they would ascend the steps to the shrine of Huitzilopochtli, and there they would be placed on their backs spread-eagled across a sacrificial stone where their chests were sliced open, and their hearts were wrenched-out from the thoracic cavity all while the victim remained awake — and under no form of analgesic. The donor-merchant was then awarded the bodies, to use them back at his home as a scrumptious main course for his banquet, along with maize for his most cherished guests. It is very obvious that behavior of this nature did not occur among the Hopi people of Arizona, thus, making it possible to recognize them as the people of one heart or the *good.*

One additional, and paramount sign of Egyptian influence on the Hopi civilization could be marked by their extensive knowledge, and use of the Orion Constellation during location of sites for towns. It is quite well known by now, and largely accepted by most scholars and modern day researchers that the ground layout of the Giza pyramids in Egypt was predetermined by the position of the Orion Constellation. In short, it represented a mirrored image on the ground of the distinct constellation of Orion in the heavens, just as the ancient Hopi produced over their desert location of the American southwest, only in a more complete fashion.

The Hopi proclaim that they were mandated by the god *Maasaw* to build 'cities' at precise locations, which would mirror all of the corresponding stars of the Orion Constellation over-head. Maasaw was a caretaker of the earth, and 'Spirit Guide'. The Hopi people of one heart — the *good*, who escaped from the underworld, and the people of two hearts — the *evil*, by climbing a tree to the surface of the earth where they encountered Maasaw near the convergence of the Little Colorado, and the Great Colorado rivers. They described his head appeared as a "raging ball of flame," and they sought his permission to live on the earth: Maasaw then dispensed bags of seeds, gourds with water, sticks to plant the 'Three Sisters' (corn, squash, and beans), and his permission provided the people would care for, and honor mother earth eternally.

The orientation of the Orion constellation on the high desert of 1.5 million acres (607028 hectares) also provided for locations marking sunrise and sunset, on both the summer and winter solstices. Just as with other astronomically astute cultures, the Hopi followed sun movements.

The three Hopi Mesas mirror the three stars of Orion's Belt, while other Puebloan sites symbolized all ancillary stars, completing the image of the Orion Constellation along with additional nearby stars; and finally, the Chaco Canyon Ruins site in New Mexico represented the star Sirius, the brightest star in the night sky. It is reasonable to question why Chaco Canyon in New Mexico, when the Hopi Nation live in Northeastern Arizona; possibly because the Hopi are considered to be descendants of the Anasazi — the architects and builders of Chaco Canyon.

Philip Coppens, author of *The Ancient Alien Question* described the cosmology of the Hopi in some detail when he wrote:

> Orion itself comprises (among others) the Betatakin Ruin in Tsagi Canyon and Keel Seel Ruin, representing the double star Rigel, or the left foot or knee of Orion. Homal'ovi Ruins State Park maps Betelgeuse, Wupatki Pueblo maps Bellatrix, and Canyon de Chelly represents Saiph, or the right foot or knee of Orion.[3]

Coppens goes on to state:

> Even the Sipapu in the Grand Canyon is mapped and corresponds with the star Pi 3 Orionis.[4]

Sipapu refers to the opening which broke through the ceiling of the underworld allowing the people of the one heart to escape from the evil ones, and enter into the Fourth World where they encountered Maasaw.

The entire ground layout of Hopi pueblos, and site locations are quite detailed in their relationship to all of the prominent astronomical features treasured, and idolized by many other ancient cultures and civilizations. Regardless of the location, whether it is the Mayan city of Teotihuacán or the three pyramids of Giza in Egypt, the Hopi of primeval times demonstrated the same exact astronomical understandings, and symbolisms. They demonstrated the use of sky-knowledge in the same manner as other more well-known civilizations, by placing their earthly locations to mirror the enigmatic constellation of Orion. Why should the Maya or Hopi have any interest in some ancient Egyptian god (Osiris) who gained fame and immortality thousands of miles away from them across lands, and sea during time immemorial? One answer might possibly be that they were descendants of the Egyptians arriving here from the east in reed boats, commanded by their W*hite Brother*, while escaping the effects of flooding from raging melt-waters, brought on by glacial meltdown — perhaps members of the Osirian Civilization. If this turns out to be the correct answer, it then strongly suggests a far more ancient civilization than scholars date them to be; and what is more, it would mean an even earlier existence if they are a descendant of the Anasazi — *the Ancient Ones.*

Saguaros Cactus (Carnegiea Gigantea)_Wikimedia_Public Domain
Exclusive to the Sonoran Desert ~ Life span — 150-200 years

There is more to America's past than appears upon the surface. A strange unrest is apparent among many of the younger historians and archaeologists of the colleges and universities, a sense that somehow a very large slice of America's past has mysteriously vanished from our public records. For how else can we explain the ever-swelling tally of the United States, Canada, and Latin America?

"The inscriptions are written in various European and Mediterranean languages in alphabets that date from 2,500 years ago, and they speak not only of visits by ancient ships, but also of permanent colonies of Celts, Basques, Libyans and even Egyptians. They occur on buried temples, on tablets and on gravestones and on cliff faces. From some of them we infer that the colonists intermarried with the Amerindians, and so their descendants still live here today."

~ ~ Barry Fell, Professor, Author
~ ~ America B.C.

The southwestern United States offers one of the most exciting enigmas, among many, which still have archaeologists, and scholars debating over today. The mystery begins with three main cultures of people who occupied areas of the great Southwest in very early times. The three civilizations were the Mogollon, Hohokam and the Anasazi, all occupying regions of Arizona, New Mexico, Utah, and Colorado, a location commonly referred to as the Four Corners, and all in about the same time period, as current dating expresses. The three civilizations have separately or jointly, left behind visible evidence, which enlightens modern science to the fact that Native American cultures did not typically dress in loin cloths, beaded headbands with bird feathers protruding outward, while hunting wild game for their squaws to cook on the open campfire. What's more, these people did not rely on animal skins for clothing or coverings for their teepees. On the contrary, most early civilizations of the eastern portion of the American continent, Mesoamerica, South America and the American Southwest, all were quite adept at weaving, and sewing.

Evidence today educates modern society that like the cultures of the eastern United States, people of the American Southwest operated in large, civilized, intelligent, and productive community nations; perhaps more advanced than those of the east. This observation often signals speculation about southwestern civilizations being the replacement cultures for the eastern societies after their dissolution. Still others surmise that perhaps some elements of the larger populations of the southwestern peoples broke away, and drifted towards the east, eventually integrating with other tribes in that location, and participating in the Adena or Hopewell cultures. The reader may recall in the legend of the Lenni-Lape that they tell of coming to the Mississippi River from the west. Could it have been as far west as Arizona? A feat of this type would not have been impossible since the distance from St. Louis, Missouri, to Phoenix, Arizona, is only 1,461 miles (2,351 km), and one must not overlook the river highways, which they could have utilized during their journey eastward.

The first major enigmatic culture, presented for our attention, is the Hohokam who once occupied a portion of the Sonoran desert around Phoenix, Arizona. The Hohokam name is from the modern Pima people of southern Arizona, and it means *Ancient Ones* in their language. Not much background or prehistory has been retrieved by archaeologists or researchers about dates or origin for the Hohokam people; therefore it was not long ago researchers still portrayed the Hohokam as typical Indian types, sometimes mixing them with images of later period plains- type nations, and assuming they had few skills, ambition, tools, and opportunities. Early scholars even noted that the Hohokam built, and used mud-stick huts for their lodging instead of teepees. Later it was learned, as archaeology advanced, the Hohokam were not the builders or users of these crudely constructed shanties, but rather they were the product of later, smaller tribal peoples, possibly even the early Pima.

Still later researchers discovered that it was the ancient Hohokam culture who was responsible for building approximately 400 miles (643.737 km) of complex irrigation canals, which served the area in, and around, what is now the city of Phoenix, Arizona, or *The Valley of the Sun*. The canals were of meticulous engineering design, with curved surfaces similar to a hard cement texture of today. The structures were found to be about 7 feet (2.133 m) deep, and around 10 feet (3.0480 m) wide. The canal design allowed for less surface area to be exposed to the desert sun, which reduced the water evaporation process over extended periods for supply. The canals were so efficiently designed, that even to this day, a portion of these ancient irrigation canals are incorporated into Phoenix's water control system, although today Phoenix's main thrust for water distribution comes from the annual Monsoon rains, usually occurring in July, August, and early September. The main Salt and Gila rivers into the Phoenix valley today, are usually only flooded during the monsoon season. At the time of the Hohokam, the rivers were used for irrigation.

David Childress, himself a native of the American west, and author of *Lost Cities of North and Central America* stated:

> ... these people aren't early Neanderthal men living in caves a million years ago in Oldavai Gorge in Africa. These are stone-age hunters who lived in Arizona 500 years ago. We mustn't think of them as people capable of mummifying their dead, carving niches, using masonry or making elaborate stone vaults. That is something that happens in ancient Europe or Asia, not in the American Southwest.[5]

The Hohokam culture is thought to be dated from about AD 200 to around AD 1450 when the archaeological record seems to end on these people. So far, most archaeologists agree the Hohokam existed for over 1,100 years, and they ranged as far north as Prescott, Arizona, south to near Tuscon, east from around the White and Black rivers over to Phoenix in the west. One mere observation, the Salt River, which comes into the Phoenix area has its origin at the convergence of the White and Black rivers in the White Mountains. Perhaps this fact might indicate an origin for the Hohokam people. The Arizona White Mountains are located in the northeastern part of Arizona near the New Mexico border, and it is part of the Arizona transition-Mogollon Rim ending in New Mexico. We also know today that this area was also inhabited around the same time by the Mogollon (named for the Rim), and the Anasazi culture. Could there be any chance that all three of these cultures were once a large nation, and for some unexplained reason separated into different groups? The answer to that question is *yes*.

The Hohokam are also known for their construction skills, which allowed them to build large pueblos, ceremonial, and sports centers in addition to structures such as Casa Grande (Big House), about halfway between Phoenix and Tuscon.

The sports complexes were mainly ball courts where teams would compete with each other using a solid rubber ball identical to the ones used by the Toltec, Maya and Zaptecs of Central America. One such rubber ball was uncovered at a Hohokam site near Toltec, Arizona, and it carried a date back to AD 900 to AD 1200. The ball obviously came from Mexico since rubber is not a product of North America, which significantly highlights a contact with people of Mesoamerica. Still this rubber ball item along with the name Toltec, for the city where the ball was discovered, leads some to speculate that the Hohokam were, in reality, descendants of the ancient Toltec's.

The ball courts on which these teams played were quite well designed, and constructed. The game itself is suspected to be the same, or very similar, to the ball game played by teams of Central America. At present more than 100 ball courts have been located. One of these courts was discovered at a place called *Snaketown*, which we will speak more about later on, and it measured out to be 185 feet (56.38 m) long by 63 feet (19.20 m) wide. At each end stood a stone marker with one additional stone marker placed at the midway point. No hoops were found, but nearby effigies of what might appear to be ball players wearing shin guards, and shoulder pads were somewhat visible.

The Hohokam people also created their own designs of jewelry, which included rings, necklaces, pendants, hairpins, bracelets, along with cheek and ear plugs fashioned from turquoise stone, jet (a substance of decayed wood materi al placed under great pressure), and seashells arriving from the coastal areas of the Pacific Ocean or the Gulf of California.

Their art work, for that time period, was state-of-the-art technology. Sea shells were used to create designs by lining out the design with pitch — the sea shell would then be dipped into a mild acid solution, believed to be made from fermented Saguaro cactus juice, which would eat away the exposed areas not covered with pitch, and thus, the artist's pattern would be exposed once the pitch residue had been removed. This etching technology is believed, by many, to pre-date any etching processes of Europe, Asia or of North America.

Hohokam etched sea shells-Wikimedia_ Public Domain

Clothing of the Hohokam was usually made of cotton, which was grown in fields irrigated by the canal system, along with maize (corn), squash, beans, and more. As a covering or coat used for cold desert nights, a poncho style garment was the item of choice. These clothing items indicate the Hohokam were skilled weavers, and possessed some early form of weaving loom to expedite the weaving tasks, although to date, none have been uncovered. Scientists know of their mode of attire by clay figurines created by the Hohokam, showing them dressed in these wardrobes wearing a type of cloth headband or, at times, turban style headwear along with earrings or cheek plugs, and in some cases bodies displaying tattoos or decorated with paint.

It remains unclear if the Hohokam society was ruled by chiefs or by shamans. In any case, this culture was sufficiently organized to plan, design, and build many types of advanced structures such as Casa Grande, which today is a ruins covered by a protective roof configuration. The ancient site once had a ditch type form of irrigation system in order to supply water to their farm land. When this author last visited the location, most of the area was closed off for renovation, but access to the adobe house was permissible. The most unique feature of the site is a round window built into one wall, which lined up precisely with the setting sun each summer solstice, clearly indicating, at least, a basic knowledge of astronomy. Also found at this site is the remains of a ball court, once used by locals for entertainment or perhaps to settle disputes. It has been noted that ball games played by some cultures in Mesoamerica ended with the losing team being put to death. It is not known if that was part of the games played in North America.

Arizona State Museum archaeologists began excavation, in 1964, on a site south of Phoenix just past Chandler, Arizona, at what is now the Gila River Indian Community, which turned out to be a fairly good size ancient city complex built by the prehistoric Hohokam Culture. The name for the site, *Snaketown,* was taken from an O'odham word, which described a "place for snakes." The site provided a wealth of knowledge about these not so well known people. More than 1,000 stone bowls were uncovered — some described as elaborate, many bone artifacts plus pottery shards, and various types of hand-flaked stone tools. The investigative team estimated the site was once home to about 1,000 to 3,000 people. Also discovered there, was the ball court already mentioned. This site also contained irrigation channels for their farm fields. Today the site is not open to the public, and it was refilled after excavation to maintain as much originality as possible. The collection of artifacts has since been relocated to the Hugugam Heritage Center, with permission from the Gila River Indian Community. Researchers believe work on the site began somewhere near the beginning of the 1st century AD, and that it progressed for a period of around 1,000 years. The site somewhat resembled the building techniques employed at Chaco Canyon, New Mexico.

Also found at this site were turquoise necklaces, and red-on-buff pieces of pottery unlike the type produced by the Anasazi. The homes located there were single-family rectangular shape, one room detached structures. These living units were occasionally built close together in groups of two to six units, which might have been family areas. Overall, the city did not reflect the spaciousness of Chaco Canyon, but for that time period, and for the north Sonoran desert location it was of considerable size, built with genuine engineering skills.

Trade enterprises of the Hohokam were vigorous with the other two main cultures, and possibly even with the Hopewell, and Mississippian cultures to the east. Other than the rubber balls used to play a game originating from Central America additional trade items have been excavated at various other sites, which show evidence of trade with cultures to the south. Gold, and silver items were among the artifacts found along with macaw bones (a colorful long-tailed parrot native to Mexico), a multitude of colorful feathers from birds further south, along with turquoise stones, copper bells, pyrite mirrors, and sea shells from an ocean approximately 500 miles (805 km) away. Trade routes by river, once water had flowed into the Valley of the Sun after melting snow filled the rivers, and tributaries to the north of them would have been the most obvious access to economical trade areas, both to the north, and to the south. With use of log dugout canoes access north to the Four Corners region would have been possible, as well as, travel by canoe south to the Sea of Cortez (the Gulf of California). Navigation by way of the Rio Grande and the Colorado rivers was also another possibility, and a very real solution for trade access with many other cultures.

Maize (corn), a product from Mexico developed from a species of wild tall grass, was a staple in the diets of all of three main southwestern cultures, including most of the smaller obscure tribes. Corn was also grown, and consumed by the Adena, Hopewell, and Mississippian cultures of the east. Maize and its persistent usage among numerous cultures over a vast range of area indicate not only elaborate trade connections, but it confirms that the food source had been in existence, in North America, for a very long time. This author spoke with a representative for Cahokia Mounds State Historical Site near Collinsville, Illinois, about the presence of maize at the site. The gentleman acknowledged that maize had been uncovered there, but he explained the maize was only used by chiefs or religious leaders, and not by the common people. He explained that maize was a rarity, not an everyday crop for feeding the population. He felt that the crop was too young of a species to have been cultivated as a staple for feeding the majority of their people. He further believed that the crop had not been in North America long enough to develop a strain vigorous enough to mass produce, and to use as an everyday economical food substance. He also negated any contact with civilizations of Mesoamerica or South America with cultures of the Mississippian people. So how then did they gain access to maize in this early plant form? No answer was received from that question.

There is evidence of long term use of maize by prehistoric Native Americans. Cultivation and consumption of maize must have been common over a number of generations as exhibited by skeletons uncovered, which displayed teeth with reduced enamel causing tooth decay. This dental problem, for the prehistoric people, was caused from tiny bits of stone mixed in with the ground corn meal, which were broken off during the grinding process. In addition, a number of female skeletons were found showing that the older women suffered from osteoporosis possibly brought on by an extensive diet of grains, along with a lack of calcium, phosphate, and vitamin D. These skeletal samples were taken from sites in the Ohio River Valley — the site of the Hopewell Tradition Mound Builders. Some of the same physical conditions were also discovered among the skeletal exhibits of the Mississippian Tradition, of which Cahokia was a part. It is also stated by nutritionists that people with diets containing more protein do not exhibit these physical characteristics. This observation can be supported by the skeletons unearthed from cultures that are mainly meat-eaters, and support their diet with food items found during foraging or obtained from small locally grown garden crops.

So with the physical evidence of skeletons exposed during archaeological digs, and the physical evidence to substantiate the cultivation and growth of maize, extending back to the early Adena culture Mound Builders, it seems to invite a theory for those cultures to have had contact, in deep prehistory, with cultures from Central America. Should this not be the case, then what other theory could have caused the people of the Adena culture to have access and crop advancement of maize? Might it have been trade contact with the cultures of the American Southwest, since they too were farmers, and consumers of maize? Or still, could the Adena culture derived from one of the Mesoamerican cultures by way of boat across the Gulf of Mexico or by a land route using river waterways to travel eastwards to the Ohio River Valley from the American Southwest? In any case, the people of the Ohio River Valley had maize in their possession, as did the Mississippians, which could not have come from anywhere other than Central America. Another mystery involving the Hohokam culture, once again reverts back to Casa Grande, the ancient Hohokam ruins, and the Pima people of the Sonoran desert. On one of the walls of adobe ruins is carved a symbol known as the *Minoan maze*. The symbol was noticed by the early Spaniards upon their arrival to the location, and they immediately questioned the local Pima people, who was then occupying the area, about the meaning of the symbol. The Pima then produced additional samples of pottery containing the maze type symbol. The Pima explained to the Spanish that the symbol represented, "The Search for Wisdom."

It is thought that this almost exact same symbol can be dated back to around the 3rd millennium BC to the island of Crete, and to the reign of King Minos — then king and son of Zeus. The object design depicted a maze or labyrinth. Archaeologist Harold Sellers during the 19th century noted the symbol was almost identical to a design used on Greek coins depicting a Minoan labyrinth. The maze symbol represented a portentous region ruled by the Bull-headed demon — *Minotaur*. Anyone dissatisfying the king would be forced into the maze where Minotaur would attack and kill the lost and disoriented victims. However, a Minoan named *Theseus* was able to learn the secrets of the maze and the Minotaur, and he then was able to slay the monster so that no other person would be killed by him.

The Pima also explained to the Spaniards that the maze symbol was used in a dart game they played called *Tculikwikut* meaning, "the House of Tcuhu" or "Tchiki." Even though there was not a lot of background information as to whom Tcuhu or Tchiki was, the Pima considered him a cultic hero, and savior similar to the Minoan hero Theseus. Did the Hohokam meet up with Minoan explorers prior to them building Casa Grande in AD 1300? The maze symbol and similarities of names with the cultic heroes leads to speculation that such an encounter could have taken place.

According to a number of scholars the Hohokam were the last to leave their ancestral homeland. By AD 1450 their once great civilization had fallen into decline. What caused the downfall of this once great culture is yet unknown; although some speculate that it was caused by drought since the Hohokam relied so heavily on their irrigation system to supply water to their farm fields. So where did they go, and why can't we find them? According to archaeologist Linda Cordell, she believes that prehistoric peoples do not just vanish. Instead she believes the Hohokam became the nucleus for the modern-day Hopi, Zuni, Pima, Papago, and the Rio Grande Pueblo people. If this theory is accurate, then as we look at these modern-day people, we are actually looking back in time to the ancient Hohokam, and their primeval ancestors. As we learned earlier in this chapter, the name of Hohokam came from the Pima people, and meant *Ancient Ones* like the Anasazi. However, perhaps the O'odham (a Uto-Aztecan people) may offer a better meaning from their language, which is "those who have gone."

Zuni pendant-Thunderbird with lowered wings

As we learned from our exploration of the Hohokam above, a possible encounter with wandering Minoans might have occurred prior to AD 1300. This possibility, though extreme, might lend support for a hypothesis argued by Professor Barry Fell. Fell stated that the language of the Zuni Nation of northeastern New Mexico is a derivation from ancient Libyan of North Africa. Of course, we also learned that Libya did not become a developed country until after the long powerful Mediterranean control of sea power, and trade routes by Egyptians, and Phoenicians had entered into a declining condition. At this time Egyptian rulers, and Phoenician merchants were calling for crew members to man the decks for exploration voyages outside of the Mediterranean Sea area, and a crew of mixed nationalities seemed to be the solution to their sailing endeavors. A time period for these changes in naval cultural crews would have been just prior to the Common Era. Fell, once President of the Epigraphic Society and Emeritus Professor at Harvard University, based his conclusion on a rock-cut inscription discovered by an archaeologist on the Zuni reservation in northeastern New Mexico. The rock-cut according to Fell, described a marriage or fertility sacrament. Fell explained that the image was written in a Libyan alphabet, which was used prior to the Moslem conquest around AD 700. After further research, Fell also was able to identify what he believed to be Libyan letters used in Zuni art. For example, Fell discovered a white leather sun-disk once used in a Zuni ceremony in 1891 containing the symbols 'T-M', which Fell identified as a formula developed in Egypt, which was a phonetic interpretation for *Atum* (Atum-Ra, symbolized as the setting sun, and its journey through the underworld until its morning rise in the east).

Fell further argued that the Zuni language is like no other family of tongues of the Amerindians. Fell's over all premise of the Zuni (A:Shiwi) language is that it derived from Libyan — a combination of Egyptian and Anatolian roots once introduced to Libya by the warring Sea People of the Mediterranean Sea around 1276 BC to 1178 BC. He believed this language was thrust upon inhabitants of Libya when the Sea People invaded Libya after their final defeat by Egypt. Fell supported his theory by stating the language is similar to Phoenician, an alphabetic form using only consonants, and in general the Zuni tongue is derived from North African dialects relating to Coptic, Middle Egyptian, and Nubian from the upper Nile River. One consideration for Fell's theory is that scholars today still have not identified who these naval raiders of the Mediterranean Sea were or from where they might have come. The question then arises — as to why these strange people would have blended all of these different languages together in such a limited period of time? Further, from all of these combined languages, and dialects would it be possible to determine what the original language of these terrifying people might have been? It seems it might have been possible to identify the one dominant language, which the others supported, and used to develop the main language. Fell stated the language has Anatolian roots, which is from Turkey — so where do these roots stem from, the Phoenicians, the Egyptians, or the Turks themselves? Perhaps modern epigraphers will unravel this mystery.

Fell also pointed out that the Zuni language uses a loan word vocabulary from the Algonquian dialects in the north, to the Mexican tongues in the south. One particular Mesoamerican language, which is used to supply loan words for the Zuni language is the Maya. The reader can see that this is quite a broad range of land area for the Zuni people to have adopted language specifics from. This knowledge most certainly confirms some type of primeval contact between many cultures either for trade, contact from hunters following big game, people escaping some form of climatic condition or for any one of a thousand other reasons; one being Fell's belief that the Zuni language origin is from the Libyans who crossed over the Atlantic Ocean sometime prior to 500 BC. Then could those Libyans have made first contact with the Algonquian, and continued crossing the North American continent into the southwest, and intermixing with the local inhabitants, and extending their travels to the south and meeting up with the Mesoamerican cultures? It seems there is no reason to disregard such a possibility.

Pre-History's Chronology Enigma

Mogollon Mimbres pottery – Distinctive Black on White_Wikimedia_Public Domain

The second major culture of the American Southwest are called the Mogollon, deriving their name from the great "Mogollon Rim," an area once occupied by these early people, which extends across northern Arizona into western New Mexico. One of the last identified settlements of the Mogollon is located about one hour north from Silver City, New Mexico, and is known as the Gila Cliff Dwellings. This author's perception of this structure is that it is somewhat similar to the Montezuma's Castle Ruins cliff dwellings located north of Phoenix, Arizona, but perhaps not as technically elaborate. Archaeologists believe the site to have been built about AD 1276, and then mysteriously abandoned somewhere around early AD 1350, having been inhabited for only about forty years. Because cliff dwellings were usually built for safety and protection of the people it is speculated that the Mogollon people fled the site due to attacks from other hostiles in the area. It has been noted that the Apache people occupied this location from very early times. In fact, the Chiricahua Apache state that Silver City (Grant County, New Mexico) is their original homeland. They call themselves *Ndeh* or *Ndee*, which means "The People." The Ndeh also state that to all others around their area they were known as "The Enemy" because of their hard fighting ways to preserve their lands and way of life. Perhaps it could have been due to battles with the Ndeh that the Mogollon was either run-out of the area or left on their own to avoid more fighting. The name Apache comes from the Pima language meaning, "Mean." In any case the archaeological record ends for these people at around AD 1400.

Overall, the Mogollon culture is not as well-known as the other major cultures of the southwest. It appears that these people kept pretty much to themselves, and limited their amount of travel. No great evidence of trade has been established to suggest they had contact with other major or lesser known cultures, in the area, other than with the Anasazi. Information about the Mogollon gathered from archaeological findings shows, in their early history period, they resided in what is described as "pit-houses," which were half-buried structures with roofs consisting of saplings and reeds. Later in their development they built kivas, and pueblos very similar to those of the Anasazi.

These mountain people hunted small game, planted maize, squash, and beans while gathering nuts and seeds in order to supplement their diet. There is some evidence that the people built houses not arranged by any planned layout in several of the mountain's valleys; perhaps to take advantage of the better quality of soil for planting, and the natural inflow of water from streams, and creeks running down from the mountain peaks during melting conditions.

From pictures hand-painted on pottery, researchers have determined that these people dressed in furs and leather robes, and played flutes made of reeds. From some of the grave-goods uncovered it is known that one of their skills consisted of making tubular shaped pipes, probably used during ceremonies. Also, they created dice-like pieces of pottery for games of chance.

What skeletons have been found showed that people living in regions where game was scarce exhibited effects of a low-protein diet. Many of the skeletons suffered from bone lesions caused by anemia and infections.

Most of the archaeological studies have produced no grand type burials with massive exotic grave-goods placed in with the dead body. With absence of this type of information it cannot be certain if this culture was led by chiefs or priests. So far, at least, there are no signs of burials, which can mark an individual as an important member of their society.

At one time archaeologists considered the Mogollon culture as a sub-group of the Anasazi. Later it was determined that these people were an entirely separate entity not only from the Anasazi, but from the other tribal nations of the southwest. Earlier times indicate the Anasazi and Mogollon cultures were not closely aligned, but as time passed the two cultures grew closer together and adopted some of the same interests.

So what makes these early mountain people so special to be considered one of the major three cultures of the American Southwest? That question is answered with — they had a special flare for creating pottery. The Mogollon pottery produced prior to AD 1000 is very distinctive from any other pottery forms of that time period. It is, and was, truly a one-of-a-kind creation, and it is referred to as *Mimbres* (Black on White), named for its creators who resided near the Mimbres River Valley in southwestern New Mexico. Early examples of this pottery form date to around AD 200. Later forms appeared by AD 1000 with new styles, and some coloring added due to different oxygen added firing techniques, which produced a reddish coloring.

The unique designs on the outside of the pottery consisted of pictures of people, animals, insects, and plants. Some others featured mythological characters such as, the hunch-backed flute player (symbol of fertility) or Spider Woman (Mother Earth). The exhibition of these symbolic images suggests contact with other tribes of the Four Corners region, namely the Zuni and Hopi Nations or perhaps in time immemorial they might have been one large nation ultimately split-off to form individual nations.

Yucca leaves split on one end created finely-tipped bristles, which allowed the artist to apply as many as fifteen straight parallel lines within a close tolerance of three-fourths of an inch (2 cm) using only one stroke. No finer bristles for paint brushes have ever been produced until synthetic ground-tipped, non-flagged, fibers were produced in the United States. The last company to produce such tipped fiber filaments was located in Kankakee, Illinois. That process has since been moved overseas and has taken on a different process of dipping instead of grinding.

The designs, it is expressed by some, symbolize order, serenity or sentiments of high *order*. Some examples appear inside of bowls, which are filled with detailed geometric designs, all placed in eye-catching patterns while others appear on the outside of pitchers or jugs. These designs might also be a reflection of the society in which they lived — neat, orderly, and religious. Researchers cannot find any signs of class distinction; in fact archaeologist Steven Le Blanc, in 1970, stated their society appeared to be Egalitarian (equality of mankind). Perhaps these complex geometric designs indicate the correctness of Le Blanc's observations. Some of the designs might have had religious significance because skeletons have been unearthed with ornately painted bowls placed on top of their heads. What symbolic importance this burial ritual might have represented is still unknown. However, the thought of the Dogon tribal (in Mali, Africa) myth of the oldest ancestor wearing a bowl on his head before entering the underworld, and being transformed by taking instructions from the Nummo seems very coincidental (see pages 103 and 104-*Our Missing Ancestors*).

More recently, since the 1970s, information about a large burial site located near Springerville, Arizona, where actor John Wayne once owned a ranch, has come to public attention. The site has become known as the catacombs of Casa Malpais. The term catacombs, though appropriate, are not as complex as those found in Rome. The underground facility does contain a series of passages, and rooms, which have been modified by members of the Mogollon culture in order to provide tombs for their dearly departed. The modifications within the catacombs consist mainly of vaulted ceilings over many existing fissures and over entry-ways that restrict easy access. The catacomb is estimated to be about two to three acres ($0.8193.7$ ha^2 to 1.2140589 ha^2) in size, and contains rooms 30 feet (9.1440 m) long, and about 20 feet (6.0960 m) high along with many other smaller rooms (all unmeasured) all containing hundreds of skeletons. Unfortunately most of the artifacts have been looted over the years.

The catacombs have never been photographed, mapped or its contents cataloged, and it is not open to the public or to professional researchers. Native American religious rights are listed as the reason.

It is estimated by some earlier researchers, who had the opportunity to inspect the site, that it might have been used as a tomb for their dead, at least, for 150 years before being abandoned.

Terrance F. Johnson

Pueblo Bonito-One of the great houses of Chaco Canyon_NASA_ Public Domain

The third and final main culture of the American Southwest is the Anasazi people. Dating for these people is varied according to which book or article is read. Most scholars seem to agree the Anasazi first appeared in the archaeological record around AD 200 or about the same time as the Mogollon and Hohokam Nations. The time of their decline or disappearance ranges from AD 900 to AD 1500.

The name Anasazi is also plagued with meaning variations. Since these ancient people resided in our prehistory, they did not have writing nor were there any ancestors available to tell us a name by which they called themselves. Most scholars seem to agree the term Anasazi is derived from the Navajo language. However, meaning or translation of Anasazi is not interpreted in the same way from one researcher to another. For example, one meaning describes the term as *Ancestor of the Enemy,* still another meaning is *Ancient Enemy,* and yet one other translation and, probably the most widely used today is *The Ancient Ones.* The meaning variations might have occurred due to a misinterpretation of the Navajo word. Navajo is a very difficult language to learn, and the Navajo people are not willing to teach their language to outsiders. The Navajo put their difficult language to good use during WW II in the South Pacific, when the Navajo U.S. Marines spoke their language over military radios when fighting the Japanese. The Japanese could not break the code language and ultimately went down to defeat. These Navajo Marines were known as, "Code Talkers."

The interpretation of 'enemy' from Anasazi comes from *zazi,* which means enemy in Navajo. The Navajo consider anyone who is not Navajo to be their enemy, and thus apply this meaning to people in many different ways. Modern Navajo still are quite hesitant about teaching non-Navajo any part of their language, and they try very hard to keep to themselves on their Nation's land in northern Arizona.

The Navajo, according to scholars, arrived in the Four Corners region long after the Anasazi had left; although some researchers blame the Navajo for attacking, and running off the Ancient Enemy. It might be more correct to agree with the term *Ancient Ones* since it is the polite form for the Anasazi, as used by the Navajo.

What is even more frustrating is that some researchers cannot agree on the origin of the Anasazi people. One theory claims that the Anasazi were red-haired civilizers who are the builders of astronomical sites, and elaborate road systems in the southwest, and were then attacked by hostiles, thus, forcing them to build, and to reside in elaborate dwellings placed into cliff sides.

Another theory hints that the Anasazi might be a people who migrated to the American Southwest from a coastal area in Peru, South America, sometime around AD 1000. These immigrants were known as the Huari, and they were forced to leave their homeland due to repeated attacks from their enemies, which coincidentally correlate with the rise of the Anasazi culture in New Mexico. This theory was probably formulated from artifactual evidence of theobromine residue (a trace-element of chocolate) found on pieces of ceramic pottery shards at Chaco Canyon Ruins site; and Chocolate, of course, being a product of Central and South America. The use of chocolate, it is suspected, was used in ceremonies by high officials or shamans during religious rituals; although evidence of chocolate residue might also indicate a long-range trade enterprise with people to the south of them.

Still one other theory for their origin is placed in Utah, U.S.A. one of the states included in the Four Corners region. Located in Utah is an ancient site called *Grand Gulch,* which is a cliff-dwelling site near Bluff City in the southeastern portion of the state. The site was first excavated by Richard Wetherill in 1893-94. Wetherill was a self-trained archaeologist who had the good fortune to excavate many of the ancient Anasazi ruins. At the Grand Gulch site Wetherill uncovered 96 skeletons exhibiting signs of mutilation, and torture in cave 7 stratigraphy, identified as Basketmakers today. Wetherill listed these human remains as older than the cliff dwellers who had also occupied these caves (eleven in all) after the remains of the people he named "Basket People." He even went so far as to list them as a separate race of people from those of the Southwestern Amerindians. Wetherill wrote a letter to Benjamin Talbot Babbitt Hyde, dated 2 February 1894, enlightening him about the facts of his find at Grand Gulch. He told Hyde, who financed this first expedition along with his brother Fredrick, about the two classes of people found there, and about their mode of burials, and belongings discovered, referring to the baskets uncovered without a sign of pottery. He told Hyde since he named the cliff dwellers it should be Hyde who has the honor of naming these new unknown people. In time, the name Basket People was changed to the Basketmakers. Benjamin Hyde and his brother also financed Wetherill's second expedition to Grand Gulch, in addition to a number of other archaeological digs.

People at the Utah site were generally referred to as the Pueblo culture. Pueblo developed upon the arrival of the Spanish, and it means *town*, which was taken from Latin meaning populous or people, hence, describing people who reside in communities.

Twenty years later, in 1914, an archaeological dig at a site in northern Arizona known to be an ancient Anasazi location turned up basket artifacts identical to those unearthed at Grand Gulch, Utah, which linked the two sites, and denoted the Utah site as the older of the two ruins. Along with the basket artifacts, and spearheads found along with the skeletal remains of those who were savagely put to death, there was an absence of bows, arrows, and pottery at the early Utah site; only atlatls were found, which are spear propelling weapons first used by hunters during the Upper Paleolithic period about 21,000 to 17,000 years ago in Europe. The earliest exhibit of an atlatl comes from the Combe Saunière site in southwestern France, which consisted of an antler hook dating to the later Solutrean period of around 18,000 years ago. Once again, the Solutrean people come into the American picture. It has been agreed by researchers that the Solutrean culture extended their tool making industries to include bone, and antler tools along with the distinct *biface* stone knapping style. Since we now have artifactual proof of the same type of spear propelling tool in Utah as was discovered in France, and dated to be around 18,000 years old, coupled with Wetherill's statement about these people being of a different race, and possibly having red hair according to one theory — might it be that the Anasazi were actually descendants of the Solutrean culture, which had been discussed in earlier chapters?

The question in the last paragraph relates quite nicely with still one other hypothesis of Anasazi origin, and that is, some believe the Anasazi derived from the ancient Clovis and possibly the Folsom cultures. This theory might have a certain amount of validity when we now add in the atlatl artifacts at Grand Gulch, and the overall fact that the Clovis and Folsom were both nomadic big game hunters whose tool industries were very similar to the Solutrean culture of France some 19,000 years ago, and also one Solutrean spearhead has already been discovered in the State of Virginia, U.S.A., and dated from the Mammoth bones found near the tip to be about 24,000 years old. The main thrust of this hypothesis argues for these nomadic hunters to have moved into a more sedentary, foraging, and small game-hunter lifestyle around AD 200. It is these people, researchers believe, who left pictographs of handprints, and fingerprints at many locations in the southwest some 28,000 years ago or around 26,000 BC.

Other interesting finds along the 75 mile (120.7 km) long canyon at Grand Gulch were a number of petroglyphs depicting images of birds, sheep, yucca plants, and people drawn in stick type figure forms. Later petroglyphs, also found at this site, showed the artists attempted to draw the human figures more accurately, and to place them in more animated poses. Possibly this may have been an indication of long term residency at this location by the early unidentified people.

Accompanying the people drawings on the rocks were images of hands, or palm prints to be more precise, with the fingers, and thumbs fully extended outward. Many Native American cultures used the hand print, in times past, as a signature. It was meant to represent something important or simply as an identifying mark of someone's presence. The open hand-print symbol was also present in the Mound Builder cultures of the east. In many Native American traditions the hand expresses a prayer or plea to the Great Spirit; perhaps the hand prints were made by the shaman during religious ceremonies, asking the Great Spirit for help and good fortune. This concept might also apply to the Mound Builder culture that created hand symbols from Mica imported from Appalachia, and were used as grave-goods in some instances.

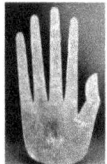

Mica hand-Hopewell-Used as grave-goods_Wikimedia Commons Public Domain

The current hypothetical argument for the Basketmakers disappearance is placed around AD 500. This dating creates a number of questions about their developmental years between the time of their vanishing, and their appearance in Chaco Canyon at around AD 850. The time for initial work on the Chaco Canyon site varies from AD 850 to AD 919. Taking all of the time variations into consideration — would 400 years be enough time for a culture of basket weavers, incapable of producing pottery, that drew humans in stick-man forms on rocks, and lived a sedentary life style to have developed into a society organized, and educated enough to produce a massive building complex that is still respected by architects, masons, and archaeologists yet today? Where and how did these ancient simple people acquire the skill, and knowledge to build structures four, and five stories tall using various forms of adobe material, with the entire complex based on layouts using astronomical knowledge? In addition to their obvious skills as builders, they managed to plan, and construct an elaborate system of roads so well designed that they rival the roads of ancient Rome. The Anasazi roadways stretched out for miles in all directions leading to sites for trade with other nations. In some cases the roads contained stairways cut into them to ascend hills in an easier manner. These "highways" measured 30 feet (9.1 m) wide, the same as Roman roads, and covered more than 400 miles (643.73 km). Ten warriors could march abreast along these expansive avenues in almost any direction outside of the San Juan Basin.

The Anasazi were responsible for building a number of sites, but Chaco Canyon located in Northwest New Mexico is the most grand, and most complex of all of their building accomplishments. This historical site first became a national monument in 1907, but today it is classified as a National Historical Park. Dates for initial building activities, by the Anasazi, varies according to the researchers providing such information. The earliest dates were supplied by archaeologist Neil Judd in the 1920s when he studied the site for the Smithsonian Institution. Along with his colleagues Frank Roberts and Gordon Vivian, they traced the earliest occupation of the canyon back to between AD 500 and AD 850 by the early Basketmakers, which seems to suggest that the Basketmakers moved directly over to Chaco Canyon from their site in Utah, and from the ancient site in northern Arizona. Support for this dating might be in the petroglyphs found at a location on the northwest end of the canyon near an unexcavated great house called, Peñasco Blanco (*White Rock*). The north canyon wall contains numerous petroglyphs and pictographs, some depicting humans in stick-man form similar to those found at Grand Gulch, Utah, painted in dark red ochre. Researchers have separated these art forms into three periods. First the rock art dated at 1500 BC to AD 200 is called Archaic. Secondly, the period from AD 500 to 1150 is referred to the Puebloan period, and these images constitute the bulk of the art work. Finally, the third period is the most recent art forms produced by the later arriving Navajo.

Other archaeologists argue for around AD 900 as the time when building first began in Chaco Canyon. The construction was extensive, well designed, well planned, and purposeful. By AD 1000 it is estimated that more than 75 small "cities" had been completed within the canyon boundaries. The San Juan Basin, which includes Chaco Canyon, extends more than 30,000 sq. miles (80,000 km^2) with the main portion of the Four Corners region covering around 4,600 sq. miles (12,000 km^2), which includes much of New Mexico, southwestern Colorado, lower southeastern Utah, and northeastern Arizona. Chaco Canyon is a 10 mile (16 km) canyon, which lies in the northwest corner of New Mexico, carved out by ancient sea beds, and centuries of erosion. Layers of rock exhibiting embedded fossils of ancient sea creatures can still be seen. Chaco Canyon is also a high-plains desert rising to an elevation of 6,200 feet (1889.7 m) with intensely hot summer days, and brutally cold winter nights. In spite of these harsh climatic conditions, human occupation of this area dates back to about 2900 BC when early nomadic people began to farm, and built small pit-houses as shelter.

In about AD 850, according to current theory, is when the grand style of building occurred at Chaco Canyon. The pit-houses were replaced by adobe stone buildings reaching to 5 and 7 story levels and containing as many as 700 rooms along with numerous kivas. Large lumber was introduced into the building concept, which had to be harvested and brought to the canyon from a distance of around 60 miles (96.5 km) away. A most recent study carried out by the University of Arizona have produced results showing that approximately 200,000 trees were cut down to use in construction of Chaco Canyon, and all were harvested from the mountaintops of the Chuska and San Mateo Mountains. This lumber figure, however, does not include species of ponderosa pine, Douglas fir, spruce, and fir trees used as roof supports on their great houses totaling 12 in all. The study also pointed out that approximately one-fourth of the timber used was from spruce and fir trees, which have not grown in the Chaco Canyon area since the end of the last glaciation period over 10,000 years ago (8000 BC). This would possibly suggest they harvested the spruce and fir trees from southern Colorado locations or from the White Mountains of Arizona, which would have extended more than the 60 estimated miles.

Stone used as surfacing material was obtained from nearby canyon walls, and estimated to be in millions of pieces, while the interior of the walls was made up of a mixture of crushed stone and finely ground pebbles compressed into a concoction resembling firm clay.

Tree-ring dating, first started by Andrew E. Douglas, an astronomer at the University of Arizona in 1901, and developed later on in the 20th century, enabled researchers to conclude that structures built at the Pueblo Bonito great house dated between AD 919 and AD 1130. This dating, however, does not place the dating for all great houses, and various additional structures.

Pueblo Bonito (Beautiful Village) is classified as a "great house," and it is probably the most notable of the twelve great houses located in Chaco Canyon. This particular structure was first studied and recorded by Lt. James Simpson, a U.S. Army surveyor and mapmaker, while on an expedition to enforce treaties with the Navajo Nation. After some time, Lt. Simpson determined the perimeter of the D-shaped layout to be 1,300 feet (396.24 m).

Later archaeological studies determined that the pueblo was constructed between AD 850 and AD 1150. Some of the buildings stood 4 to 5 stories tall, and consisted of approximately 50 rooms along with 45 small kivas, and 2 large kivas. Kiva is a Hopi word, which is used to designate a special room or structure mainly reserved for religious or other social ceremonies.

Richard Wetherill, explorer of the Grand Gulch site in Utah, arrived at Chaco Canyon in 1895, and immediately formed an excavation party, which unearthed the first reported burial of an Anasazi body. Buried with the body was a quiver containing 81 arrows, various pottery items, more than 300 wooden staffs, and an effigy stone portraying a bird with turquoise stone inlay.

In a second room of the same structure another burial was discovered, only this time the corpse was thought to have been a high-official. The body was found with bands of turquoise pendants, and beads wrapped around both wrists, and both ankles. Additionally, two pendants containing 4,000 pieces of turquoise stone were placed around the neck and stomach.

Another interesting discovery, at the site location, involved pottery shards that were decorated using a color scheme of black on white. From what we learned earlier, black on white was created by the Mogollon culture, signifying Mimbres pottery invented by the Mimbres River Valley people. Any further details about the pottery are currently not available. The discovery could possibly indicate a trade relationship between the two nations or perhaps, an artist copied the style of the Mogollon. Without details of the pottery we will never know since Anasazi pottery was made by creating clay rope-strings, and layering these strings in a circle one upon another until the desired configuration had been achieved. When the clay had dried, and formed tightly together the surface of the pottery item would be rubbed smooth, and then painted.

The entire multitude of structures built within the canyon appears to indicate a high level of astronomical knowledge. One example of this knowledge is represented by the placement of the style-D pueblos. Some archeoastronomers have argued that the Anasazi had extensive awareness of the cyclic and seasonal patterns of the sun, moon and stars. They not only built living quarters and kivas, but they also built celestial observatories in order to survey the heavens. This knowledge did however, spill over into the great houses with the lines of the walls placed exactly to display the arcs of the sun, and moon, as they rise and fall overhead while particular interest is placed on the importance of the solstices and the equinoxes. Further investigations have reported that some of the larger rooms, within the great houses, would have split in half as the rays of the sun streamed through window openings.

Probably the most publicized archaeoastronomy example of Chaco Canyon is a petroglyph referred to as the Sun Dagger, which illustrates the in depth celestial knowledge retained by these master builders. The Sun Dagger consists of two spiral petroglyphs carved into a vertical cliff face near the upper band of Fajada Butte, which rises to about 380 feet (115.82 m) high. Fajada, in Spanish, means "banded" referring to the stacked layers of cliffs, which creates the butte. In front of these two spirals stand three large slabs of sandstone with an estimated weight of about 4 tons (1,000 kg) each, measuring about 6 to 10 feet (1.8 -3.0 m) tall, close to 3 feet (0.9 m) wide, with a varying thickness of 8 to 20 inches (20.32 to 50.8 cm). The movement of the sun and moon were tracked, including the solstices and equinoxes, on a daily basis by a light pattern dubbed a *dagger* created by the rays of the sun through, and around the three large stones. This dagger of light would move across the spirals as the angle of the sun or moon would change. On the summer solstice the dagger of light falls directly over the center of the large spiral, and then descending visibly to the right of center on the succeeding days. This light dagger assumes a different location at each solstice and equinox. In order for the Anasazi to track these movements there is evidence to indicate they once had constructed a 750 foot (228.6 m) ramp up to the viewing location, which, it is believed, has since eroded away over time.

Directly behind the great houses, about 30 feet (9.144 m) away, refuse heaps known as middens were found, which like most dumping areas were used to discard most everything. Only within these middens, of the Anasazi, human skeletal remains were discovered along with shells, broken pottery shards, and animal bones. At first, this might seem that the Anasazi had no respect for their dead or in one other respect, the bones were from an enemy killed in battle or even from a slave not worthy of ritual burial; but these conclusions would be incorrect. The Anasazi believed in an afterlife, and further believed that all existing items including inanimate objects possessed a use in the afterlife. Therefore, the middens were deemed to be a sacred location for the spiritual afterlife of all things. Of course, this relates closely to the Archaic Maritime culture.

The entire Chaco Canyon complex had been designed, planned and developed to be connected physically, mentally, and spiritually to the cosmos. Some researchers believe that each great house, each kiva, each individual house, each wall, and each directional placement for buildings was intentionally integrated into a design to project order, knowledge, peace, understanding, and a connection with all things, living or dead, and a personal relationship with the heavens above. Everything at Chaco Canyon had an actual or symbolic purpose. The collective process had to have been visualized prior to the first stake being driven into the ground to mark a location for any type of structure. Anna Sofaer, author of *Chaco Astronomy* believes even the elaborate road system was designed as a cosmographic expression. Using the Great North Road as an example, Sofaer stated:

Finding no evidence of residential structures on the road or of other functional use, we concluded that it was built to commemorate the direction north and a dramatic topographic feature of the north...[6]

The Chaco ruins contained thousands of small houses, and they like all other structures in the canyon are oriented to the sun, moon and four cardinal points. Their main source of water came from the San Juan Basin of the Colorado Plateau.

Around AD 900, some speculate, drought conditions developed, which might have lasted for fifty years. If this theory is correct it could be one explanation for the *Outliers,* believed to be the last structures built in the canyon area. The outliers were about a 2 or 3 day walk from the main complex, and they were constructed as smaller versions of the great houses. Their purpose might have been to disperse the population owing to drought conditions.

The Anasazi seems to have the longest evidence of prehistory of all of the ancient cultures of the American Southwest. As a Nation, they are also probably the most technologically astute of all the rest. Even though archaeologists place their appearance around AD 200, it has been clearly established that their ancestors, the Archaic-Early Basketmakers, extended back to about 7000 BC. It is truly mysterious how a people with so few skills, and knowledge could have risen to a level of master builders with an in depth understanding of the cosmos without assistance from some other more advanced civilization. Perhaps if the Anasazi were descendants of the Solutrean culture of ancient France, then it just could be their knowledge had been passed along to them from people who had journeyed far, and learned to advance their knowledge and skills in order to survive the great fluctuations, which occurred over the thousands of years of glaciation. This is a possibility which researchers are not seeing or not looking for. Could it really have been that these so-called ancient, underdeveloped, technologically unskilled, archaic people are the ones responsible for such a highly advanced planned complex like Chaco Canyon; and could have designed, envisioned, planned, developed, and created all aspects of Chaco Canyon without writing or the use of mathematical symbols? Why would these people have built such wide roads? Could they have been built to move large trees into their canyon to use in construction of the great houses, without using wheels? One of our answers to the questions of all prehistoric peoples must lie in their construction of roads. The ancient Egyptians built many long roads, which science is just now discovering through the use of satellite imagery, the mysterious Nazca lines of South America, the long, wide passageways with earth-embankments of the Hopewell Tradition all seem to be a sign of our deep antiquity.

Why did this nation of builders, and early scientists leave Chaco Canyon after investing that much time, and thought into its meticulous construction? Perhaps, as some believe, it was drought conditions, which forced the people to abandon their homes or maybe over population, and lack of food. In any event, where did they go? The answer to that question might be answered by the Hopi, Ute, Zuni, and the Pueblo people along the Rio Grande River in Mexico who all claim they are descendants of this once High-Civilization.

Perhaps though, the greatest enigma surrounding the Anasazi is whether they are the descendants of the Solutrean, Clovis, Folsom and Red Paint People? There seems to be substantial similarities to suggest that there is an interconnection among these individual peoples separated by time and space. As scientists and other independent researchers continue their investigations, prehistory waits patiently for the results.

Today, as the explorer removes the stones from her ancient structures, he finds here and there one, whose inner surface is carved with curious devices and inscription, showing that it once had a place in older and demolished edifices. She had then her libraries also, in which the knowledge of her sages was preserved. Tombs of the librarians have been discovered, dating back at least five hundred years before Homer sang in the cities of Greece, and inscribed "To the chief of books."

"*Long since, the line of the Pharaohs became extinct, and no prince or king — so the prophet said — shall ever sit on her throne again or sway the scepter over the land of the Nile. How old she seems! And yet old Egypt was of yesterday, compared with the men of the drift, the reindeer period, or the preglacial times of Scandinavia, Scotland, France, England and the Pyrenees.*"

~ ~ A. J. Conant, Author
~ ~ *Foot-Prints of Vanished Races*

Chapter 12

The Fertile, Moist Sahara

Some reader might recall that in my last book attempts were made to explain how an advanced civilization, from deep antiquity in Europe, could have sailed their way to Egypt, and once there, rendered an impact of enlightenment, and vision to those early tribes people residing in the Nile Valley long before time was recorded. As a simple review for the readers who might not have read *Our Missing Ancestors* the Experimental Hypothesis argued that a much superior civilization, having its origins in Europe, and predating any modern form of Egyptian culture, were the mysterious people who are responsible for the many megalithic structures, astronomical knowledge, and mathematical proficiency found in many locations around the world. It was explained that since the Mediterranean Sea was a fertile, lush basin of farm land, towns, and early societies, it would not have been a route most suitable for a seafaring race of people to have selected as a water-way for world exploration. Therefore, due to climatic conditions of North Africa prior to the end of the last glacial period, it would have been possible for a sea going people to have followed natural water-ways across what is now known as the Sahara Desert. That time prior to an end to the glacial periods the Sahara, along with the entire North African continent came under immense periods of monsoon rainfall, causing flooding, creation of lakes, streams, and rivers all across North Africa from Morocco to the Nile River valley. My premise was that these seafarers used these natural watery highways to sail their shallow draft, curved prow (bow) and stern long ships across the area now known as the Sahara Desert, probably meeting up with, and influencing local tribes' people along the way.

Support for moist, humid-like conditions covering North Africa already exists in records held by geologists, and archaeologists that have studied these ancient time periods for many different reasons. Also mentioned in my book were two large lakes, that supported settlements of tribal people, which have been identified by archaeologists and researchers. Of course, these lakes no longer exist, but fortunately many artifacts did remain allowing for modern day studies.

Today, geologists have stumbled upon even greater evidence of numerous water-ways across North Africa, which have survived for millennia, each having been created by the Earth's glacial and geological time periods. While drilling for oil in some outlying areas of the Sahara, fossil water was brought to the surface exposing ancient underground supplies of water. In some locations the water tested was given a date of 1,000,000 years old. The newly discovered under-ground water basins have been given the name 'Nubian Sandstone Aquifer'. These water basins have been detected in parts of today's, Sudan, Chad, Libya, and Egypt.

When the water is brought to the surface, it is hot, indicating that it is located deep underground, and it can climb to around 150° F. (65° C). The heating of the water is accomplished by the Earth's natural internal heat caused by the hot mantel layer. Some of the water is brought to the surface from a distance of close to 3/4 of a mile (1.2 km) down. Hematite, an orangish-red mineral of iron, has been noticed clinging to the sides of holding tanks, disclosing the fact that this water has been in that location for a very long time.

The water once provided mainly by monsoon rains, was captured by layers of sandstone rock acting like a porous sponge to hold the water in place creating a pooling effect. Precession is pinpointed as the main cause for the monsoon rains, which occurs approximately every 26,000 years. The sandstone rock containing this water was then enclosed by layers of clay, which aided in forming a seal for the water while protecting it from the hot desert sun. Fault lines occurring in the clay surroundings established the desert Oasis — found sparingly over the floor of the desert sands.

This underground supply of fossil water is considered to be the largest supply in the world covering almost 78,000 sq. miles (2020 km^2), which is about twenty times greater than the Great Lakes of North America. Experts calculate its quantity to be at 148,301 tons of water (136263.342 kg). This supply, no matter how great, will not last over time. Doctor Fatma Abdel Rahman Attia, head of the Groundwater Sector in the Ministry of Water Resources and Irrigation, has established a search for more existing, yet undiscovered, fossil water basins in North Africa. It is also part of her responsibility to use the water wisely while establishing new towns away from the current overcrowding of Cairo and other cities along the Nile River. It has been estimated that what water amounts have been accumulated over one million years can be used up in less than one hundred years. If that should occur, it will mean North Africa will have to wait for about another 15,000 years for precession to happen again, and bring new amounts of monsoon rains to replenish the depleted supplies.

These water resources are not renewable. They are not supplied by underground rivers or streams. They are, quite simply, the remains of Egypt's one time ancient lakes and rivers. They are evidence of the once great water-ways, which provided the highways of travel for the Dynamic Civilization. Today's advanced technology confirms the paths of ancient rivers of Egypt, now hidden beneath the desert sands. These massive water-ways give substantial support for a hypothesis of a Dynamic Civilization — *Our Missing Ancestors*

Appendix

The name Aztalan poignantly reminds us of a time when Euro Americans refused to acknowledge that the native population was capable of such wonders or even that North American Indians had a deep history that connected them to the land. The name also now symbolizes a fascinating and important time in Native American history that molded much of what was to come later. Indeed, the legacy of the Mississippians and Woodland people can be found around us today in the form of corn agriculture. Wisconsin still derives its identity from this crop, and it appears prominently on the state quarter issued in 2004. In this light, Aztalan can be recognized as the state's first farming town.
~ ~ *Robert A. Birmingham & Lynne G. Goldstein*
~ ~ *Aztalan, Mysteries of an Ancient Indian Town*

Aztalan

Upon entering Aztalan State Park the first impression seems rather routine — business like; pay your fee, collect the available brochures, then figure out which way to travel. While doing so one catches a glimpse of a portion of high stockade fencing in the field ahead, in the background of the first large park general information sign. The vision immediately creates excitement and questions. What does the stockade fence signify? Why is it placed in that location? A quick flip through the park booklet does not bring answers.

    A park attendant pulling into the parking area directed my son, Derek, and I to the last parking area to begin the walking tour of the partially excavated and restored ancient Mississippian archaeological site. Once we arrived at the parking area it became instantly obvious that this walking tour would be eventful, knowledgeable, exciting, and would provide many photos for my son, a freelance photographer in Chicago, Illinois.

    We started our tour at a self hand-cranked audio machine, which imparted general information about the site and the people who might have once called this settlement home. During the audio presentation, the only view available is a low level side view of the largest platform earthen mound at the site. Even though this gigantic mound, labeled number six in the guide booklet, is not the beginning point of the tour, the impressive sight alone calls for your attention and misdirection. So therefore, Derek and I began our exploration counter-clockwise.

The truncated (platform) mound was nowhere the size of Monk's Mound at Cahokia near Collinsville, Illinois, another, but grander, Mississippian archaeological location. In fact, the mound might not even be one-half the size of Monk's Mound, but since Mound #6 had been restored it is not possible to know exactly how large the original size might have been.

The first noticeable exhibit, as one approaches from the gradual slope in the rear of the mound, is the high stockade fencing complete with ramparts or look-out stations placed at various points along the fence area. Just as at Cahokia, and at other Mississippian locations, it is not clear if the stockade or palisade were built for defense or for some other unexplained purpose. In most instances, no sign of attacks have been discovered at any of the site areas.

The posts, again similar to Cahokia, were placed into the ground close together, and cemented into place using possibly a mixture of clay, grass, pebbles, and other accessible materials. Unlike Cahokia, where stockade fence surrounded the two mile (3.2 km) ceremonial district, requiring somewhere close to 20,000 logs, the stockade at Aztalan was only used to enclose the north, west, and south sides of the village layout; the eastern area was bordered by the Crawfish River. Also, at the habitation area along side of the river, a smaller stockade was erected to encircle the huts and living space, which has as yet, not been restored. In total, the stockade walls enclosed the twenty-one acre (8 ha 4984.0 m^2) village, and was buttressed by thirty-two rectangular watch-towers evenly spaced along the entire wall. Originally, a thick layer of clay blended with grass coated the posts, giving an appearance of an adobe finish. The exterior coating served two purposes; to prevent timber rot and lessen the chance of fire destroying the wall.

The stockade to the rear of the southwest platform mound originally was joined with the southern stockade wall, which extended upward verging with the backside of the large mound where it led into a structure built on the rear of the top flat area of the mound. The building could have possibly been a location for the shaman or maybe a house for the chief and his family. The building of structures on top of the flat mounds was common practice among the Mississippian Tradition. The walls, also at this location, formed ingress to the plaza area.

From a point directly behind the platform mound, it was but a few quick climbing steps up the hill to reach the flat top of the mound. Once on top, it was an automatic reflex to turn in all directions in order to establish a position, and to take in sights of the ancient village. Looking down range towards the north end of the village, another flat top mound was recognizable, which according to the guide booklet totaled out to around 382 yards (350 m) or almost four American football fields away. Suddenly, a statement by David Childress came to mind from his book *Lost Cities of North and Central America* when he visited this site. Childress commented, "I was immediately impressed by the two main pyramids facing each other across a broad plaza. It was like a miniature version of Teotihuacán in Mexican, a pyramid of the Sun facing a Pyramid of the Moon."[1] Derek instantly began snapping off pictures and making comments about never believing this, had he not witnessed the sight for himself; while I flipped through the booklet for measurements of the mound which were not included.

According to information found in the book *Aztalan* the Southwest Mound, labeled #6 in the tour guide booklet, stands 16 feet high (4.88 m) consisting of two tiers. The base is rectangular in form, and measures out to be 185 feet x 130 feet (56.39 m x 36.62 m). It contains a top square-shaped tier found to be 75 feet (22.86 m) at the base on all sides, which slants inward to about 40 feet (12.19 m) at the top. At one time a thick layer of colored clay coated the top of the mound area, also found at other Mississippian sites. (See photos at end of chapter)

In comparison, Monk's Mound at Cahokia has a base expanding out to 14 acres (5.66 ha^2), and stands 100 feet high (30.48 m). It has been estimated that it took 22 million cubic feet (0.62 m^3) of earth to complete construction of the largest truncated mound of the Mississippian Tradition.

From the front top of the mound there are wooden steps leading down from both tiers. Steps were also found at Monk's Mound; although at some point a winding trail-way was used.

One other interesting fact, between the Southwestern Mound at Aztalan and Monk's Mound at Cahokia, is that the mound at Aztalan faces due east, while Monk's Mound faces south. This is, also, the case with the second flat-topped mound listed as #4 in the guide book. The placement for the front of the mound facing east exhibits knowledge of the passage of the sun, and like other Mississippians, they also placed great importance on the rising sun. Since these people followed the sun, it might well be expected that they also had knowledge of astronomy. However, so far, there has been no evidence of a Woodhenge type structure, such as the one at Cahokia. The only explanation for this can be such a structure has not yet been uncovered since the entire site has not been completely excavated including the Southwestern Mound.

Prior excavation in 1951 had revealed that the mound was built in stages. It was determined that the first stage consisted of a large ceremonial post placed at the center and then burned. This ritual was common practice within the Mississippian Tradition. From there layers were built upon layers, covering over existing structures, again, a common occurrence of the Mississippian Mound Builders.

The Plaza

The area centered within the village is designated as the *Plaza Area*. This area was set aside to allow community participation for ceremonies and religious activities. The Aztalan plaza measures around 492 feet (150 m) between the large flat-topped pyramid and mound labeled #1 just across from it going east. It then stretches north for about 1,148 feet (350 m) while narrowing down to nearly 328 feet (100 m) at the north end. One estimate of people residing at Aztalan around AD 1100 to AD 1200 is 350 in total. What seems questionable about this estimate, taken from the hand-cranked audio device at the tour commencement, is the fact that the area appears to be very large to only accommodate 350 people. From a perspective of standing on top of the large pyramid at the southwest corner, it seemed 350 people would probably not even fill one-half of the plaza area. If this observation is correct, the question would be — why would they have created such a large land area for their main plaza? Were there more people than the estimated 350? Or did they invite neighboring tribes to the festive activities?

The plaza was L-shaped and completely enclosed, as was the plaza at Cahokia. At the Aztalan site, the plaza was bordered by the western double walls of the habitation area, and by the eastern wall of the elite precinct placed on the higher ridge across the plaza. Researchers attribute this layout to symbolize *water-to-sky*, that of the watery-underworld up to the *sky-sprit* of the heavens, representing the Mississippian universe. The interior walls portioning off the elite precinct were different than the usual wall construction. These walls consisted of single-post-construction without the clay covering. Additional massive walls separated the village into three distinct zones, the residential, the elite, and the common plaza. Through the design and use of semi-concentric rings formed by the walls, all of the people had access to the Crawfish River.

One unusual feature of the common plaza vicinity was the discovery of what came to be called storage-pits, placed on the north end of the plaza. The pits were observed during a dry-period of the late 1980s when dark ovals appeared in the grass. After opening fourteen of the pits, archaeologists determined that these were community storage pits which were larger than the pits found in the habitation area. The builders of these pits skimmed off 3 feet (0.9 m) of top soil, and then formed the pit into three tiers. It is suspected that the soil removed was used to construct the northwest platform mound, labeled number 4 in the trail guide book.

The Gravel Knoll

Directly east of the large platform mound, which stands in the southwestern corner of the village, is a natural glacial knoll listed as #1 on the trail guide map. This mound was either constructed differently or over the years was reworked due to necessity. All of the identified mounds within the complex were built using piled up earth. Conversely, Mound #1 was a natural moraine created by the Late Wisconsinan glacial which contained gravel that was dragged along by the huge ice pack. As the people used the knoll, they automatically made changes to suit their needs. One such need was for a garbage pit (midden), which contained numerous freshwater mussel shells, probably obtained from the Crawfish River over many years. Fire pits were also uncovered inside of the knoll at different locations other than at the midden area.

Still at one other digging area, at about waist deep, more shells were found along with animal bones, pottery, and charcoal, which seemed to indicate this spot was used for cooking. In fact Lynne Goldstein, anthropologist and co-author of *Aztalan* believes that the entire manipulation of the knoll was related solely for the purpose of food preparation, eating and disposal. No human bones or signs of burials were discovered at the gravel knoll; once thought to be the "large oval mound" described by Sterling in his 1838 investigation.

To the east of the gravel knoll near the river, numerous trash pits (middens) were found, with fire scars nearby. These middens, just as those found on the island of Téviec off the coast of Brittany, France, and in numerous burial locations of the Red Paint People, plus the Anasazi midden mounds of Chaco Canyon, all contained human skeletal evidence which were mixed in with shells, broken pottery, animal bones, and other sediment. Could there have been a connection among all of these entities? It seems there is good justification to believe there was a onetime association. After all, what are the odds that different groups of people, in different parts of the world, over thousands of years could have adopted the same practice of placing human bones in garbage deposits? As the saying goes — you do the math.

The discovery of the human bones mixed with refuse, led anthropologist Samuel A. Barrett of the Milwaukee Public Museum to believe the people who once resided there were cannibals. Barrett's archaeological dig occurred in 1919 – 1920, which was too early to have any knowledge of the Red Paint People or the findings at Chaco Canyon, which explained the belief of these various groups of people, that all living things and all inanimate objects have a purpose in the afterlife. Therefore by combining all of these items together, it would be easy for those who passed on to retrieve what would be needed.

Also located, by Barrett, in the habitation area were "bathtub-shaped" cubicles what appeared to have been used for the purpose of cremations. The cubicles were made of clay, and contained a narrow firebox with partially burned human bones intermixed with charcoal and ash. Researches now believe that cremation was an earlier form of body disposal, which was replaced with ritual style burials. No Carbon-14 dates are currently available to inform us of a definite time period. One other explanation for the cremation chambers might have been they were used to quickly clean flesh away from the bones for bundling and reburial purposes, also a common practice of the Mississippians.

In most cases skulls were kept separately for adoration by relatives, while saving certain bones and discarding others. According to the authors of *Aztalan*, what is so unusual is the large amount of bone fragments, and bone parts exhibiting breaks and cuts, which were discarded. According to the authors this is a mystery for future study; but one thing is clear, cannibalism was not the reason.

The Mound of the Dead

The Mound of the Dead stands in the northwest corner of the village complex, and it is designated as Mound #4 on the trail guide map. Currently the mound appears as a one level flat-top structure with wooden steps, facing east, leading up to the top. However in its original state, the mound possessed two tiers, and it was constructed in stages. It is estimated to have been, at least, 9 feet high (2.7 m), and measuring out at 105 feet x 92 feet (32.0 x 28.0 m) at the base. As with the other mounds of the village this mound is oriented to the four cardinal points, with the long axis oriented to a north-south direction.

The mound has not been thoroughly excavated; however researchers did uncover a structure measuring 12 feet x 5 feet (3.6 x 1.5 m) believed to be a charnel house (a skeletal storage area). This addition, it is believed, was built during the second stage on the west side of the mound in a southeast to northwest orientation, lining to the solstices, with an entryway placed on the southeast side. Because of the burials, the mound also is known as a *mortuary mound*.

Charnel houses were usually built for the ruling class of chiefs and their families. The charnel house addition to Mound #4 was covered over by a wattle and daub mixture similar to the covering used on the houses of the chiefs located on the flat portion of the truncated mounds. As a rule, the charnel houses were occasionally burned and rebuilt or simply emptied out with the bones then cleaned and reburied in another location. The Mound 4 charnel house contained charred skeletal remains of ten men and women, laid adjacent to the long bones of an additional skeleton bundled together with a cord-like material. All of the bodies were positioned side-by-side, resting on a mat woven from cattails, with grave-goods consisting of a bag of hickory nuts, a shell tempered round pot, and small pieces of fabric. Unfortunately, this mound was subjected to the forces of apathetical civilization.

The Southwest Enclosure

Directly behind the large truncated mound, bordering the stockade wall on the Westside, and extending to a short distance farther west to around 326 feet (100 m), is an area once enclosed from just south of the large pyramid, north to about 1,300 feet (400 m), and widening to around 650 feet (200 m) at the north end. The enclosure was on the highest terrain of the village, and it was only accessible through a wing gate of the main stockade fence. The enclosure was approximately five-acres (2.0 ha), and it bordered a portion along the main stockade of the elite precinct. The exterior stockade was constructed in the same manner as the main stockade fence, complete with regularly spaced watchtowers with no exiting gateways to the outside.

Most of the enclosure has been excavated. The results of the investigation are unclear of what once existed within the five-acre area other than one conical mound, a rise, thought to be another conical mound with a long tail, and perhaps what might have been the remnants of another wall, which ran the entire length of the complex. From Barrett's research of the early 1920s, he listed additional lines of posts, large storage pits, and several burials near the wall — one without a head, which was a common practice of the Mississippians. What exactly was the reason for building the five-acre area is still only speculation. In 2003, electro-magnetic conductivity technology was used to measure the soil underground for changes, and what was discovered were possible large features, which have not yet been scrutinized. Probably, the small-high area was used for special rituals involving the leaders or other elite members.

The Northeast Platform Mound

Listed as Mound #3 in the trail guide booklet, this mound has been greatly destroyed by looters, and plowing activity over time. It stands close to the northeast corner of the habitation area, and at one time was a low rectangular platform mound with a large structure built on top. Researchers identify this mound as almost identical to the Natchez temple mound, produced by the Natchez Mound Builders near Natchez, Mississippi, approximately one hundred years before Aztalan.

Found at the mound location were artifacts of charcoal and white sand, which seemed to suggest that the mound was used to maintain a continuous sacred fire, controlled by specially selected warriors, called *guardians*. In some cases, the guardians would face death if the fire went out. In some instances bones of the chiefs and sacred artifacts were kept at the site. The white sand was a sacred purifying substance used by many Native Americans. At times there would be a need to extinguish the flame. When this occurred, the fire area would be cleaned, and relined with the white sand before building a new fire in that location.

The mound, fortunately, was described by Increase A. Lapham, a surveyor and antiquarian who published *The Antiquities of Wisconsin* in 1855. Lapham pointed out that the mound stood 5 feet (1.5 m) high on the east end, it was wedge-shaped, oriented to an east-west direction, and it sloped downward towards the plaza area, where a stockade double-wall might have stood between the mound and the plaza.

Originally the area was 45 feet x 90 feet (13.7 x 27.4 m) in size with the top layer of soil removed, and a vertical open-walled structure was built that probably included a thatched roof. Later the wooden walls were dismantled and the earthen platform was constructed. During a second stage of building, another structure was built on top of the raised platform, which contained an area for the *eternal* fire.

Trade

The villagers at Aztalan, as with other Mississippian towns, had a regular trade business with other cultures in neighboring and far-ranging states. They used copper tools thought to have come from northern Michigan and pipestone from Minnesota. They procured large clam shells of a species native to the Illinois and Mississippi Rivers to use for hoes and pottery making. Unique stones from areas along the southern Mississippi River were brought in; while bartering for more local items of arrowheads, beads, and area pottery obtained from other Late Woodland tribes living in the region.

Burials

One unusual fact at Aztalan is that there were never conical or circular mounds containing mass burials found at the village site, unlike the ones discovered at Cahokia and at other Mississippian archaeological sites. Of course, the common use of charnel houses were used for the chiefs and his lineage, but possibly the many small conical mounds found in the area points to a practice of individual family type burial practices; perhaps a move away from the established Mississippian customs and rituals. We know cremation was used, but as it appears it was used in a limited way. There seems to be no signs of mass cremations, or of cremation areas inside of mounds such as those recorded by antiquarians at the Ohio River Valley Hopewell locations.

Cannibalism

If the Aztec people of Mesoamerica came to the Aztalan site after encountering the Spanish invasion, it must be observed that their cannibalistic ways had been reversed. Although researchers unearthed many cut, broken, and fragmented human bones at the site, they argue that these were not the result of a cannibalistic culture. Even though, human bones were pulled from fire-pits, found in the habitation area, or discarded into refuse heaps, does not demonstrate a cannibalistic society. Some answers for these findings are that bone preparation for bundling and reburial purposes can account for some of the activities. Another answer for bones and bone pieces can be explained by the fact that some of the human bones were not selected, for some unknown reason, for burial, reburial, or bundling; so they were simply discarded. One final answer to the mystery can be answered by the belief of some ancients that all things living, dead or even inanimate, have a useful purpose in the afterlife. So by combining all of these items, the people in the afterlife would be able to have everything they will need for a happy eternity. More information on this topic is available in Chapters 10 and 11 of *Pre-History's Chronology Enigma*.

Dispersal

By around AD 1450 the Hopewell / Mississippian Traditions were all but history. The man-made earthen mounds sat as extant symbols of a one time superior civilization that mysteriously disappeared into the unknown of prehistorical times, just as the once great Egyptian society in northeastern Africa. Along with these visible inexplicable configurations, many similarities exist between the two enigmatic cultures which cannot be disregarded. Likewise, the comparison of Mesoamerican and Mississippian Tradition cannot be overlooked or discounted. The Mississippians, just as the ancient Egyptians, Adena, Hopewell, Maya, Olmec, and Aztec, seemed to simply disperse into thin air, leaving no detailed written explanations, only structural symbols of their society, culture, and existence for modern man to ponder.

History is always asking — why did they leave — where did they go — what caused their decline? It might be the answer rests with the fact that all great cultures are doomed to collapse and extinction. The reasons are varied and numerous, but they probably apply to all civilizations both past, present and future. It, more than likely, depends on the people themselves. The more education people have, the more life experiences people possess, a decline in fear of tyrants, the will to escape poverty and rise to higher levels, the attainment of *Hope* and *Self-Empowerment* all are responsible for the changes to human civilization. Perhaps, the overall motivation for a culture to grow and change is; *somewhere out there, something better can be found.*

Aztalan Archaeological Site
Aztalan State Park
Near Lake Mills, Wisconsin, U.S.A.

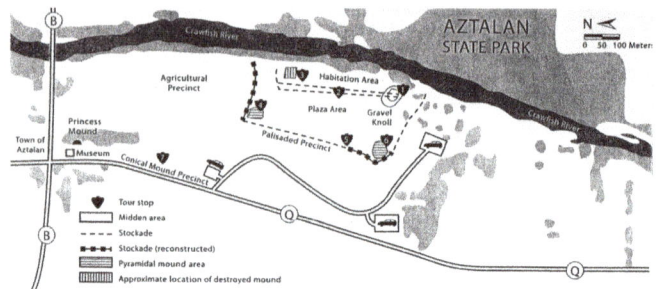

Tour Guide Map from Site Booklet

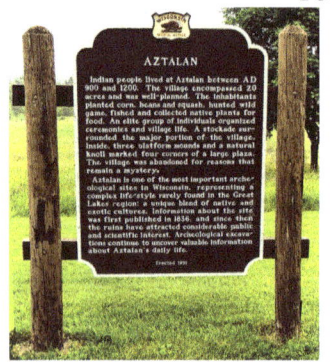

Park Entry Sign

Conical Mound Precinct Image 1

Conical Mound Precinct Image 2

Habitation Area South End near Mound 1

Habitation Area North End near Mound 4

Mound 1 (Gravel Knoll) from base in Plaza area

Photos by Derek W. Johnson, Chicago, Il (customimagephotos@gmail.com)-2014

Aztalan Archaeological Site Continued:

Mound #1 Panoramic view from top of Mound 6

Mound #4 from Plaza looking North

Mound #4 looking west from Stockade

Mound #4 - top looking west

Mound #4-Looking North from Mound 6

Mound #6 panoramic view from top of Mound #1

Photos by Derek W. Johnson, Chicago, Il (customimagephotos@gmail.com)-2014

Aztalan Archaeological Site Continued:

Mound #6 from base looking west

Mound #6 from Plaza area looking southwest

Mound #6 from south Plaza area

Mound #6 -Tier 1 with Stockade Fence

Stockade Fence — South End

Stockade behind Mound #6-looking west

Princess mound full view

Princess mound sign

The Photographer, Derek W. Johnson

Photos by Derek W. Johnson, Chicago, Il (customimagephotos@gmail.com)-2014

Footnote
1 David Childress, *Lost Cities of North and Central America,* p.362.

Footnotes

Footnotes

Chapter Three

1 John Haywood, *Dark Age Naval Power*, p. 1.

2 A. J. Conant, *Foot-Prints of Vanished Races*, p. 8.

3 Ibid., p. 9.

4 Lionel Casson, *The Ancient Mariners*, p. 4.

5 Ibid., p. 6.

6 Robert Gardiner, *The Earliest Ships*, p.16.

7 Ibid., p. 39.

Chapter Four

1 John Baldwin, *Pre-Historic Nations*, p. 271.

2 Philip Coppens, *The Ancient Alien Question*, p. 109.

3 Erich von Däniken, *Signs of the Gods*, p. 103.

4 Ibid., p. 82.

5 Marc Van De Mieroop, *A History of Ancient Egypt,*. p. 21.

6 Denise Bessert-Schmandt, *How Writing Came About*, p. 6.

7 Lionel Casson, *The Ancient Mariners*, p. 18.

8 Barry Fell, *America B.C.,* p. 174.

9 David Childress, *Lost Cities of Atlantis, Ancient Europe & The Mediterranean*, p. 103.

10 John Baldwin, *Pre-Historic Nations*, p. 366.

11 David Childress, *Lost Cities of Atlantis, Ancient Europe & The Mediterranean*, p. 146.

12 Philip Coppens, *The Lost Civilization Enigma*, p. 54.

Chapter Five

1 Michael Cremo and Richard Thompson, *The Hidden History of the Human Race,* p. 40.

2 Ibid., p. 40.

3 Ibid., p. 36.

4 Douglas Kenyon, *Forbidden History,* p. 19.

5 Vilhelm Moberg, *A History of the Swedish People*, p. 30.

6 Miloš M. Bogdanović and Marija Lj. Bogdanović, *Reconstruction of Speech and Language of the Cro-Magnon Man 2004*, p. 1.

7 Ibid., p. 1.

8 The Enigma of Pelasgians and Etruscans, p.1.

9. Johns Baldwin, *Pre-Historic Nations*, p. 392.

Chapter Six

1 Ivan Van Sertima, *They Came Before Columbus,* pgs. 5-6.

2 Ibid., p. 28.

3 Graham Hancock, *Fingerprints of the Gods*, p. 162.

4 David Childress, *Lost Cities of North & Central America*, p. 362.

5 Graham Hancock, *Fingerprints of the Gods*, p. 167.

6 Ibid., p.167.

7 John Baldwin, *Pre-Historic Nations,* pgs. 394-395.

Chapter Seven

1 Graham Hancock, *Fingerprints of the Gods*, p. 56.

2 David Childress, *Lost Cities & Ancient Mysteries of South America*, p.139.

3 Ibid., p. 98.

4 Erich von Däniken, *Twilight of the Gods,* p. 70.

Chapter Eight

1 www.resurrectisis.org/IceAge.htm, p. 1.

2 Ibid., p.1.

3 Patrick Huyghe, *Columbus Was Last,* p. 16.

4 Graham Hancock, *Fingerprints of the Gods*, p. 222.

5 Patrick Huyghe, *Columbus Was Last,* p. 16.

Chapter Nine

1 Charles River Editors, *The History and Culture of the Mound Builders*, p. 6.

2 Robert Silverberg, *The Mound Builders,* p. 181.

3 A. J. Conant, *Foot-Prints of Vanished Races*, p. 98.

4 Charles Phillips, *Aztec & Maya, The Complete Illustrated History*, p. 215.

5 Time Life Books, *Mound Builders and Cliff Dwellers*, p.15.

Chapter Eleven

1 Patrick Huyghe, *Columbus Was Last,* p. 27.

2 www.indianlegend.com/hopi/hopi_001.htm

3 Philip Coppens, *Lost Cities of North and Central America*, p. 303.

4 Ibid., p. 280.

5 David Childress, *Lost Cities of North and Central America*, p. 303.

6 Anna Sofaer, *Chaco Astronomy,* p. xv.

BIBLIOGRAPHY

Baldwin, John D., *Pre-Historic Nations.* New York: Forgotten Books, 2012.

Birmingham, Robert A. and Goldstein, Lynne G., *Aztalan.* Wisconsin: Wisconsin Historical Society Press, 2005.

Casson, Lionel, *The Ancient Mariners.* Princeton, New Jersey: Princeton University Press, 1991.

Charles River Editors, Native American Tribes: *The History And Culture of The Mound Builders.* San Bernardino, CA, 2014.

Childress, David Hatcher, *Lost Cities of Atlantis, Ancient Europe & The Mediterranean.* Kempton, Illinois: Adventurers Unlimited Press, 1996.

Childress, David Hatcher, *Lost Cities of North & Central America.* Kempton, Illinois: Adventures Unlimited Press, 1992.

Childress, David Hatcher, *Lost Cities & Ancient Mysteries of South America.* Kempton, Illinois: Adventures Unlimited Press, 1989.

Conant, A.J., *Foot-Prints of Vanished Races.* Davenport, Iowa: Gustav's Library, 1879.

Coppens, Philip, *The Lost Civilization Enigma.* Pompton Plains, NJ: The Career Press, 2013

Coppens, Philip, *The Ancient Alien Question.* Pompton, NJ: New Page Books, 2012.

Cremo, Michael and Thompson, Richard L., *The Hidden History of the Human Race.* Los Angeles, California: Bhaktivedanta Book Publishing, 2008.

Farrell, Joseph P., *Genes, Giants, Monsters and Men.* Port Townsend, WA: Feral House, 2011.

Fell, Barry, *America B.C.* New York, N.Y.: Pocket Books, 1976.

Fell, Barry, *Saga America.* New York, N. Y.: Times Books, 1980.

Gardner, Robert, *The Earliest Ships.* London, England: Conway Maritime Press, 1996.

Hancock, Graham, *Fingerprints of the Gods.* New York, N.Y.: Three Rivers Press, 1995.

Hapgood, Charles H., *Maps of the Ancient Sea Kings.* Kempton, Illinois: Adventures Unlimited Press, 1996.

Haywood, John, *Dark Age Naval Power.* New York, N.Y.: Routledge, 1991.

Huyghe, Patrick, *Columbus Was Last.* Jefferson Valley, N. Y.: Anomalist Books, 1992.

Johnson, Terrance F., *Our Missing Ancestors/ A Dynamic Civilization.* College Station, TX: Virtual Book Worm, 2013.

Joseph, Frank, *The Lost Worlds of Ancient America.* Pompton Plains, NJ: The Career Press, 2012.

Kavasch, E. Barrie, *The Mound Builders of Ancient North America.* London, NE: iUniverse, Inc. 2004.

Kenyon, Douglas J., *Forbidden History.* Rochester, Vermont: Bear & Company, 2005.

Kresiberg, Glenn, *Lost Knowledge of the Ancients.* Rochester, Vermont: Bear & Company, 2010.

Lourie, Peter, *The Lost World of the Anasazi.* Honesdale, PA: Boyds Mill Press, 2003.

Moberg, Vilhelm, *A History of The Swedish People*, Volume 1. Minneapolis, MN: First University of Minnesota Press, 2005.

Pemberton, John, *Myths and Legends.* New York, N.Y.: Chartwell Books, Inc., 2012.

Phillips, Charles, *The Complete Illustrated History Aztec & Maya.* New York, N.Y.: Metro Books, 2012.

Pye, Michael & Dalley, Kirsten, *Lost Civilizations & Secrets of the Past.* Pompton Plains, NJ: Career Press, 2012.

Reeves, Arthur Middleton, *The Norse Discovery of America.* Blacksburg, VA: A & D Publishing, 2010.

Schmandt-Bessert, Denise, *How Writing Came About.* Austin, TX: University of Texas Press, 1992.

Schoch, Robert M., *Forgotten Civilization.* Rochester, Vermont: Inner Traditions, 2012.

Sertima, Ivan Van, *They Came Before Columbus.* New York, N.Y.: Random House, 2003.

Shaw, Ian, *The Oxford History of Ancient Egypt.* New York, N.Y.: Oxford University Press, 2003.

Silverberg, Robert, *The Mound Builders.* Greenwich, Conn.: Ohio University Press, 1970.

Sofaer, Anna, *Chaco Astronomy.* Santa Fe, New Mexico: Ocean Tree Books, 2008.

Sitchin, Zecharia, *When Time Began.* New York, N.Y.: Harper, 1993.

Van De Mieroop, Marc, *A History of Ancient Egypt.* Chichester, West Sussex: Wiley-Blackwell & Sons Publication, 2011.

Von Dänikin, Erich, *Chariots of the Gods.* New York, N.Y.: Berkley Books, 1999.

Von Dänikin, Erich, *Signs of the Gods.* London: Souvenir Press Ltd., 2010.

Von Dänikin, Erich, *Twilight of the Gods.* Pompton Plains, NJ: New Page Books, 2010.

INDEX

A

Adena, 127, 128, 130 -132, 140, 149, 150, 155, 166, 178, 183, 184, 212
Afton interglacial, 14
Alamanni, 74
Alaska, 4, 8, 10, 13, 115 - 117, 156, 163, 164
Algonquian, 157, 166, 167, 168, 186
Alligewi, 123, 124, 134
America, 3, 49, 68, 80, 113, 61, 162, 164, 165, 168, 182
American, 3, 13, 19, 65, 85, 90, 94, 113, 114, 127, 130, 132, 135, 152, 157, 161, 162, 164, 178, 179, 184, 187, 188, 190, 191, 198, 204, 205
Americas, 85, 93, 94, 113, 118, 130, 162 - 167, 177, 178
    Central America, 79, 80, 82, 84, 86 - 89, 91, 94, 95, 117, 135, 164, 174, 179, 180, 182, 184, 206
    Mesoamerica, 39, 82 - 86, 89, 92 - 94, 96, 107, 117, 121, 122, 135, 139, 142, 175, 178, 180, 181, 183, 184, 186, 212
    Native American, 4, 118, 123 – 125, 128, 129, 132 – 134, 136, 140, 141, 143, 149, 151, 156, 157, 161, 162, 164, 165, 178, 183, 189, 193, 204, 211
    North America, 3 – 5, 7, 8, 13 – 18, 20, 22 – 24, 27, 44, 50, 65, 80, 82, 87, 88, 91, 98, 100, 104, 105, 113 – 119, 121 – 127, 129, 132, 133, 135, 136, 142, 143, 146, 149, 150, 155, 156 – 158, 161 – 165, 168, 170, 173, 174, 180 – 183, 186, 201, 204
    South America, 1, 13, 39, 50, 65, 82 – 85, 93 – 96, 101, 103, 105 – 108, 115, 117, 118, 121, 122, 135, 162 – 164, 173, 178, 183, 191, 198
Amorica / Brittany, France, 70, 74, 75, 151, 208
Anasazi, 49, 91, 130, 152, 176 – 178, 180, 182, 185, 187, 188, 190 – 198, 208
Angeln, 61
Apache, 187
Aryan, 65, 66, 69 – 73
Asthenosphere, 15, 21
Aztalan, 87, 88, 174, 175, 204 – 212, 214 – 216
Aztec, 81, 83, 87 – 89, 91, 92, 95, 107, 139, 142, 171, 173 – 175, 185, 212

B

Baltic Sea, 6, 12, 25, 29, 44, 51, 61
Barrett, Samuel A., 208, 210
Basketmakers, 191, 193, 194, 198
Basque, 10, 64 – 68, 73, 134, 165, 178
Bellamy, Schindler Prof., 97, 103
Beothuk Nation, 156
Bering Strait, 8, 115, 117, 127, 162, 164
    Beringia, 115 – 117, 161, 164
    Land Bridge, 8, 13, 115 – 117, 161, 162, 163
Big Mound, 136, 171
Brackenridge, Henry 128, 171
Burkitt, M. C., 58
Byblos, 39, 43, 44

C

Cahokia, 136 – 140, 142, 143, 147, 183, 205 -207, 211
Canada, 10, 13, 15, 17, 19, 20, 65, 66, 81, 98, 116, 117, 135, 142, 150, 152, 154, 156, 161, 164, 166 – 168, 178
Caral, 93,104, 105
Casa Grande, 180, 181, 184
Casa Malpais, 189
Celts / Kelts, 26, 49, 69, 70 – 76, 78, 163, 165, 178
Chaco Canyon, 176, 182, 190, 191, 193 – 198, 208
Chauci, 27, 60, 61
Clarke, Grahame Prof., 155
Clovis Tradition, 115, 125 – 127, 131, 145, 146, 192, 198
Columbus, Christopher, 3, 4, 65, 79, 80, 81, 83, 84, 90, 113, 116, 118, 125, 161 – 164
Convergent margins, 21
Cordell, Linda, 185
Cro-Magnon, 8 – 10, 64, 66 – 68, 151
Cush / Kush / Nubian, 44, 51, 52, 70, 72, 73, 86, 186, 200

D

Danube Script / Vinča, 46, 47, 56
Davenport Calendar Stele, 133, 134
Death Valley, 20
Delaware Nation, See Lenni- Lenape
Denmark (Also see Jutland), 7, 11, 29, 30, 61, 64, 72, 151, 158
Dickson Mound, 141
Doggerland, 8, 9, 12

E

Egypt / Egyptians, 26, 31 – 35, 38 – 45, 47 – 53, 84 – 86, 89, 90, 97, 99, 102, 103, 108, 125, 132 – 135, 137, 139, 163, 165 – 168, 170 – 175, 177, 178, 185, 186, 198 – 201, 212
Eriksson, Leif, 80, 81, 132
Etruscan, 71, 73
Europe, 1, 3, 5 – 11, 13, 16, 17, 22, 24 – 30, 33, 46 – 49, 54, 57 – 62, 64 – 76, 78, 79, 103, 106, 107, 114, 122 – 126, 131 – 134, 151, 152, 155 – 159, 162, 163, 165, 168, 178, 179, 181, 192, 199

F

Fell, Barry Prof., 49, 50, 133, 134, 157, 162, 163, 165, 166, 178, 185, 186
Fitzhugh, William Dr., 154
Flandrian Transgression, 9
Folsom Culture, 125, 127, 145, 192, 198
Foster, J. W., 135, 136

G
Gass, M. Rev., 133
Gaul, 72, 74 – 76
Gila Cliff Dwelling, 187
Gimbutas, Marija, 47, 56
Grand Gulch, Utah, 191, 192, 194, 195
Greeks / Greece, 32, 38, 42 – 44, 46, 47, 49 – 51, 53, 70, 71, 73, 74, 76, 136, 184, 199
Greenberg, Joseph, 162

H
Hamlin, Augustus, 150, 152
Heckewelder, John, 124, 132
Hittite, 49 - 51
Hohokam, 178 – 182, 184, 185, 190
Holocene, 6, 7, 9, 77
Holsteinian interglacial, 5
Hopewell Tradition, 126, 130 – 132, 134, 135, 140 – 142, 148, 166, 167, 178, 182, 183, 193, 198, 212
Hopi Nation, 49, 88, 91, 171 – 178, 185, 188, 195, 198
Humboldt von, Alexander, 87, 88

I
Illinoian glacial, 13 – 17, 19, 23, 116
Inca, 93 – 96, 98, 101, 102, 104 – 106
Inuksuk, 154
Iroquois Nation / Mengwe, 123, 124, 168

J
Jutland (also see Denmark), 6, 29, 61, 62

K
Kankakee, 17, 18, 189
Kansan glacial, 14
Kehoe, Alice, 81
Kincaid, G. E., 169, 170, 173
Kukulcán, 87, 139
Kush, (see Cush)

L
Lago Mare Event, 37, 38
Lake Titicaca, 95, 96, 98 – 102, 105
Lapps / Laplanders (see Sámi)
Lenni-Lenape / Delaware Nation, 123, 124, 132, 134, 167, 178
Levant, 31, 37, 42 – 44, 52, 54
Libyans, 49, 51, 71, 133, 134, 165, 174, 178, 185, 186, 200

M

Maillard, Pierre, 167
Maize / Corn, 102, 104, 135, 171, 175, 183, 184, 187, 204
Malta, 38, 40 – 42, 54
Marfan syndrome, 107, 108
Maasaw, 176, 177
Maritime Archaic Culture (see Red Paint People), 150, 154 – 158, 197
Maya, 82, 84, 86, 87, 92, 95, 118, 135, 137 – 139, 142, 177, 180, 186, 212
Mediterranean Sea, 9, 37, 38, 40, 42 – 47, 50, 52, 53, 85, 86, 133, 134, 151, 157, 159, 163, 185, 186, 199
Mengwe (see Iroquois)
Messinian Event, 37
Mexica (see Aztec)
Mexico, 19, 38, 81 – 85, 87 – 89, 91, 95, 115, 127, 131, 134, 135, 138, 139, 143, 165, 176, 178, 180, 182 – 185, 187, 198
Micmac Nation, 156, 166, 168
Millon, Rene Prof., 90
Mimbres pottery, 187, 188, 196
Mindel glaciation, 5
Minoan, 47, 48, 50, 52, 184, 185
Mississippian Tradition, 133, 134, 142, 183, 205, 206, 212
Moche Culture, 107, 108
Mogollon Culture, 178, 180, 187 – 190, 196
Moir, Ried J., 58
Monk's Mound, 136, 139, 140, 147, 205, 206
Moraine, 6, 18, 208
Mound City, 138
Mountains,
   Alps, 6, 11, 61, 73, 75
   Andes, 6, 13, 53, 94, 95, 98, 101, 102, 105, 106
   Pyrénées, 6, 10, 64, 75, 199
   Sierra Nevada, 18, 20
   Ural, 63 – 66, 163, 164
   White, 180, 195

N

Native American Graves Protection and Repatriation Act, 141
Navajo, 65, 171, 190, 191, 194, 195
Nebraskan glacial, 5, 14
Nelin, Gustavo, 81
Nubian (see Cush)
Nubian Sand Stone Aquifer, 200

O

Ojibwe Nation / Chippewa, 167, 174
Olmec, 82 – 86, 88, 89, 92, 142, 212

Ometeotl, 139
Orion, 90, 175 – 177,
Osiris, 38, 39, 40, 53, 84, 133, 139, 177

P
Patagonia, 98, 106 – 108
Pelasgians, 69 – 73
Pfeiffer, Robert, 136
Phoenicians, 32, 43 – 45, 49 – 51, 70, 84, 86, 163, 185, 186
Pima Nation, 88, 171, 179, 184, 185, 187
Pleistocene Epoch, 5, 10, 18, 19, 57, 59, 77
Pliocene age, 57, 58, 77
Posnansky, Arthur Prof., 96 – 98, 100, 103
Potawatomi, 129, 167

Q
Quetzalcoatl, 81, 83, 84, 87, 89, 90, 95, 96, 139

R
Red ochre, 132, 149 – 156, 158, 166, 194
Red Paint People (also see Maritime Archaic Culture) 152, 156, 157, 161, 166, 198, 208
Renfrew, Colin, 47
Rivers,
   Adour, 65
   Crawfish, 88, 205, 207, 208
   Colorado, 106, 169, 171, 172, 176, 178, 182
   Danube, 46, 47, 73
   Des Plaines, 18
   Gila, 179, 182, 187
   Huron, 124
   Illinois, 18, 140, 141, 211
   Kankakee, 17, 18, 189
   Lena, 116, 163
   Mississippi, 16 – 18, 38, 124, 132 – 138, 140 - 142, 171, 174, 178, 211
   Missouri, 19
   Mur, 73
   Niagara, 17
   Nile, 16, 32, 33, 37, 40, 42, 137, 186, 199, 200, 201
   Ohio, 17, 18
   Rio Grande, 182, 185, 198
   Salt, 179, 180
   Snake, 20
   St. Lawrence, 167
   Styx, 38
   Teays, 17, 18
   Thames, 7

White, 180
　　Yenisei, 163
Riss glaciation, 5, 6
Rockwell Mound, 140, 148
Rogers, Richard, 165
Romans, 27, 28, 33, 43, 59, 60, 64, 72, 74, 75
Ryan-Pitman Theory, 9

S

Sacsayhuamán, 105
Sahara Desert, 200
Sámi (Lapps/ Laplanders), 62, 63, 65, 67, 69, 162
Sangamonian interglacial, 7, 16, 17
Saxons, 33, 34, 61, 70, 102, 137, 152
Schlemmer, Alfred, 90
Serpent Mound, 129, 173
Siberia, 4, 6, 8, 10, 13, 65, 115 – 117, 120, 162, 163, 168
Slate, 157, 158
Snaketown, 180, 182
Sofaer, Anna, 197
Solutrean Culture, 68, 69, 115, 125, 127, 131, 145, 152, 162, 192, 198
Spiderwoman, 172, 173, 175, 188
Stanford, Dennis, 68, 69
Storegga side, 9
Système Eémien, 7, 16

T

Tampico Mound, 141
Tenochtitlán, 88, 174
Teotihuacan, 88 – 90, 95, 96, 177, 206
Téviec Island, 151, 152, 155, 208
Tiahuanaco, 53, 85, 95 – 101, 105
Tolstoy, Paul, 84
Tuck, James, 154

V

Vinča script (see Danube script), 46, 47, 56
Vinland, 80, 132, 150
Viracocha, 95, 96, 98, 101, 109
Vistulian glaciation, 6

W

Wabanaki Nation, 166, 167
Watson Brake Culture, 127
Weichselian glaciation, 6, 17, 33

Wetherill, Richard, 191, 192, 195
Willerslev, Eske Prof., 28
Wisconsinan glacial, 5, 16 – 19, 100, 114 – 117, 126, 127, 208
Würm glaciation, 5 – 7, 10, 11, 17

Y
Yarmouthian interglacial, 14, 15
Younger Dryas glacial, 7, 9, 22, 100

Z
Zuni, 49, 50, 157, 185, 186, 188, 198

www.ingramcontent.com/pod-product-compliance
Lightning Source LLC
Chambersburg PA
CBHW041243240426
43670CB00024B/2965